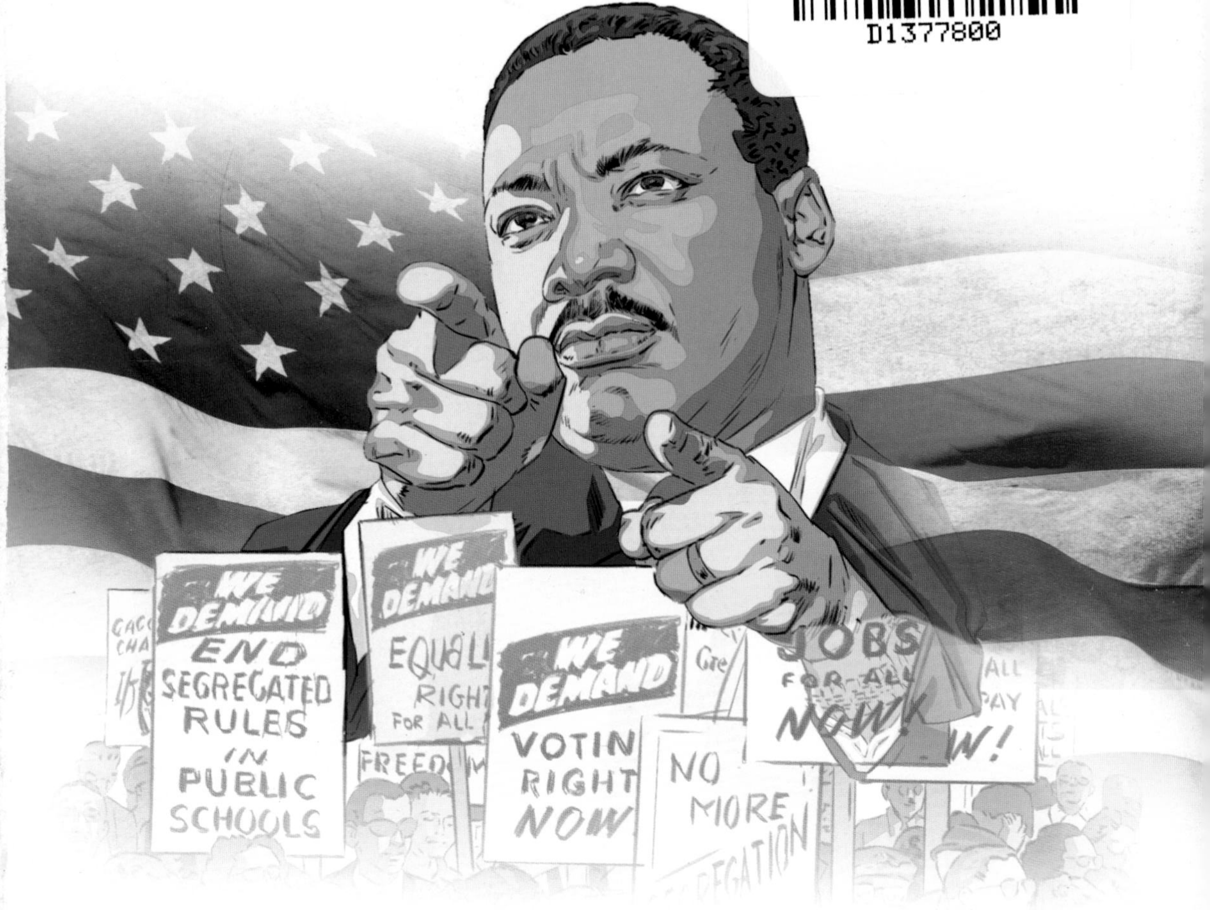
WE DEMAND
END SEGREGATED RULES IN PUBLIC SCHOOLS
WE DEMAND
RIGHT FOR ALL
WE DEMAND
VOTIN RIGHT NOW
NO MORE
JOBS FOR ALL NOW!

MARTIN LUTHER KING JR.

LET FREEDOM RING

CAMPFIRE®

KALYANI NAVYUG MEDIA PVT LTD

MARTIN LUTHER KING JR.
LET FREEDOM RING

Script
Michael Teitelbaum & Lewis Helfand

Edits
Suparna Deb & Aditi Ray

Line Art
Naresh Kumar

Color
Vijay Sharma & Pradeep Sherawat

Desktop Publishing
Bhavnath Chaudhary

CAMPFIRE®

www.campfire.co.in

Published by Kalyani Navyug Media Pvt Ltd
101 C, Shiv House, Hari Nagar Ashram, New Delhi 110014, India
ISBN: 978-93-80028-69-9

Printed in India

ABOUT THE AUTHORS

MICHAEL TEITELBAUM

As a child, Michael Teitelbaum loved baseball, radio, music, and comic books. After graduating from Adelphi University, New York, with a BA in Communications, Michael worked in radio and the stressful world of advertising before joining the publishing industry as an editor of comic books and children's books and magazines. Michael is the writer and project editor of 'Breaking Barriers: In Sports, In Life', an education program of Scholastic, Inc. He has written many books based on popular characters such as Spider-Man, Superman, Batman, and Kermit the Frog. His latest fiction includes *The Scary States of America*. His latest non-fiction book is *Jackie Robinson: Champion for Equality*, a biography of the great baseball player and civil rights leader.

LEWIS AARON HELFAND

Lewis Aaron Helfand has been interested in cartoons, animation, and comics from a young age, and by the age of twelve, had turned to writing in that medium as an amateur. His career, however, was a far cry from his passion. At the age of twenty-four, Lewis had been editing phonebooks for a year and a half and felt no closer to his lifelong goal of writing comic books. So, one day, he decided to quit his job. Lewis then spent the next two months working day and night to write and draw his first independent comic book, *Wasted Minute*. With the first issue received well, he was soon collaborating with other artists, and released four more issues over the next few years. Outside the field of comics, Lewis works as a freelance writer and reporter for a number of US print and online publications. He has covered everything from sports and travel to politics and culture for magazines such as *Renaissance*, *American Health and Fitness*, and *Computer Bits*.

ABOUT THE ARTIST

NARESH KUMAR

A resident of New Delhi, India, Naresh describes himself as a seeker who is continuously trying to learn as much as he can, and his art is an expression of his curiosity towards the world. A firm believer in humanity, Naresh brings an experienced hand to the drawing board, and his photo-realistic style captures the subtle emotions of his characters. His work features in a number of titles from Campfire, which include *Robinson Crusoe*, *A Christmas Carol*, *The Adventures of Huckleberry Finn*, *Frankenstein*, *Kidnapped*, and *Sinbad: The Legacy*.

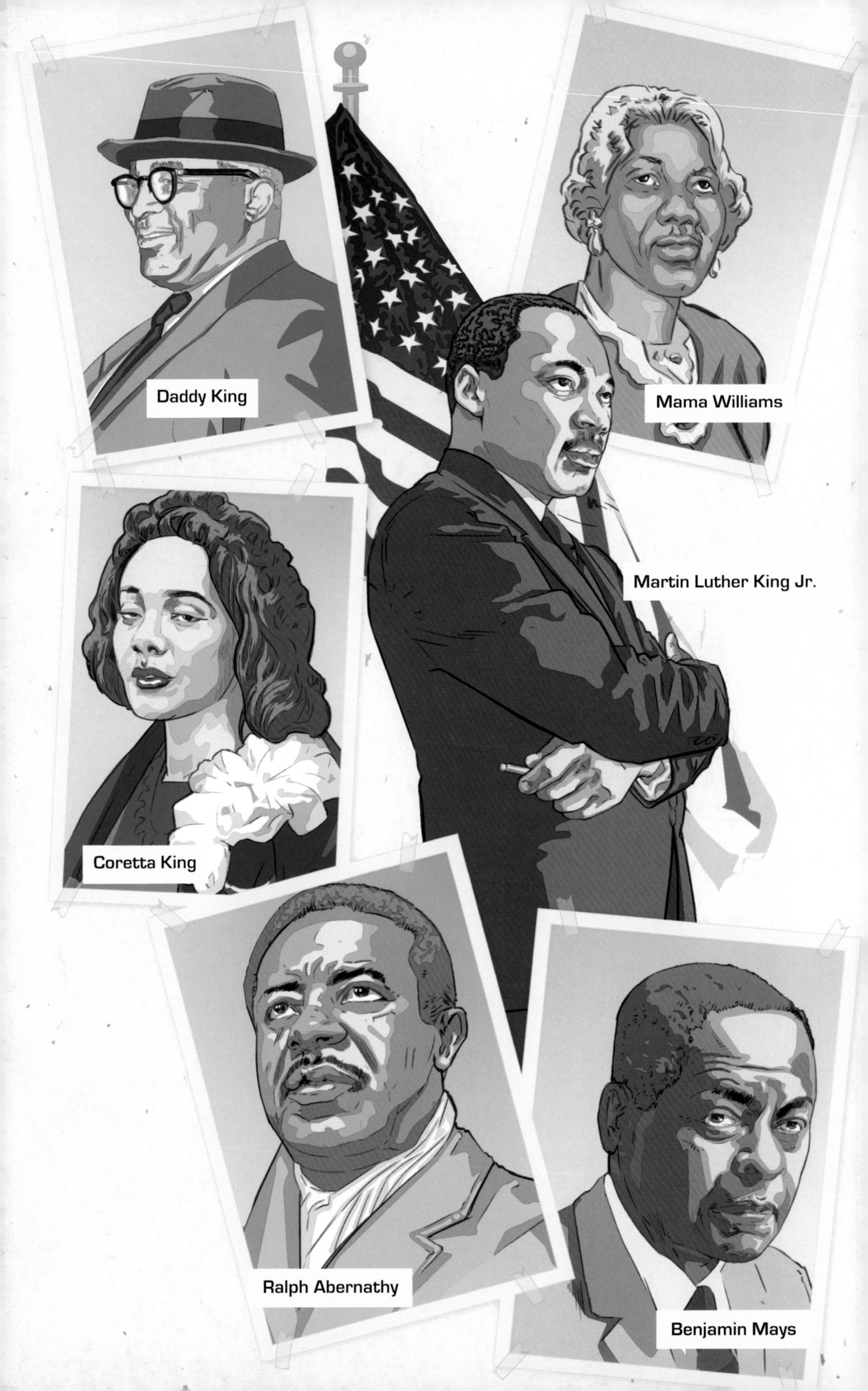
Daddy King
Mama Williams
Martin Luther King Jr.
Coretta King
Ralph Abernathy
Benjamin Mays

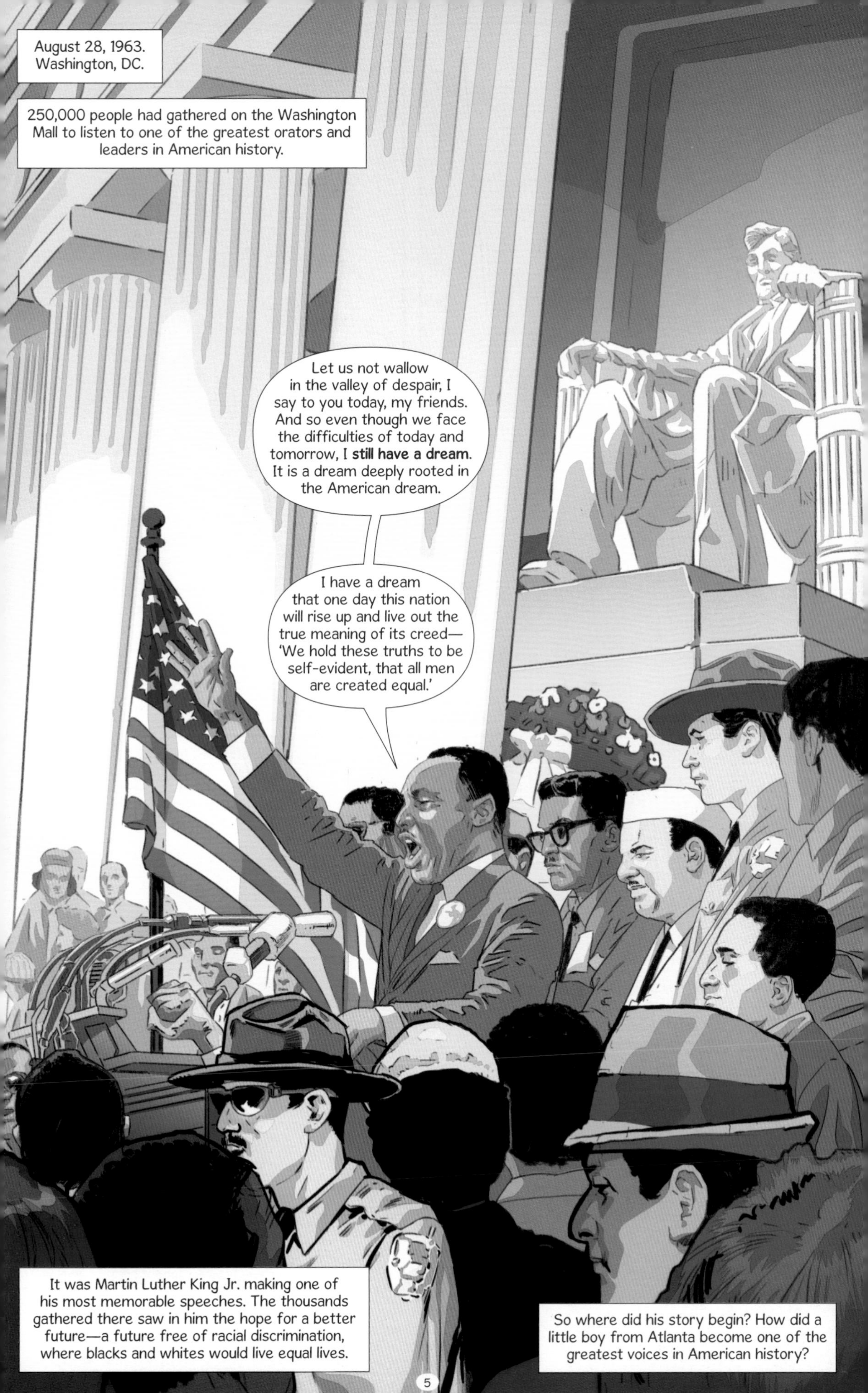
August 28, 1963.
Washington, DC.
250,000 people had gathered on the Washington Mall to listen to one of the greatest orators and leaders in American history.
Let us not wallow in the valley of despair, I say to you today, my friends. And so even though we face the difficulties of today and tomorrow, I **still have a dream**. It is a dream deeply rooted in the American dream.
I have a dream that one day this nation will rise up and live out the true meaning of its creed—'We hold these truths to be self-evident, that all men are created equal.'
It was Martin Luther King Jr. making one of his most memorable speeches. The thousands gathered there saw in him the hope for a better future—a future free of racial discrimination, where blacks and whites would live equal lives.
So where did his story begin? How did a little boy from Atlanta become one of the greatest voices in American history?

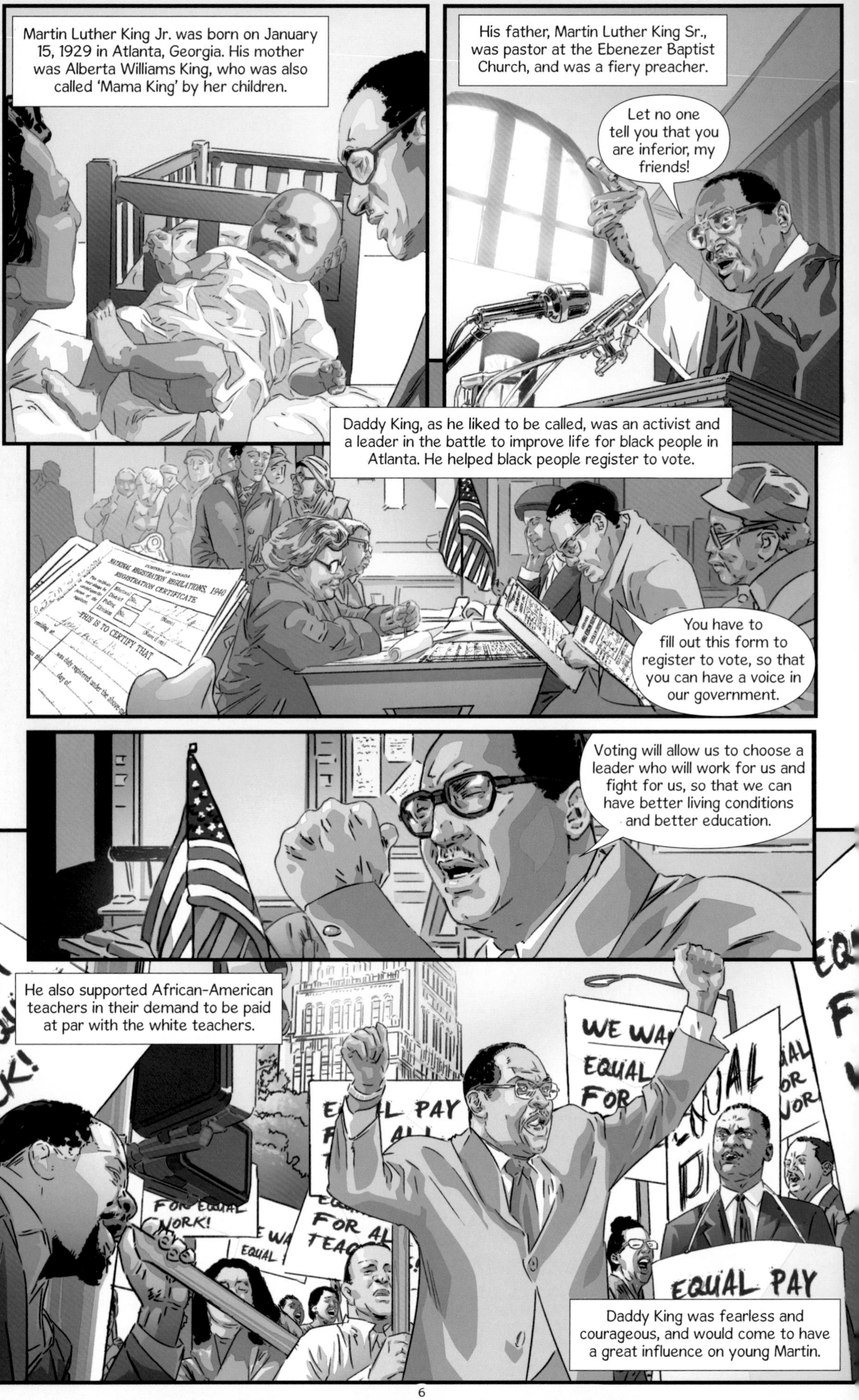

Martin Luther King Jr. was born on January 15, 1929 in Atlanta, Georgia. His mother was Alberta Williams King, who was also called 'Mama King' by her children.
His father, Martin Luther King Sr., was pastor at the Ebenezer Baptist Church, and was a fiery preacher.
Let no one tell you that you are inferior, my friends!
Daddy King, as he liked to be called, was an activist and a leader in the battle to improve life for black people in Atlanta. He helped black people register to vote.
NATIONAL REGISTRATION REGULATIONS, 1940
REGISTRATION CERTIFICATE
THIS IS TO CERTIFY THAT
You have to fill out this form to register to vote, so that you can have a voice in our government.
Voting will allow us to choose a leader who will work for us and fight for us, so that we can have better living conditions and better education.
He also supported African-American teachers in their demand to be paid at par with the white teachers.
EQUAL PAY
FOR EQUAL WORK!
EQUAL PAY
Daddy King was fearless and courageous, and would come to have a great influence on young Martin.

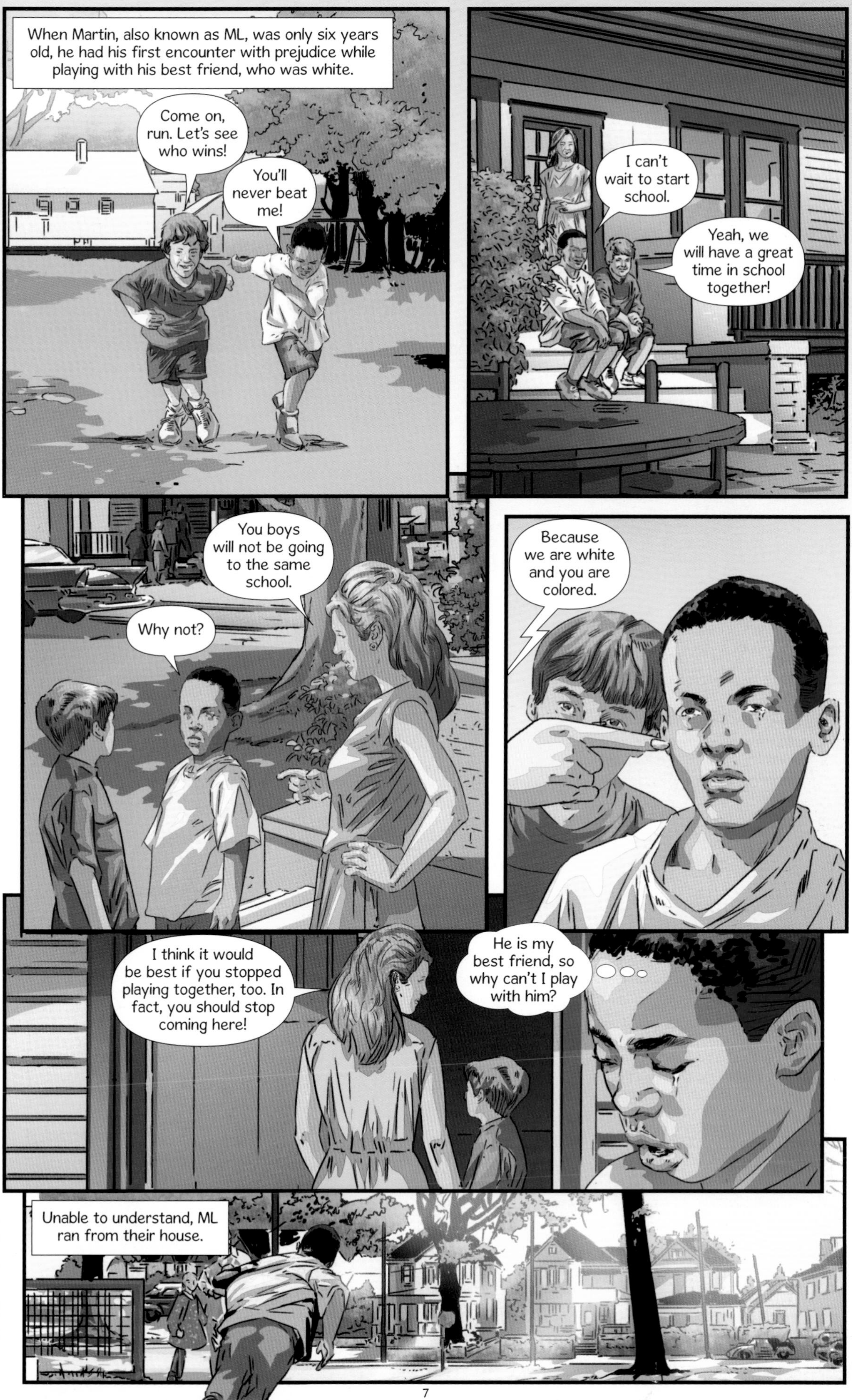
When Martin, also known as ML, was only six years old, he had his first encounter with prejudice while playing with his best friend, who was white.
Come on, run. Let's see who wins!
You'll never beat me!
I can't wait to start school.
Yeah, we will have a great time in school together!
You boys will not be going to the same school.
Why not?
Because we are white and you are colored.
I think it would be best if you stopped playing together, too. In fact, you should stop coming here!
He is my best friend, so why can't I play with him?
Unable to understand, ML ran from their house.

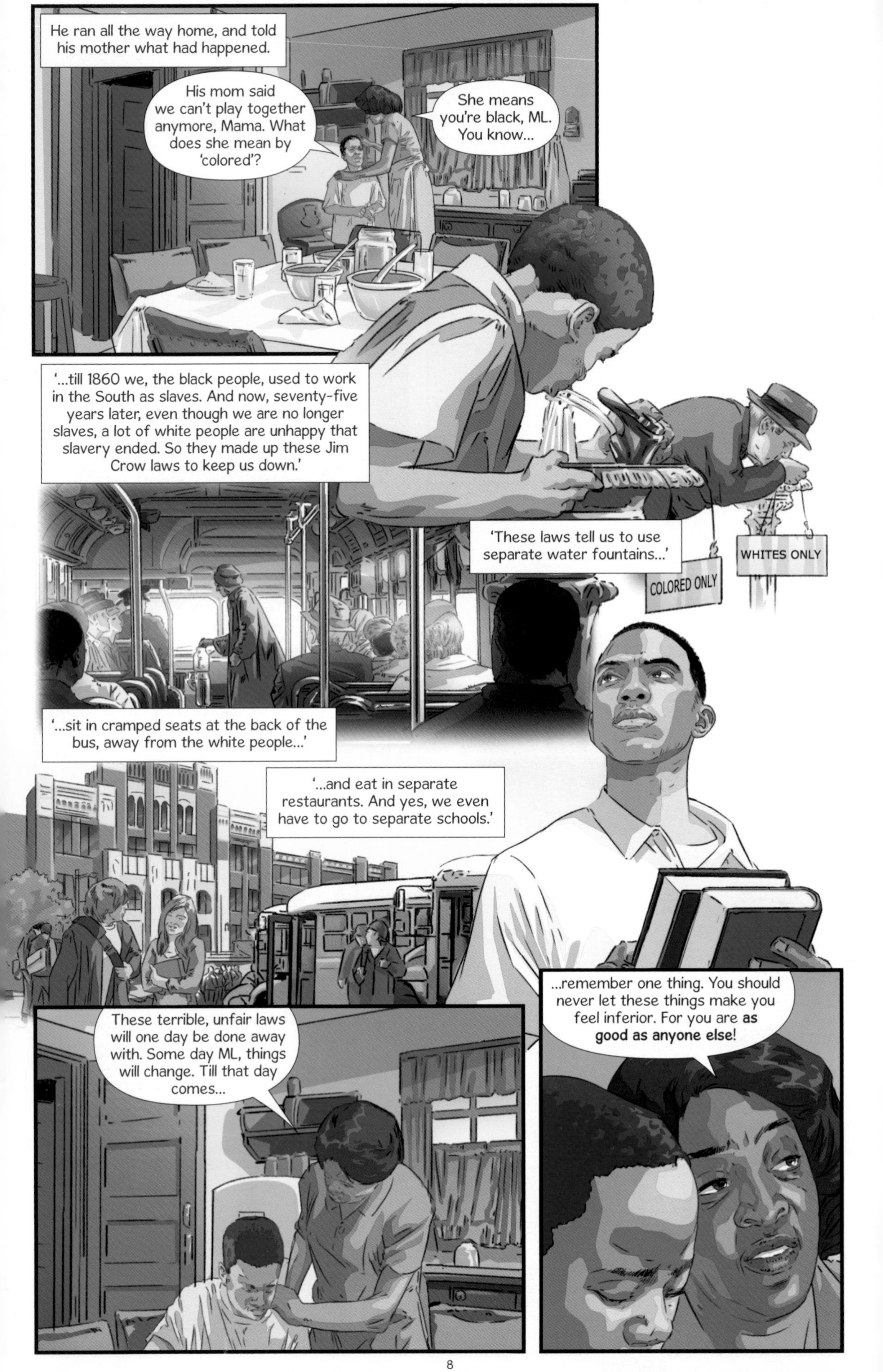
He ran all the way home, and told his mother what had happened.
His mom said we can't play together anymore, Mama. What does she mean by 'colored'?
She means you're black, ML. You know...
'...till 1860 we, the black people, used to work in the South as slaves. And now, seventy-five years later, even though we are no longer slaves, a lot of white people are unhappy that slavery ended. So they made up these Jim Crow laws to keep us down.'
'These laws tell us to use separate water fountains...'
WHITES ONLY
COLORED ONLY
'...sit in cramped seats at the back of the bus, away from the white people...'
'...and eat in separate restaurants. And yes, we even have to go to separate schools.'
These terrible, unfair laws will one day be done away with. Some day ML, things will change. Till that day comes...
...remember one thing. You should never let these things make you feel inferior. For you are **as good as anyone else**!

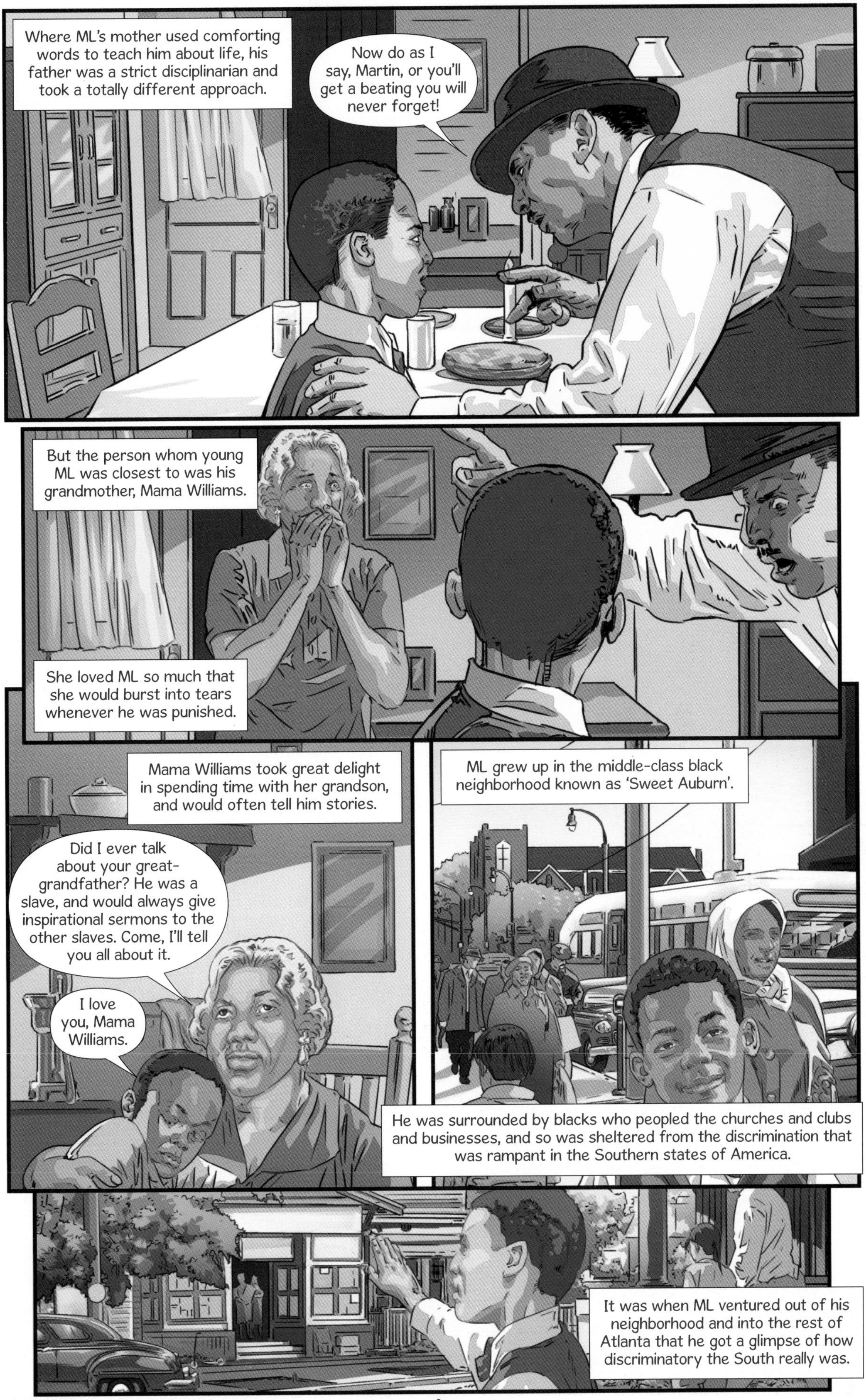
Where ML's mother used comforting words to teach him about life, his father was a strict disciplinarian and took a totally different approach.
Now do as I say, Martin, or you'll get a beating you will never forget!
But the person whom young ML was closest to was his grandmother, Mama Williams.
She loved ML so much that she would burst into tears whenever he was punished.
Mama Williams took great delight in spending time with her grandson, and would often tell him stories.
Did I ever talk about your great-grandfather? He was a slave, and would always give inspirational sermons to the other slaves. Come, I'll tell you all about it.
I love you, Mama Williams.
ML grew up in the middle-class black neighborhood known as 'Sweet Auburn'.
He was surrounded by blacks who peopled the churches and clubs and businesses, and so was sheltered from the discrimination that was rampant in the Southern states of America.
It was when ML ventured out of his neighborhood and into the rest of Atlanta that he got a glimpse of how discriminatory the South really was.

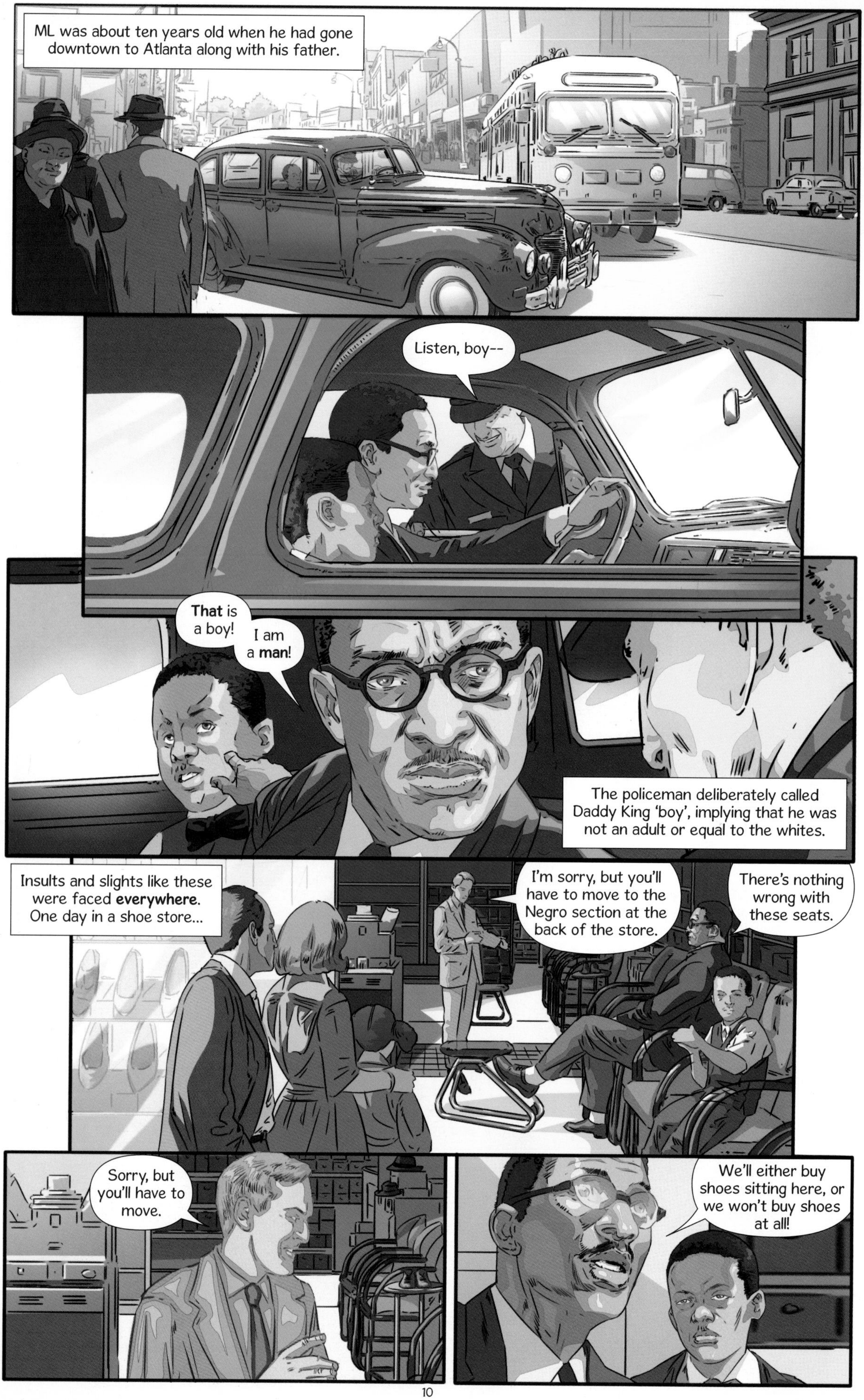
ML was about ten years old when he had gone downtown to Atlanta along with his father.
Listen, boy--
That is a boy!
I am a man!
The policeman deliberately called Daddy King 'boy', implying that he was not an adult or equal to the whites.
Insults and slights like these were faced everywhere. One day in a shoe store...
I'm sorry, but you'll have to move to the Negro section at the back of the store.
There's nothing wrong with these seats.
Sorry, but you'll have to move.
We'll either buy shoes sitting here, or we won't buy shoes at all!

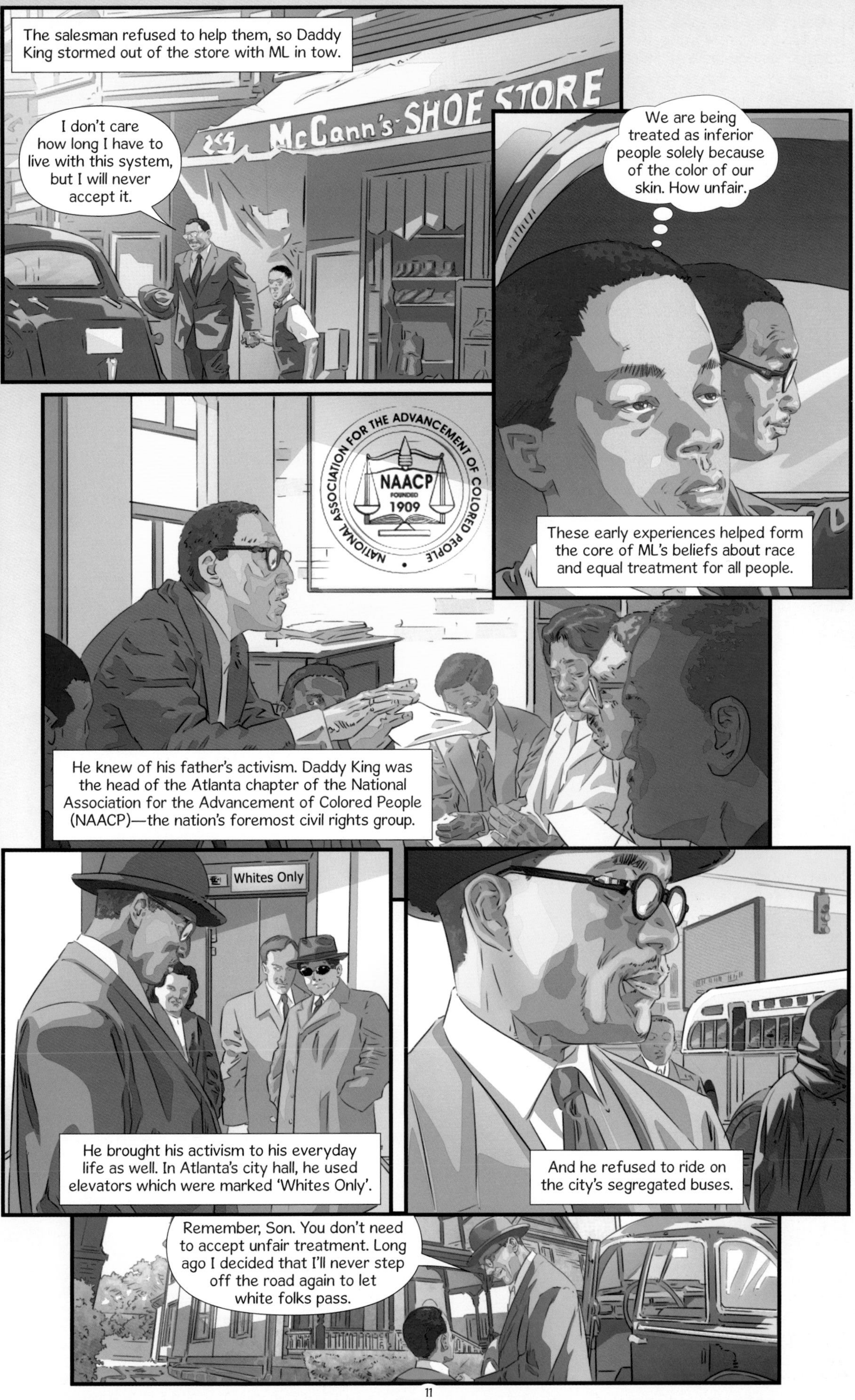
The salesman refused to help them, so Daddy King stormed out of the store with ML in tow.
McCann's SHOE STORE
I don't care how long I have to live with this system, but I will never accept it.
We are being treated as inferior people solely because of the color of our skin. How unfair.
These early experiences helped form the core of ML's beliefs about race and equal treatment for all people.
NATIONAL ASSOCIATION FOR THE ADVANCEMENT OF COLORED PEOPLE
NAACP
FOUNDED
1909
He knew of his father's activism. Daddy King was the head of the Atlanta chapter of the National Association for the Advancement of Colored People (NAACP)—the nation's foremost civil rights group.
Whites Only
He brought his activism to his everyday life as well. In Atlanta's city hall, he used elevators which were marked 'Whites Only'.
And he refused to ride on the city's segregated buses.
Remember, Son. You don't need to accept unfair treatment. Long ago I decided that I'll never step off the road again to let white folks pass.

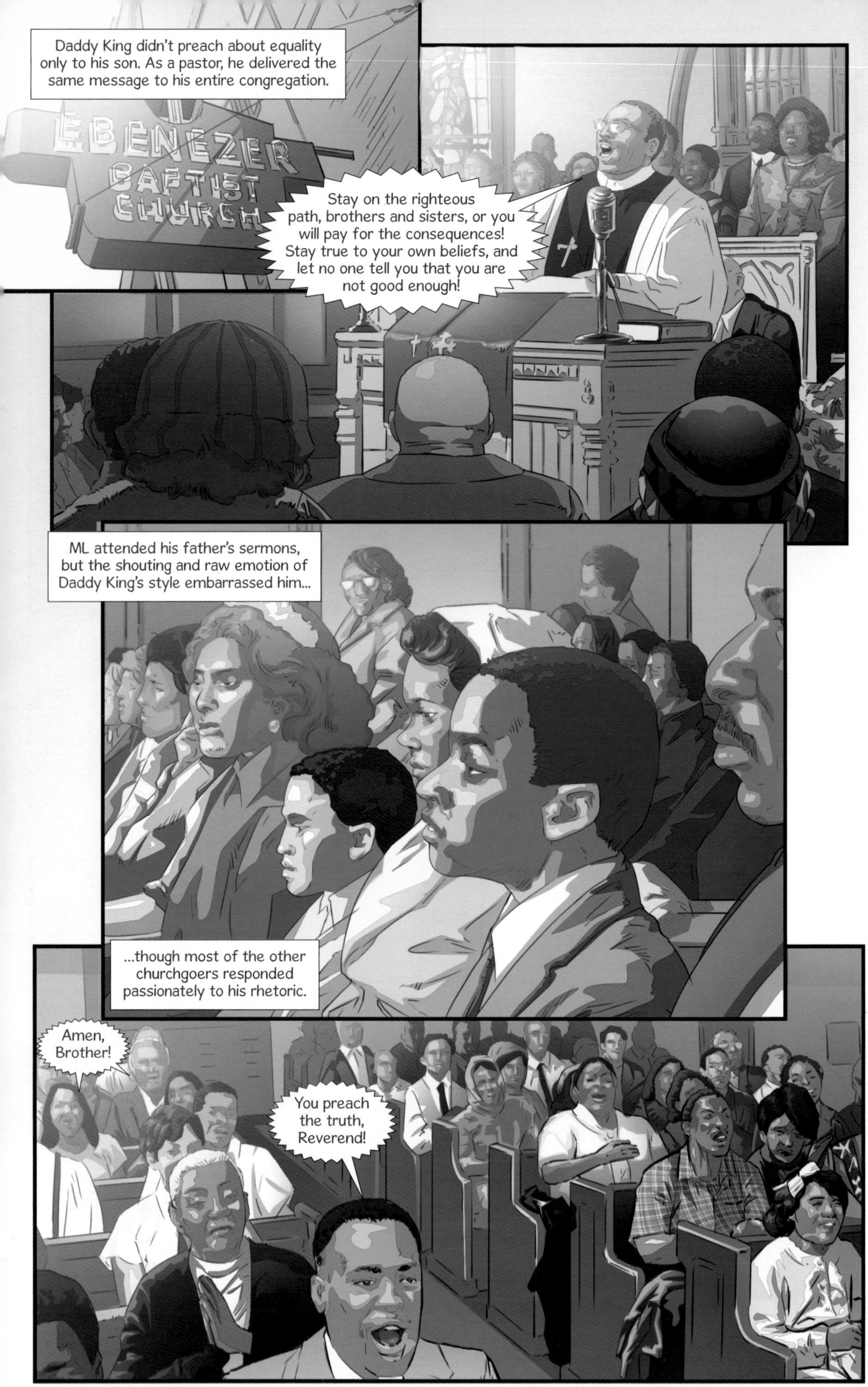
Daddy King didn't preach about equality only to his son. As a pastor, he delivered the same message to his entire congregation.
EBENEZER BAPTIST CHURCH
Stay on the righteous path, brothers and sisters, or you will pay for the consequences! Stay true to your own beliefs, and let no one tell you that you are not good enough!
ML attended his father's sermons, but the shouting and raw emotion of Daddy King's style embarrassed him...
...though most of the other churchgoers responded passionately to his rhetoric.
Amen, Brother!
You preach the truth, Reverend!

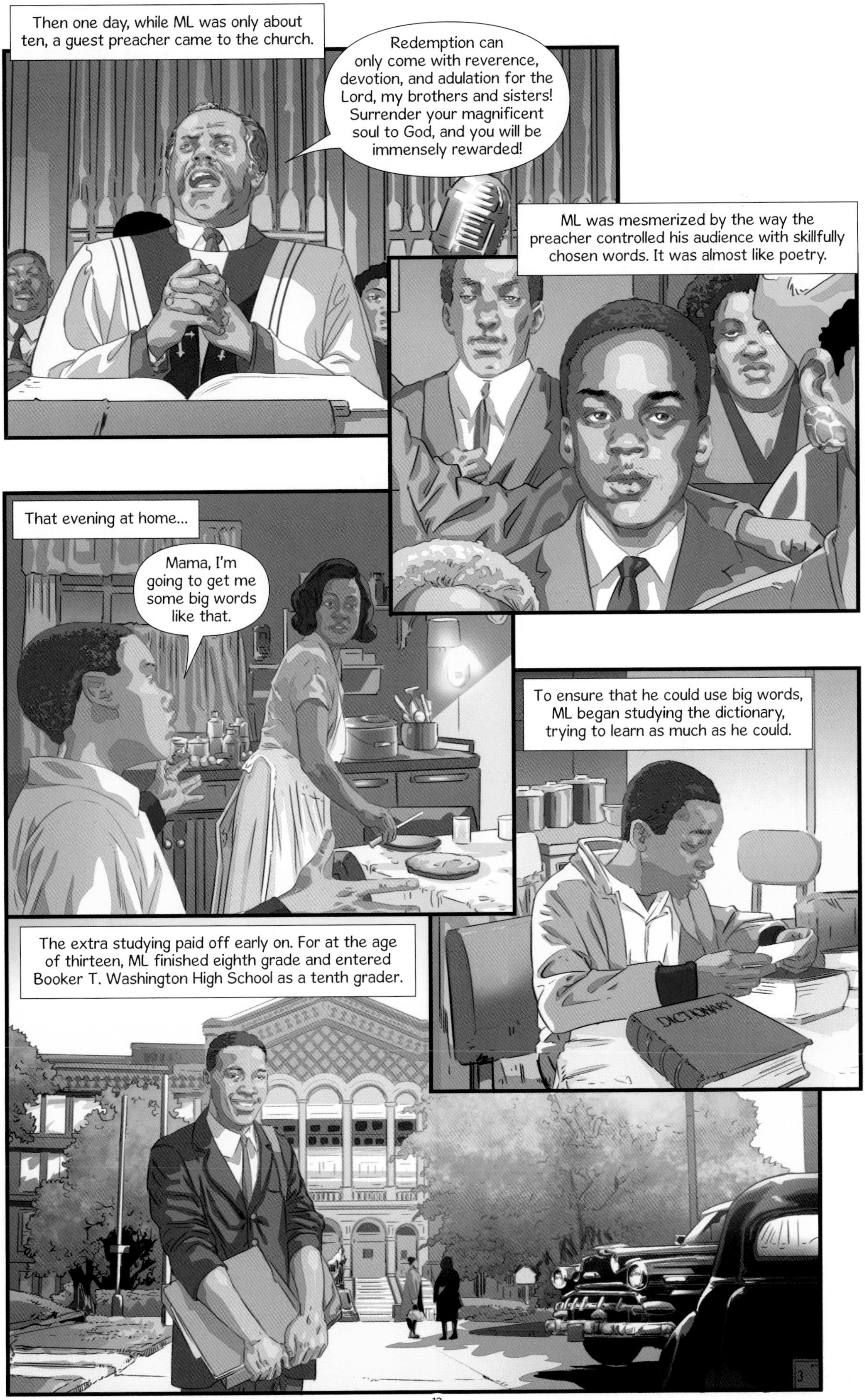
Then one day, while ML was only about ten, a guest preacher came to the church.
Redemption can only come with reverence, devotion, and adulation for the Lord, my brothers and sisters! Surrender your magnificent soul to God, and you will be immensely rewarded!
ML was mesmerized by the way the preacher controlled his audience with skillfully chosen words. It was almost like poetry.
That evening at home...
Mama, I'm going to get me some big words like that.
To ensure that he could use big words, ML began studying the dictionary, trying to learn as much as he could.
DICTIONARY
The extra studying paid off early on. For at the age of thirteen, ML finished eighth grade and entered Booker T. Washington High School as a tenth grader.

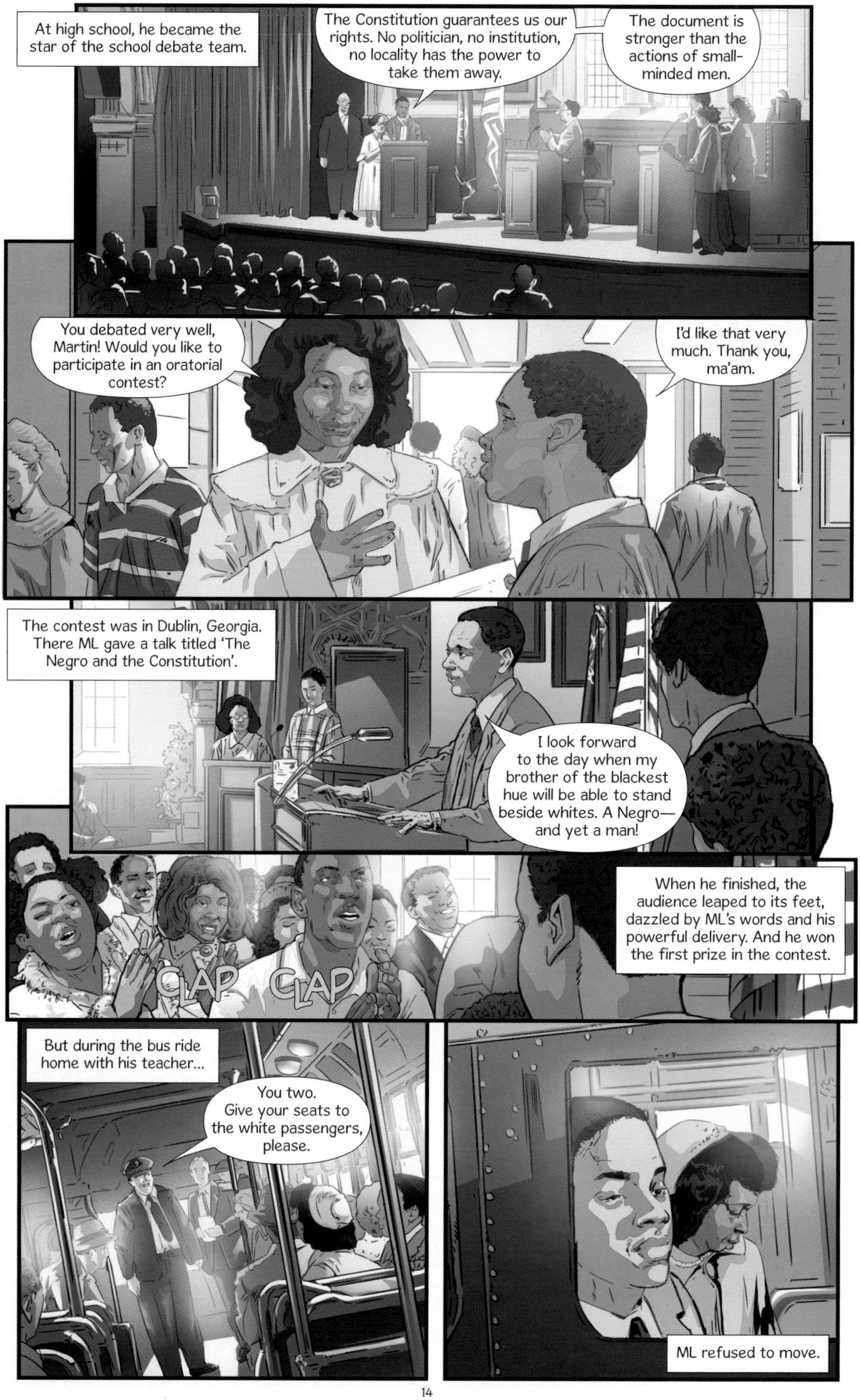
At high school, he became the star of the school debate team.
The Constitution guarantees us our rights. No politician, no institution, no locality has the power to take them away.
The document is stronger than the actions of small-minded men.
You debated very well, Martin! Would you like to participate in an oratorial contest?
I'd like that very much. Thank you, ma'am.
The contest was in Dublin, Georgia. There ML gave a talk titled 'The Negro and the Constitution'.
I look forward to the day when my brother of the blackest hue will be able to stand beside whites. A Negro— and yet a man!
CLAP CLAP
When he finished, the audience leaped to its feet, dazzled by ML's words and his powerful delivery. And he won the first prize in the contest.
But during the bus ride home with his teacher...
You two. Give your seats to the white passengers, please.
ML refused to move.

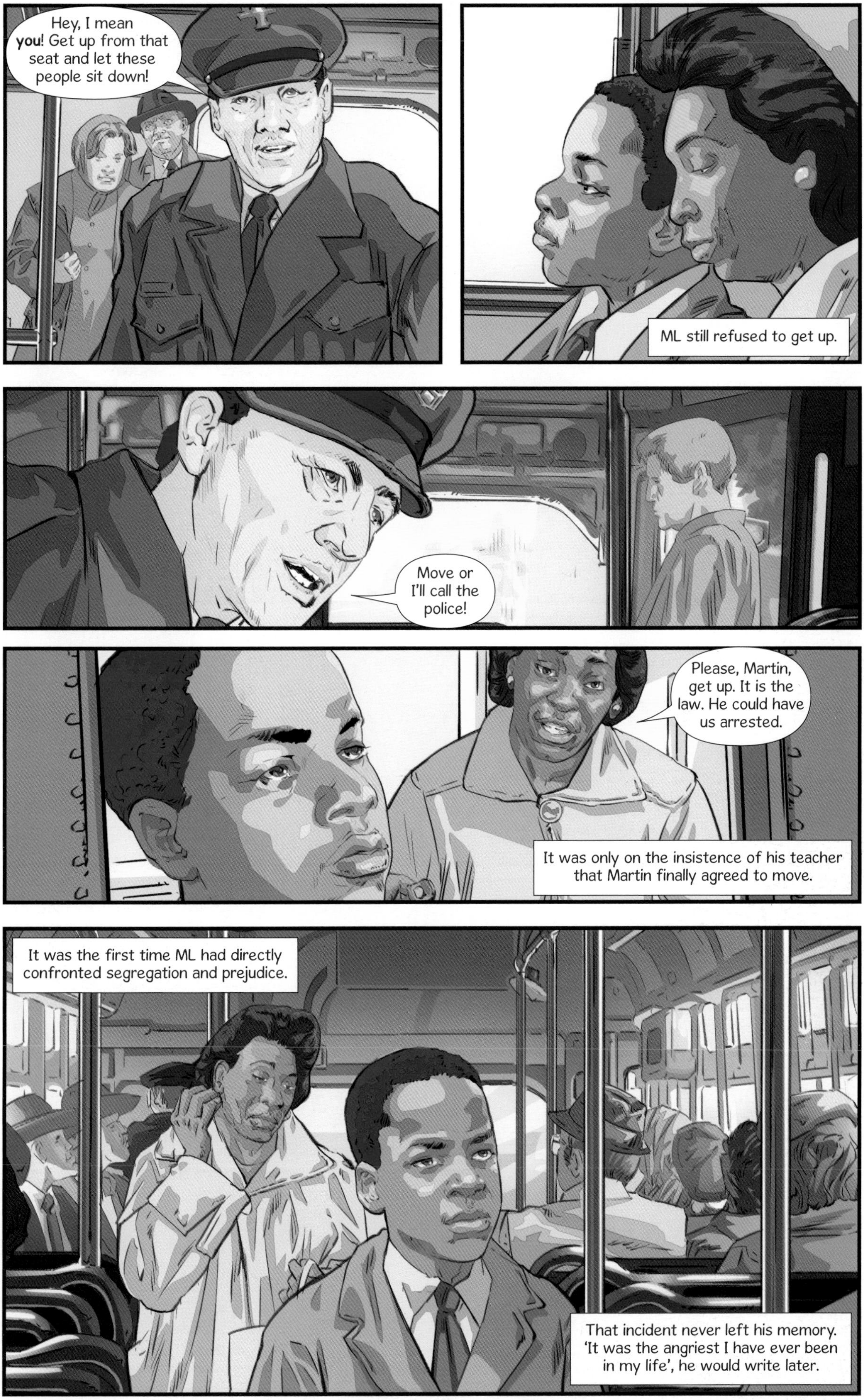
Hey, I mean **you**! Get up from that seat and let these people sit down!
ML still refused to get up.
Move or I'll call the police!
Please, Martin, get up. It is the law. He could have us arrested.
It was only on the insistence of his teacher that Martin finally agreed to move.
It was the first time ML had directly confronted segregation and prejudice.
That incident never left his memory. 'It was the angriest I have ever been in my life', he would write later.

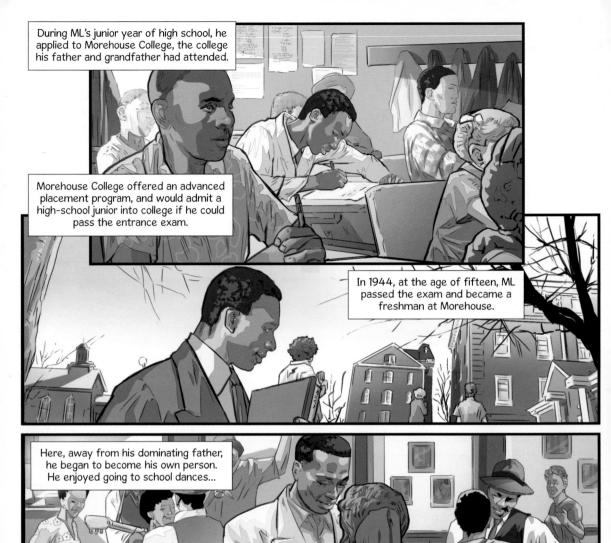

During ML's junior year of high school, he applied to Morehouse College, the college his father and grandfather had attended.

Morehouse College offered an advanced placement program, and would admit a high-school junior into college if he could pass the entrance exam.

In 1944, at the age of fifteen, ML passed the exam and became a freshman at Morehouse.

Here, away from his dominating father, he began to become his own person. He enjoyed going to school dances...

...dating women...

...playing cards...

...and going to parties...

...all things his father disapproved of and considered as sins.

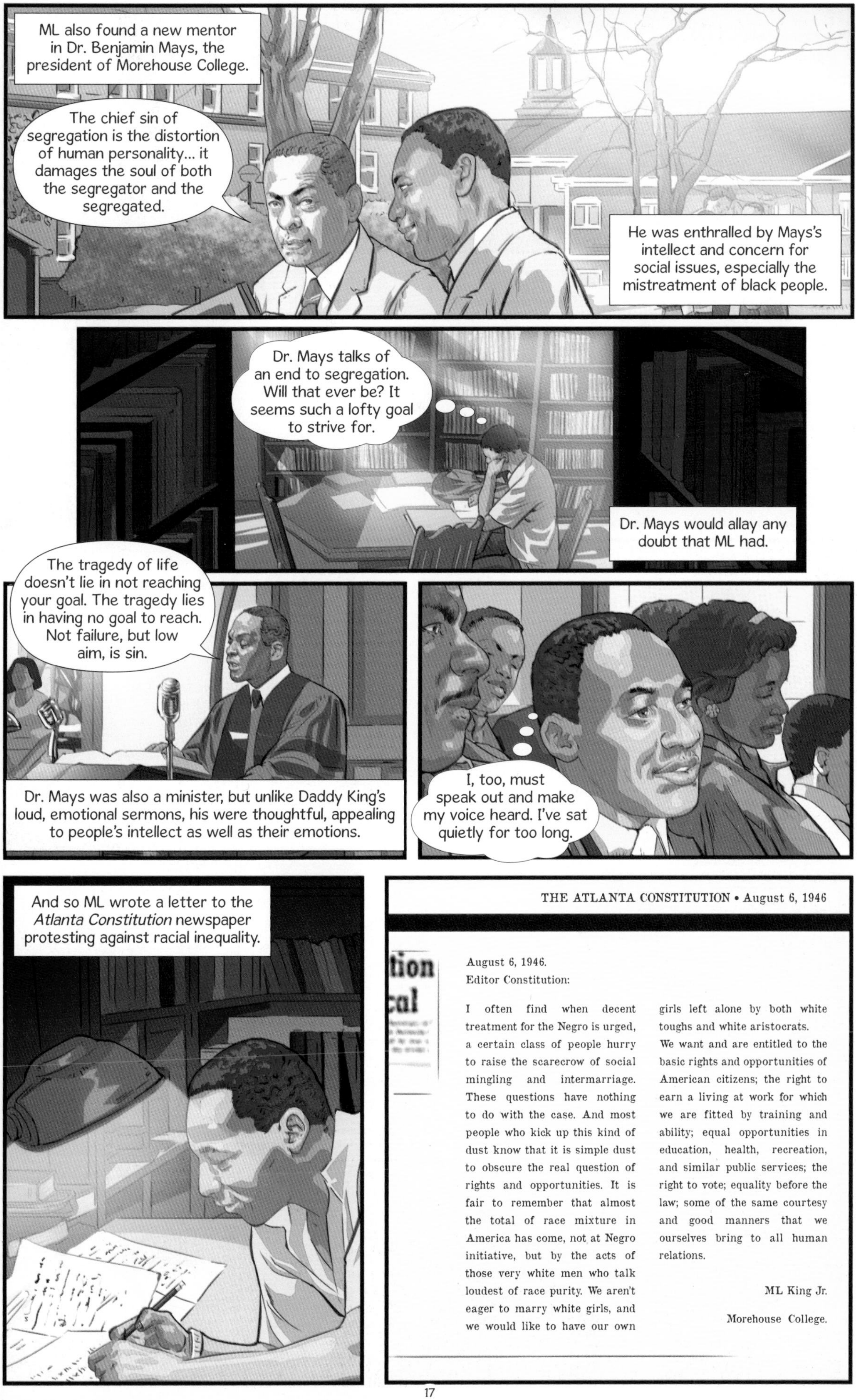
ML also found a new mentor in Dr. Benjamin Mays, the president of Morehouse College.
The chief sin of segregation is the distortion of human personality... it damages the soul of both the segregator and the segregated.
He was enthralled by Mays's intellect and concern for social issues, especially the mistreatment of black people.
Dr. Mays talks of an end to segregation. Will that ever be? It seems such a lofty goal to strive for.
Dr. Mays would allay any doubt that ML had.
The tragedy of life doesn't lie in not reaching your goal. The tragedy lies in having no goal to reach. Not failure, but low aim, is sin.
Dr. Mays was also a minister, but unlike Daddy King's loud, emotional sermons, his were thoughtful, appealing to people's intellect as well as their emotions.
I, too, must speak out and make my voice heard. I've sat quietly for too long.
And so ML wrote a letter to the *Atlanta Constitution* newspaper protesting against racial inequality.
THE ATLANTA CONSTITUTION • August 6, 1946
August 6, 1946.
Editor Constitution:
I often find when decent treatment for the Negro is urged, a certain class of people hurry to raise the scarecrow of social mingling and intermarriage. These questions have nothing to do with the case. And most people who kick up this kind of dust know that it is simple dust to obscure the real question of rights and opportunities. It is fair to remember that almost the total of race mixture in America has come, not at Negro initiative, but by the acts of those very white men who talk loudest of race purity. We aren't eager to marry white girls, and we would like to have our own girls left alone by both white toughs and white aristocrats.
We want and are entitled to the basic rights and opportunities of American citizens; the right to earn a living at work for which we are fitted by training and ability; equal opportunities in education, health, recreation, and similar public services; the right to vote; equality before the law; some of the same courtesy and good manners that we ourselves bring to all human relations.
ML King Jr.
Morehouse College.

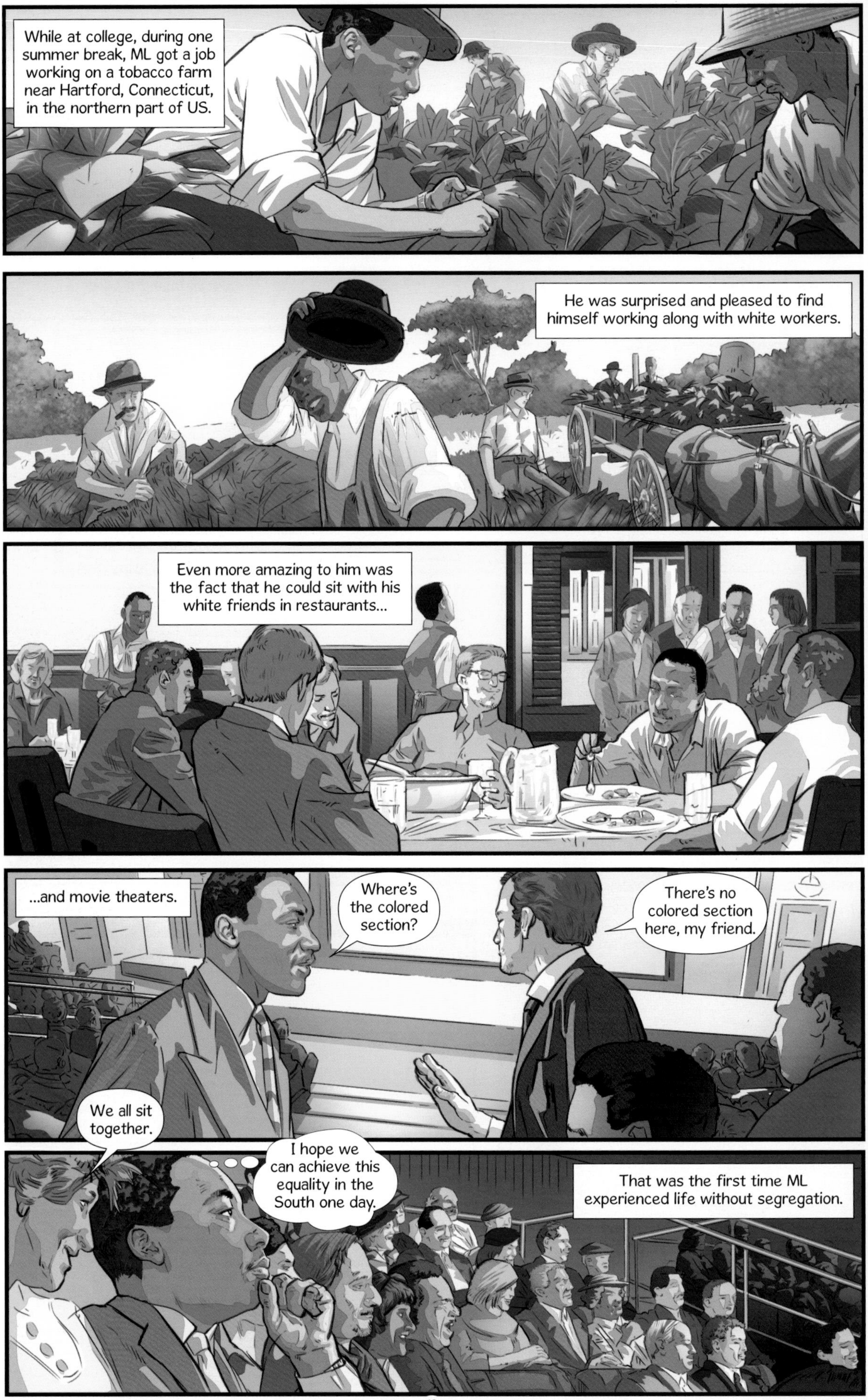
While at college, during one summer break, ML got a job working on a tobacco farm near Hartford, Connecticut, in the northern part of US.
He was surprised and pleased to find himself working along with white workers.
Even more amazing to him was the fact that he could sit with his white friends in restaurants...
...and movie theaters.
Where's the colored section?
There's no colored section here, my friend.
We all sit together.
I hope we can achieve this equality in the South one day.
That was the first time ML experienced life without segregation.

But on the train back to Atlanta, ML got a sharp reminder of the racial inequalities of life in the South.

This is Hartford! All aboard for the train to Washington, DC!

In Hartford, at the start of his trip, ML sat with white passengers.

In Washington, DC, ML changed trains.

WASHIN

COLORED ONLY

On the second train, he was forced to sit in a 'Colored Only' car, segregated from the white passengers.

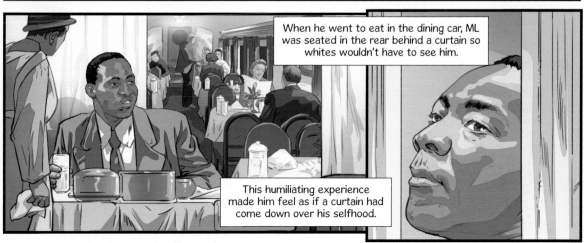

When he went to eat in the dining car, ML was seated in the rear behind a curtain so whites wouldn't have to see him.

This humiliating experience made him feel as if a curtain had come down over his selfhood.

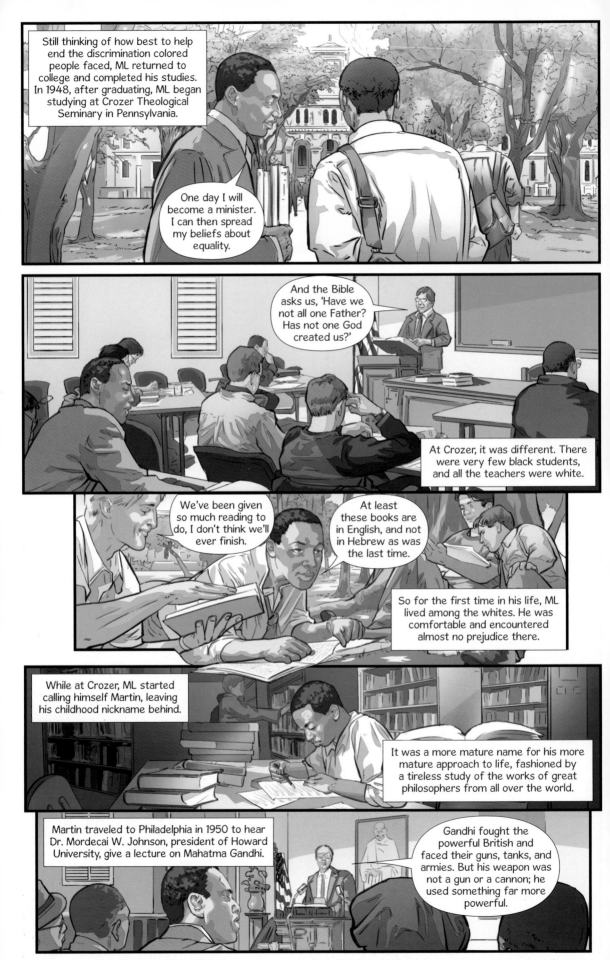

Still thinking of how best to help end the discrimination colored people faced, ML returned to college and completed his studies. In 1948, after graduating, ML began studying at Crozer Theological Seminary in Pennsylvania.

One day I will become a minister. I can then spread my beliefs about equality.

And the Bible asks us, 'Have we not all one Father? Has not one God created us?'

At Crozer, it was different. There were very few black students, and all the teachers were white.

We've been given so much reading to do, I don't think we'll ever finish.

At least these books are in English, and not in Hebrew as was the last time.

So for the first time in his life, ML lived among the whites. He was comfortable and encountered almost no prejudice there.

While at Crozer, ML started calling himself Martin, leaving his childhood nickname behind.

It was a more mature name for his more mature approach to life, fashioned by a tireless study of the works of great philosophers from all over the world.

Martin traveled to Philadelphia in 1950 to hear Dr. Mordecai W. Johnson, president of Howard University, give a lecture on Mahatma Gandhi.

Gandhi fought the powerful British and faced their guns, tanks, and armies. But his weapon was not a gun or a cannon; he used something far more powerful.

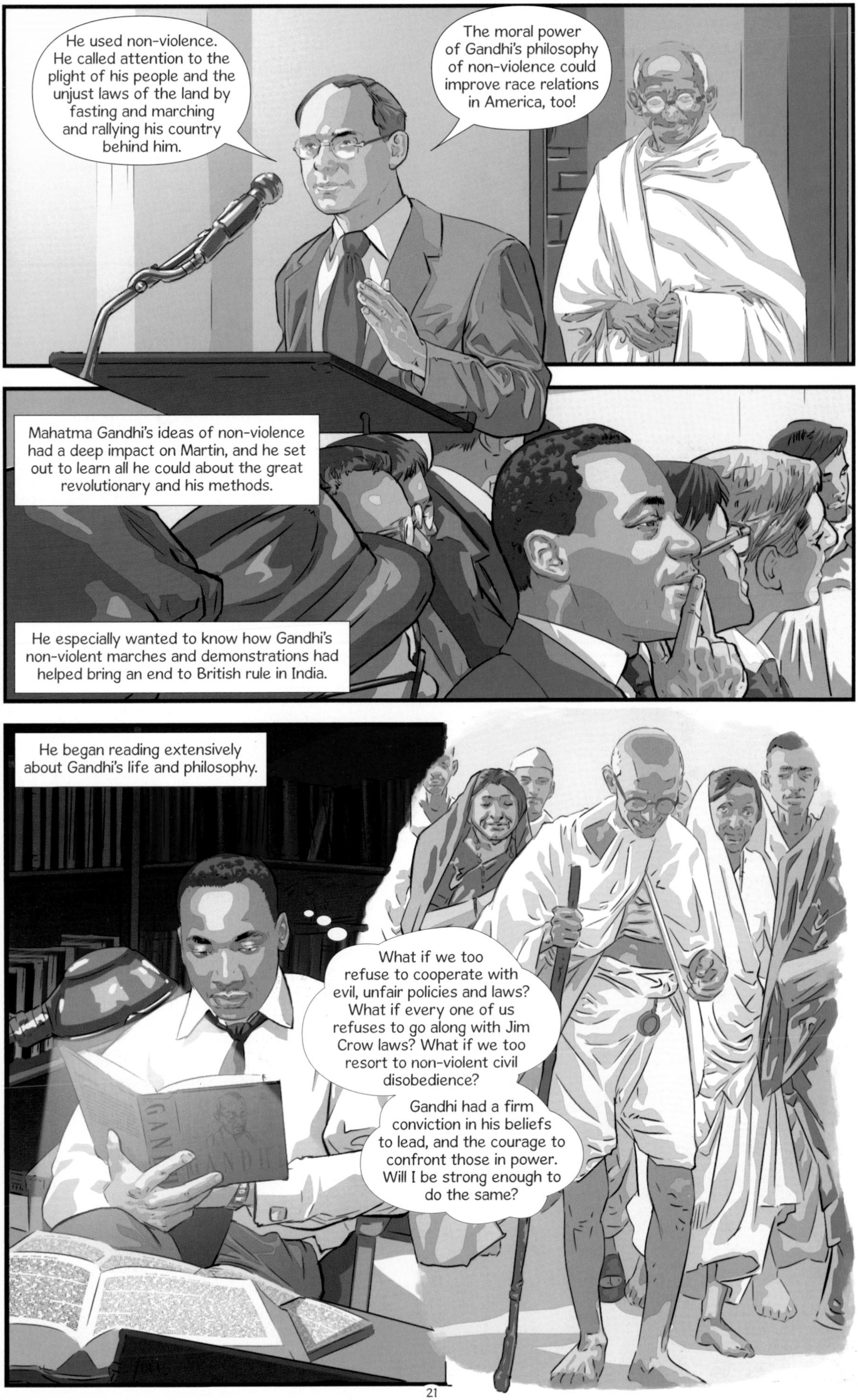

He used non-violence. He called attention to the plight of his people and the unjust laws of the land by fasting and marching and rallying his country behind him.
The moral power of Gandhi's philosophy of non-violence could improve race relations in America, too!
Mahatma Gandhi's ideas of non-violence had a deep impact on Martin, and he set out to learn all he could about the great revolutionary and his methods.
He especially wanted to know how Gandhi's non-violent marches and demonstrations had helped bring an end to British rule in India.
He began reading extensively about Gandhi's life and philosophy.
What if we too refuse to cooperate with evil, unfair policies and laws? What if every one of us refuses to go along with Jim Crow laws? What if we too resort to non-violent civil disobedience?
Gandhi had a firm conviction in his beliefs to lead, and the courage to confront those in power. Will I be strong enough to do the same?

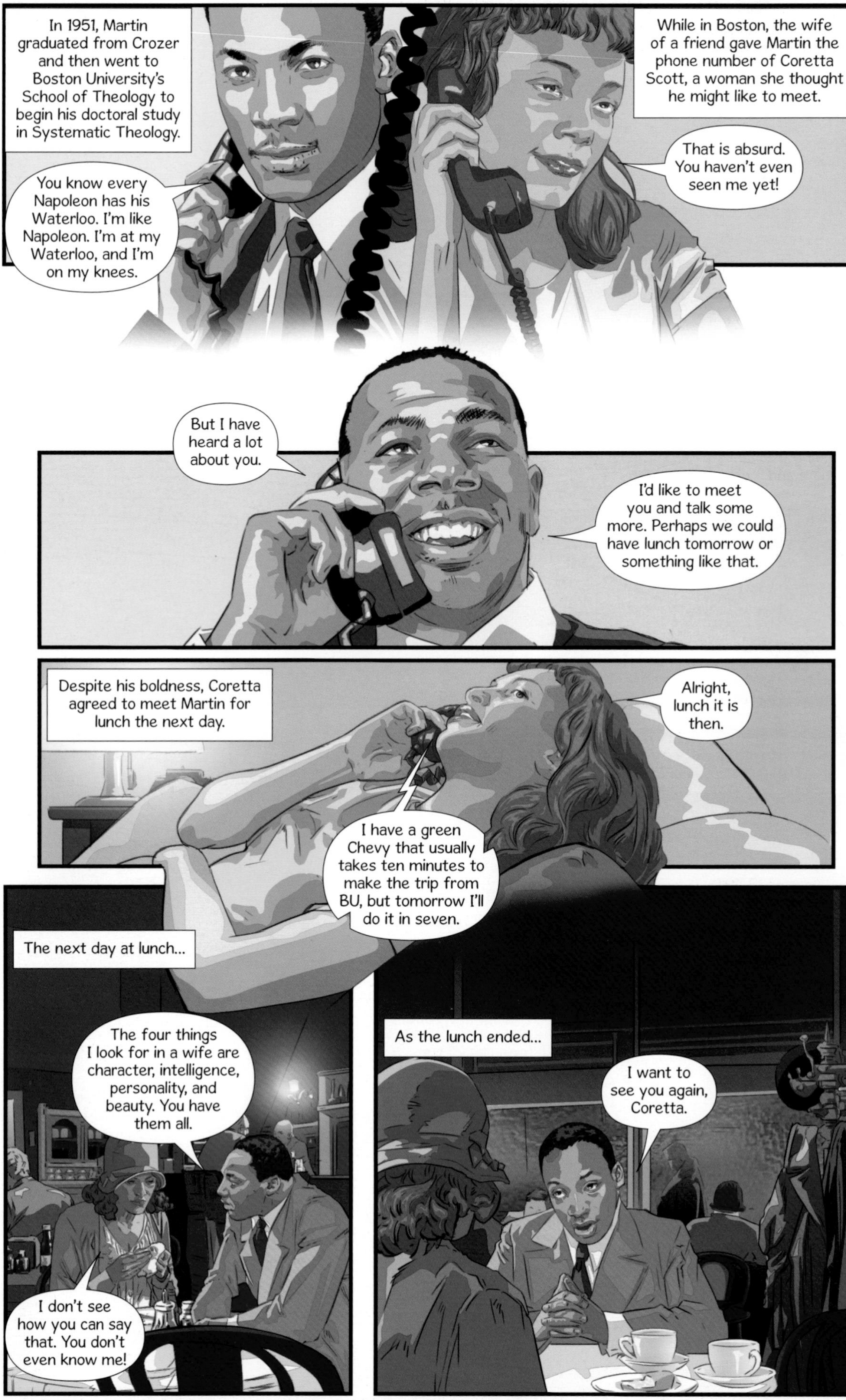
In 1951, Martin graduated from Crozer and then went to Boston University's School of Theology to begin his doctoral study in Systematic Theology.
While in Boston, the wife of a friend gave Martin the phone number of Coretta Scott, a woman she thought he might like to meet.
You know every Napoleon has his Waterloo. I'm like Napoleon. I'm at my Waterloo, and I'm on my knees.
That is absurd. You haven't even seen me yet!
But I have heard a lot about you.
I'd like to meet you and talk some more. Perhaps we could have lunch tomorrow or something like that.
Despite his boldness, Coretta agreed to meet Martin for lunch the next day.
Alright, lunch it is then.
I have a green Chevy that usually takes ten minutes to make the trip from BU, but tomorrow I'll do it in seven.
The next day at lunch...
The four things I look for in a wife are character, intelligence, personality, and beauty. You have them all.
I don't see how you can say that. You don't even know me!
As the lunch ended...
I want to see you again, Coretta.

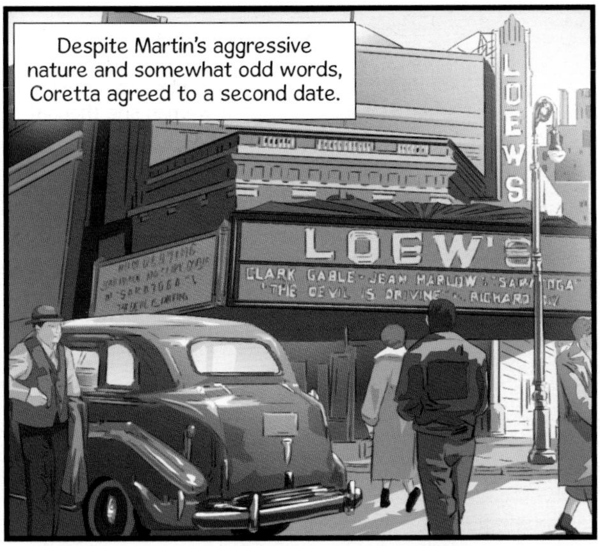
Despite Martin's aggressive nature and somewhat odd words, Coretta agreed to a second date.
LOEWS
LOEW'S

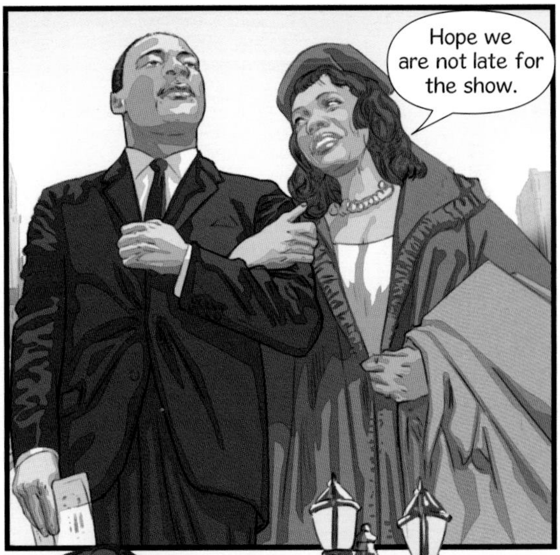
Hope we are not late for the show.

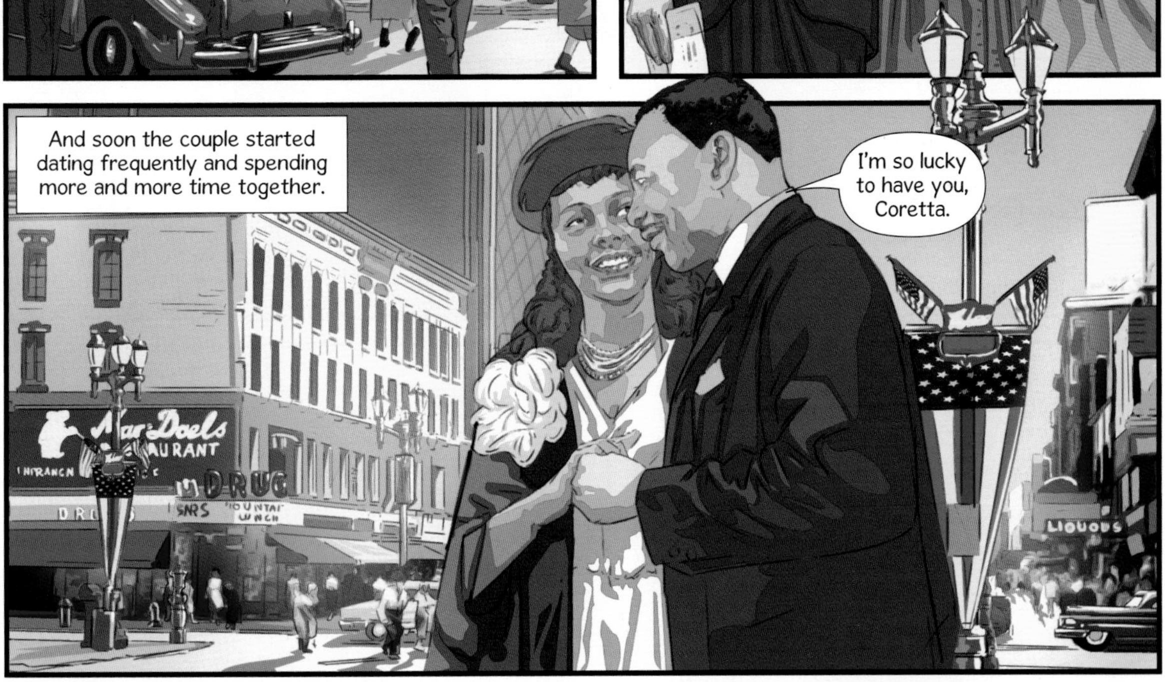
And soon the couple started dating frequently and spending more and more time together.
I'm so lucky to have you, Coretta.
DRUG

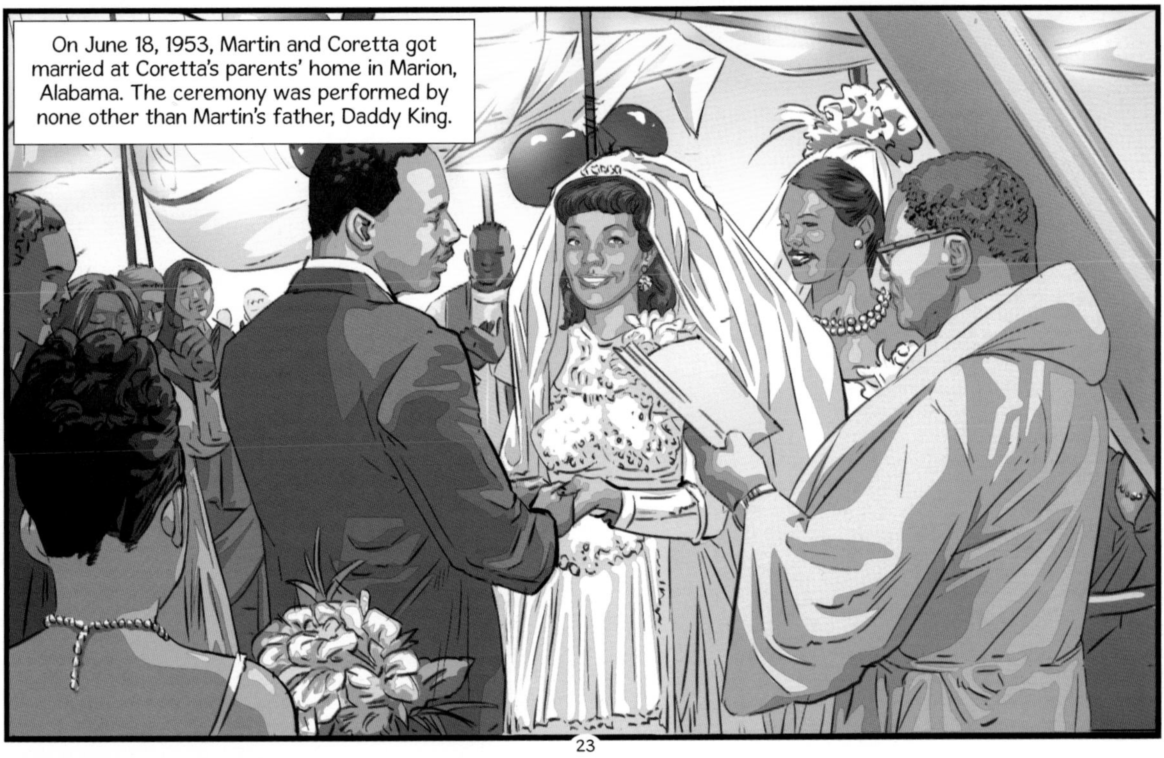
On June 18, 1953, Martin and Coretta got married at Coretta's parents' home in Marion, Alabama. The ceremony was performed by none other than Martin's father, Daddy King.

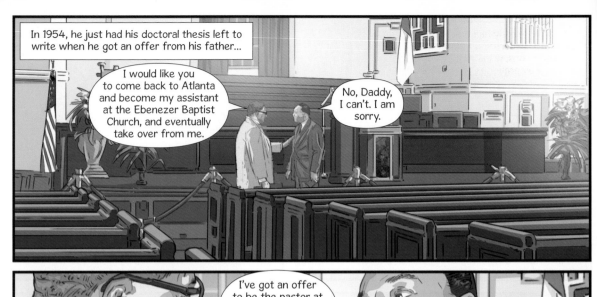

In 1954, he just had his doctoral thesis left to write when he got an offer from his father...

I would like you to come back to Atlanta and become my assistant at the Ebenezer Baptist Church, and eventually take over from me.

No, Daddy, I can't. I am sorry.

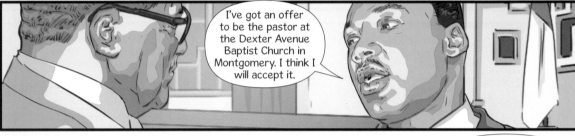

I've got an offer to be the pastor at the Dexter Avenue Baptist Church in Montgomery. I think I will accept it.

That's a big church, with people who think they know more than you do! They'll make you miserable!

But those are exactly the kind of people I need to help in the fight against racial injustice—people with power and influence.

I've decided. I'm going to Montgomery.

Once in Montgomery, Martin visited Ralph D. Abernathy, a local pastor whom he had met while interviewing for the Dexter Avenue job.

I'm glad you got the job, Martin. I'm excited to have someone like you in our community.

And I'm excited to be here, Ralph.

Abernathy would soon become one of Martin's steadfast partners in the Civil Rights Movement.

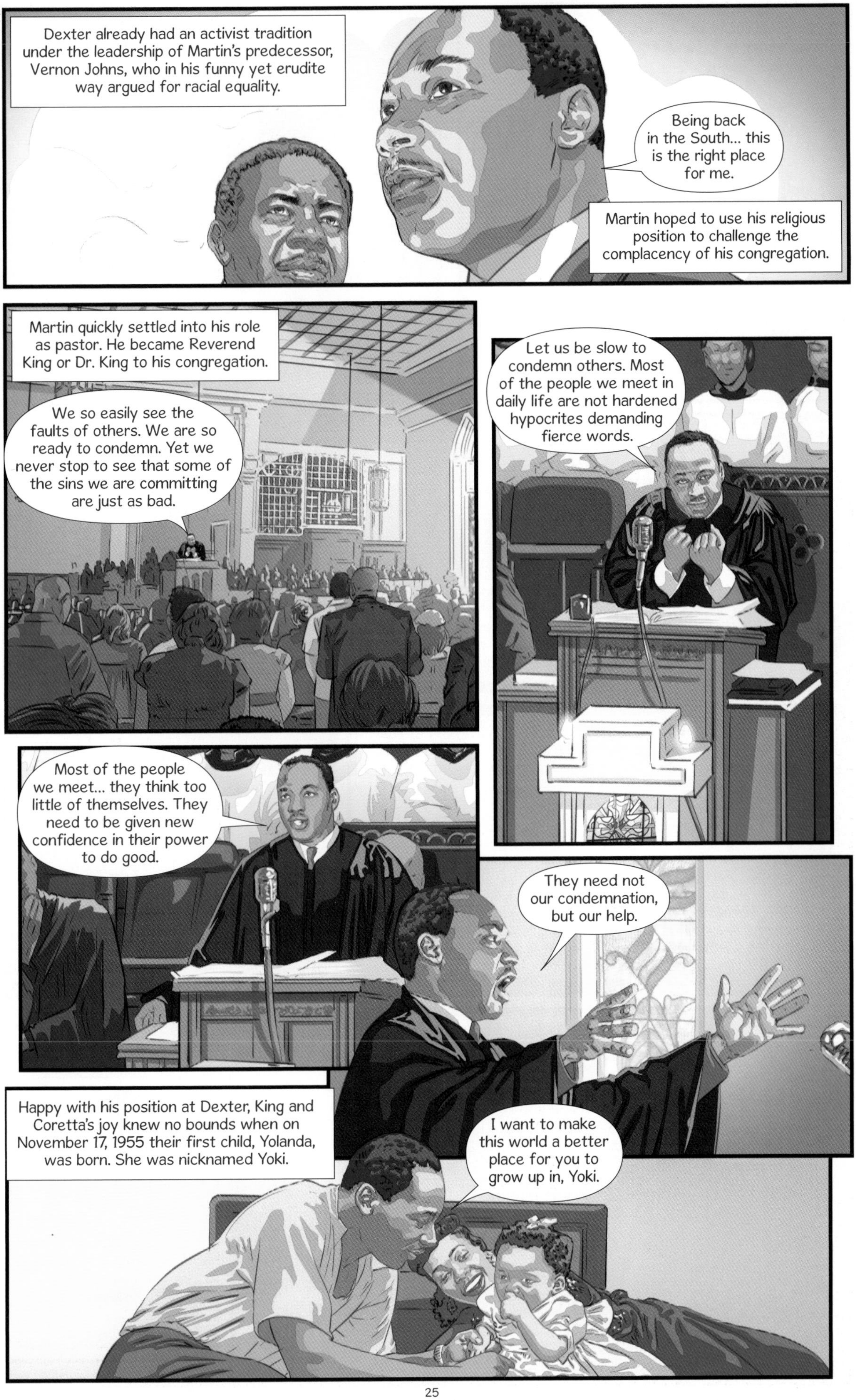

Dexter already had an activist tradition under the leadership of Martin's predecessor, Vernon Johns, who in his funny yet erudite way argued for racial equality.
Being back in the South... this is the right place for me.
Martin hoped to use his religious position to challenge the complacency of his congregation.
Martin quickly settled into his role as pastor. He became Reverend King or Dr. King to his congregation.
We so easily see the faults of others. We are so ready to condemn. Yet we never stop to see that some of the sins we are committing are just as bad.
Let us be slow to condemn others. Most of the people we meet in daily life are not hardened hypocrites demanding fierce words.
Most of the people we meet... they think too little of themselves. They need to be given new confidence in their power to do good.
They need not our condemnation, but our help.
Happy with his position at Dexter, King and Coretta's joy knew no bounds when on November 17, 1955 their first child, Yolanda, was born. She was nicknamed Yoki.
I want to make this world a better place for you to grow up in, Yoki.

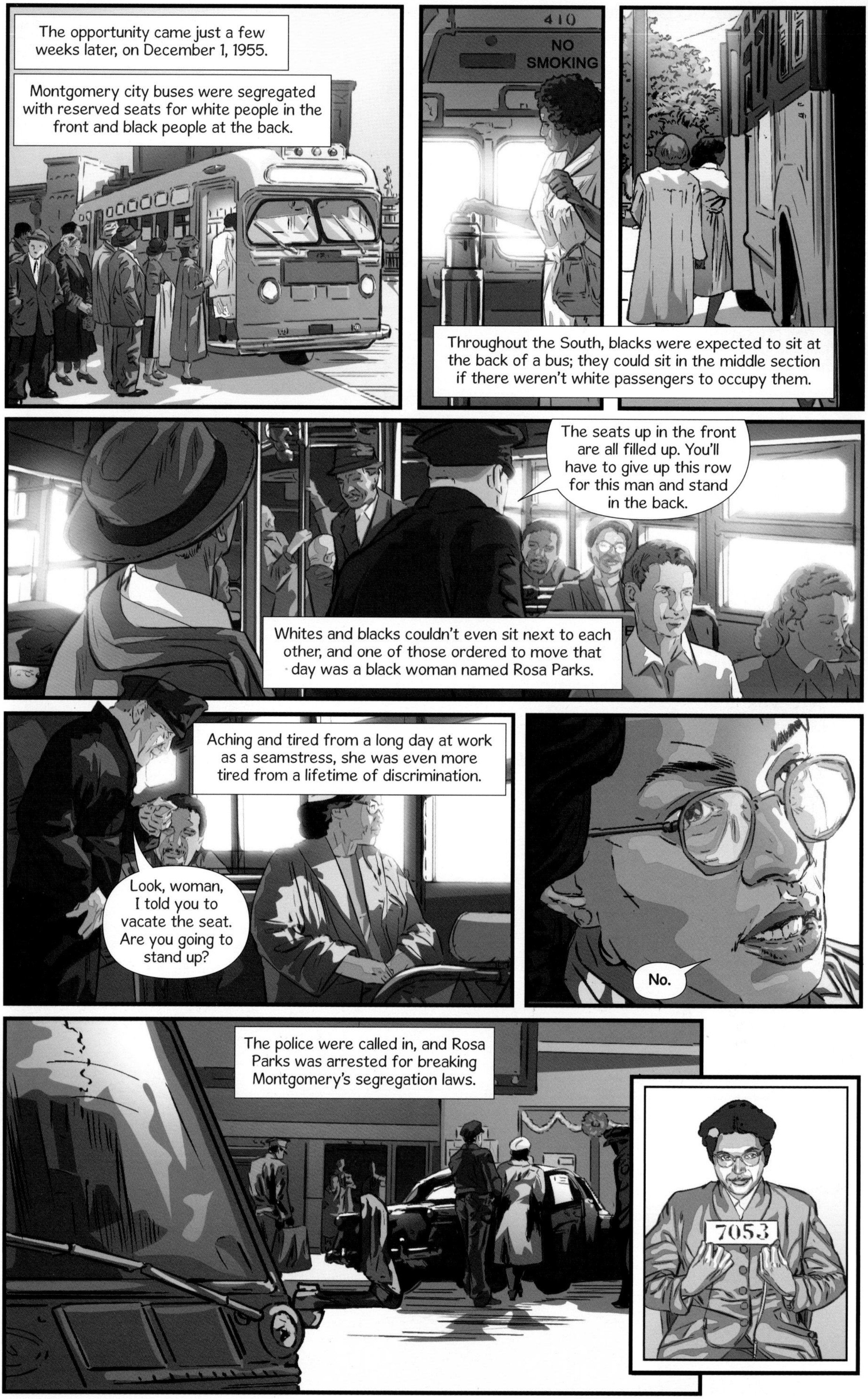
The opportunity came just a few weeks later, on December 1, 1955.
Montgomery city buses were segregated with reserved seats for white people in the front and black people at the back.
410
NO SMOKING
Throughout the South, blacks were expected to sit at the back of a bus; they could sit in the middle section if there weren't white passengers to occupy them.
The seats up in the front are all filled up. You'll have to give up this row for this man and stand in the back.
Whites and blacks couldn't even sit next to each other, and one of those ordered to move that day was a black woman named Rosa Parks.
Aching and tired from a long day at work as a seamstress, she was even more tired from a lifetime of discrimination.
Look, woman, I told you to vacate the seat. Are you going to stand up?
No.
The police were called in, and Rosa Parks was arrested for breaking Montgomery's segregation laws.
7053

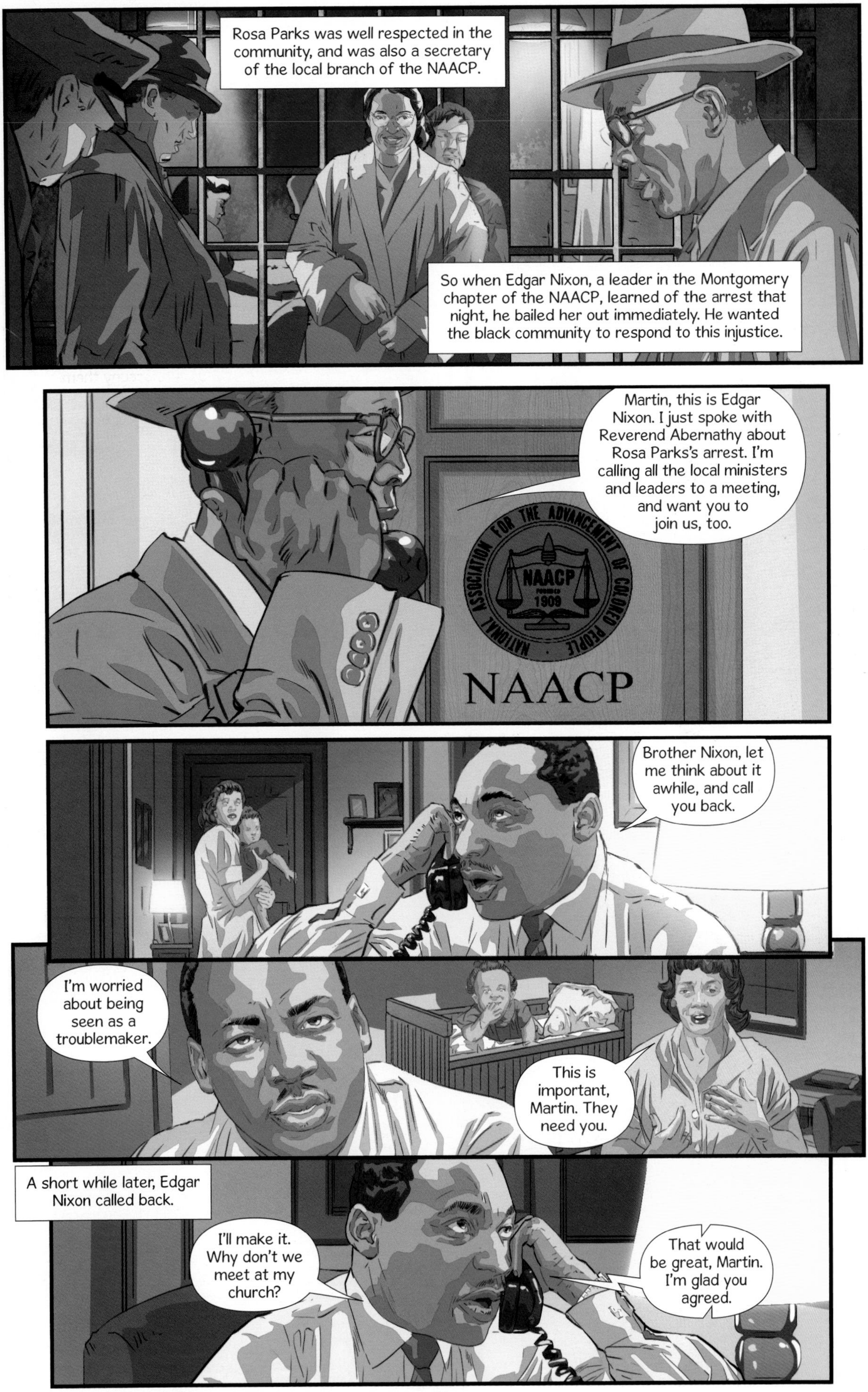
Rosa Parks was well respected in the community, and was also a secretary of the local branch of the NAACP.
So when Edgar Nixon, a leader in the Montgomery chapter of the NAACP, learned of the arrest that night, he bailed her out immediately. He wanted the black community to respond to this injustice.
Martin, this is Edgar Nixon. I just spoke with Reverend Abernathy about Rosa Parks's arrest. I'm calling all the local ministers and leaders to a meeting, and want you to join us, too.
NATIONAL ASSOCIATION FOR THE ADVANCEMENT OF COLORED PEOPLE
NAACP
1909
NAACP
Brother Nixon, let me think about it awhile, and call you back.
I'm worried about being seen as a troublemaker.
This is important, Martin. They need you.
A short while later, Edgar Nixon called back.
I'll make it. Why don't we meet at my church?
That would be great, Martin. I'm glad you agreed.

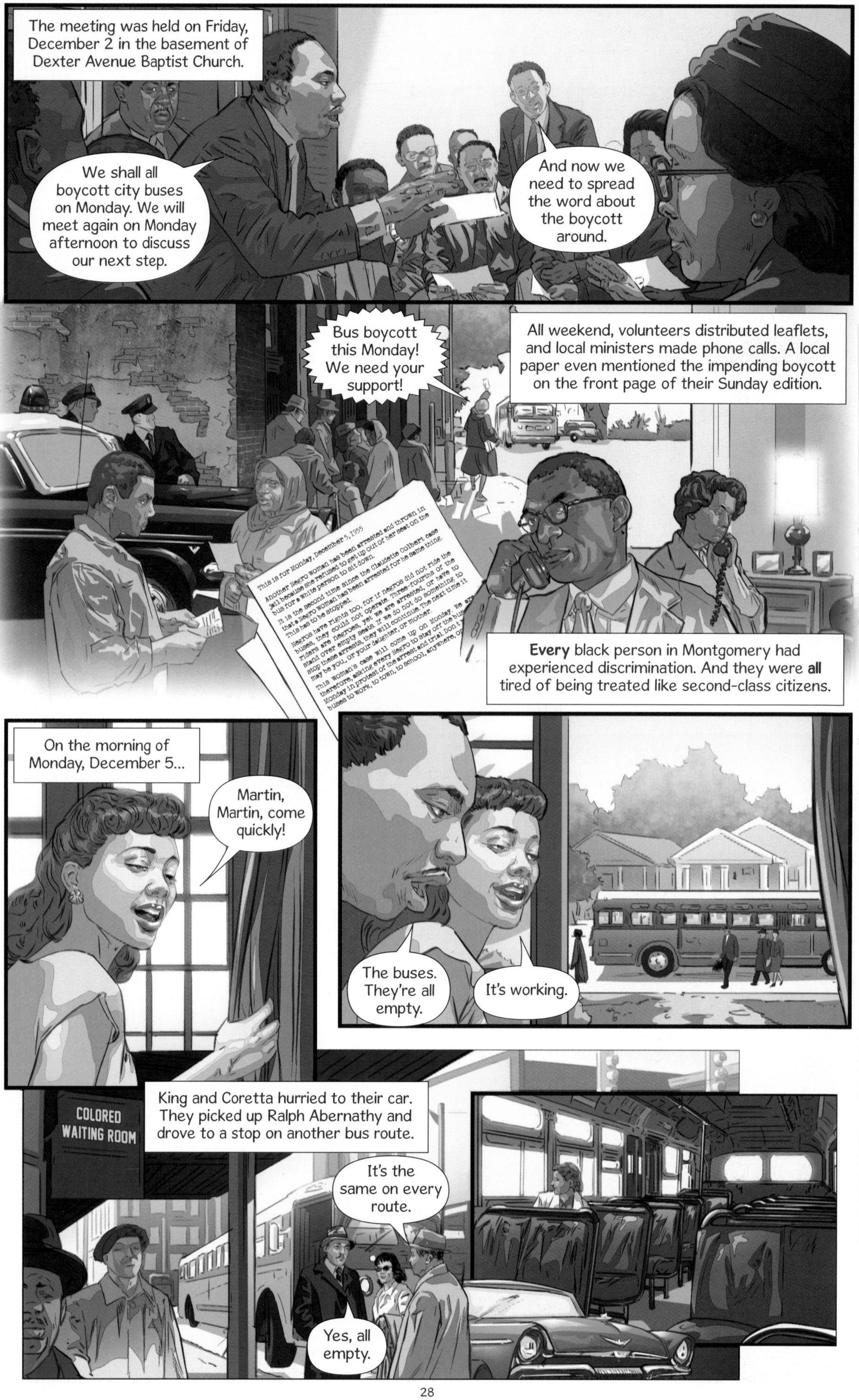

The meeting was held on Friday, December 2 in the basement of Dexter Avenue Baptist Church.
We shall all boycott city buses on Monday. We will meet again on Monday afternoon to discuss our next step.
And now we need to spread the word about the boycott around.
Bus boycott this Monday! We need your support!
All weekend, volunteers distributed leaflets, and local ministers made phone calls. A local paper even mentioned the impending boycott on the front page of their Sunday edition.
This is for Monday, December 5, 1955
Another Negro woman has been arrested and thrown in jail because she refused to get up out of her seat on the bus for a white person to sit down.
It is the second time since the Claudette Colbert case that a Negro woman has been arrested for he same thing. This has to be stopped.
Negros have rights too, for if negros did not ride the buses, they could not operate. Three-fourths of the riders are negroes, yet we are arrested, or have to stand over empty seats. If we do not do something to stop these arrests, they will continue. The next time it may be you, or your daughter, or mother.
This woman's case will come up on Monday. We are
therefore, asking every Negro to stay off the bus
Monday in protest of the arrest and trial. Don't r
buses to work, to town, to school, anywhere, on
Every black person in Montgomery had experienced discrimination. And they were all tired of being treated like second-class citizens.
On the morning of Monday, December 5...
Martin, Martin, come quickly!
The buses. They're all empty.
It's working.
King and Coretta hurried to their car. They picked up Ralph Abernathy and drove to a stop on another bus route.
COLORED WAITING ROOM
It's the same on every route.
Yes, all empty.

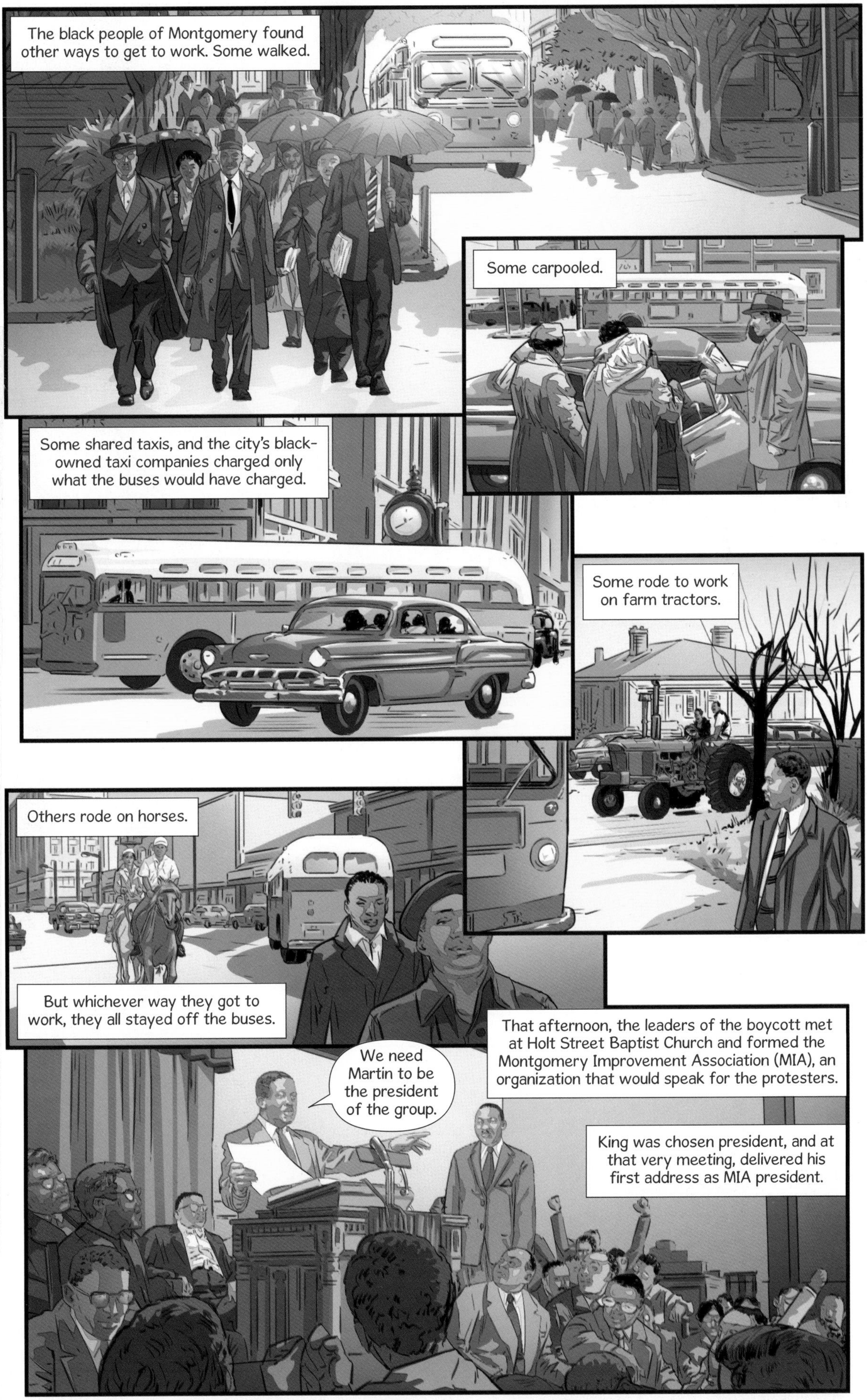

The black people of Montgomery found other ways to get to work. Some walked.
Some carpooled.
Some shared taxis, and the city's black-owned taxi companies charged only what the buses would have charged.
Some rode to work on farm tractors.
Others rode on horses.
But whichever way they got to work, they all stayed off the buses.
That afternoon, the leaders of the boycott met at Holt Street Baptist Church and formed the Montgomery Improvement Association (MIA), an organization that would speak for the protesters.
We need Martin to be the president of the group.
King was chosen president, and at that very meeting, delivered his first address as MIA president.

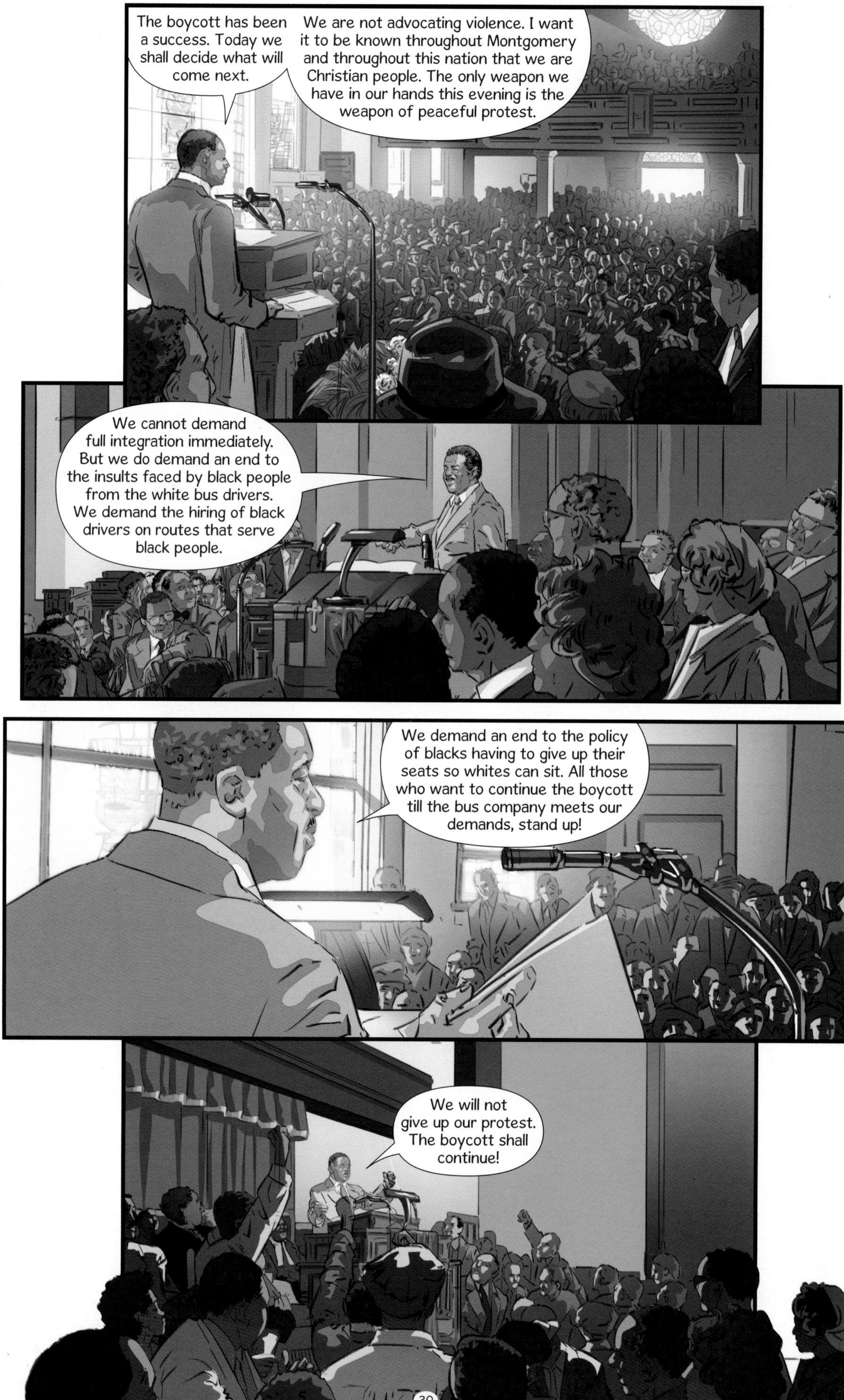
The boycott has been a success. Today we shall decide what will come next.
We are not advocating violence. I want it to be known throughout Montgomery and throughout this nation that we are Christian people. The only weapon we have in our hands this evening is the weapon of peaceful protest.
We cannot demand full integration immediately. But we do demand an end to the insults faced by black people from the white bus drivers. We demand the hiring of black drivers on routes that serve black people.
We demand an end to the policy of blacks having to give up their seats so whites can sit. All those who want to continue the boycott till the bus company meets our demands, stand up!
We will not give up our protest. The boycott shall continue!

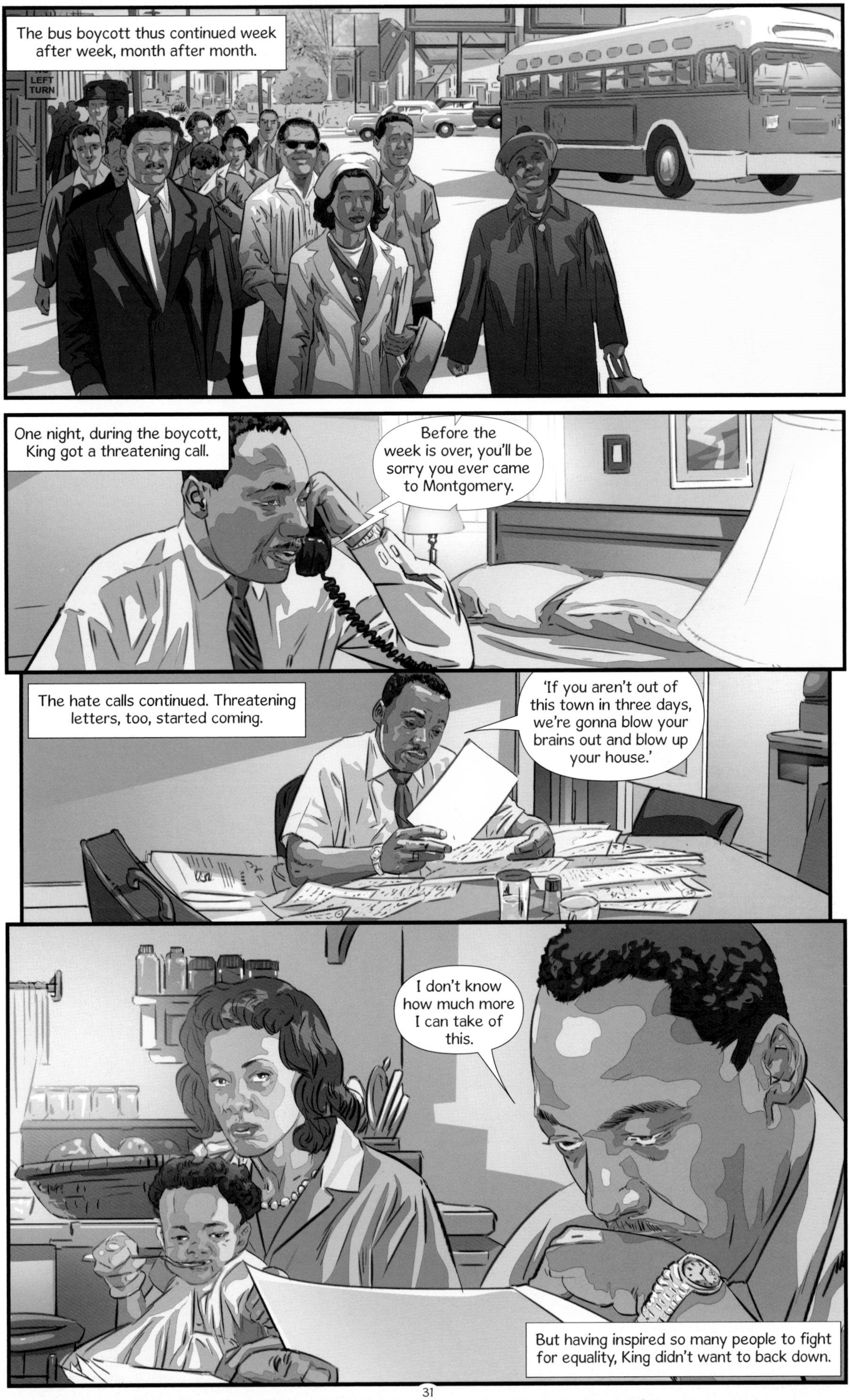
The bus boycott thus continued week after week, month after month.
NO LEFT TURN
One night, during the boycott, King got a threatening call.
Before the week is over, you'll be sorry you ever came to Montgomery.
The hate calls continued. Threatening letters, too, started coming.
'If you aren't out of this town in three days, we're gonna blow your brains out and blow up your house.'
I don't know how much more I can take of this.
But having inspired so many people to fight for equality, King didn't want to back down.

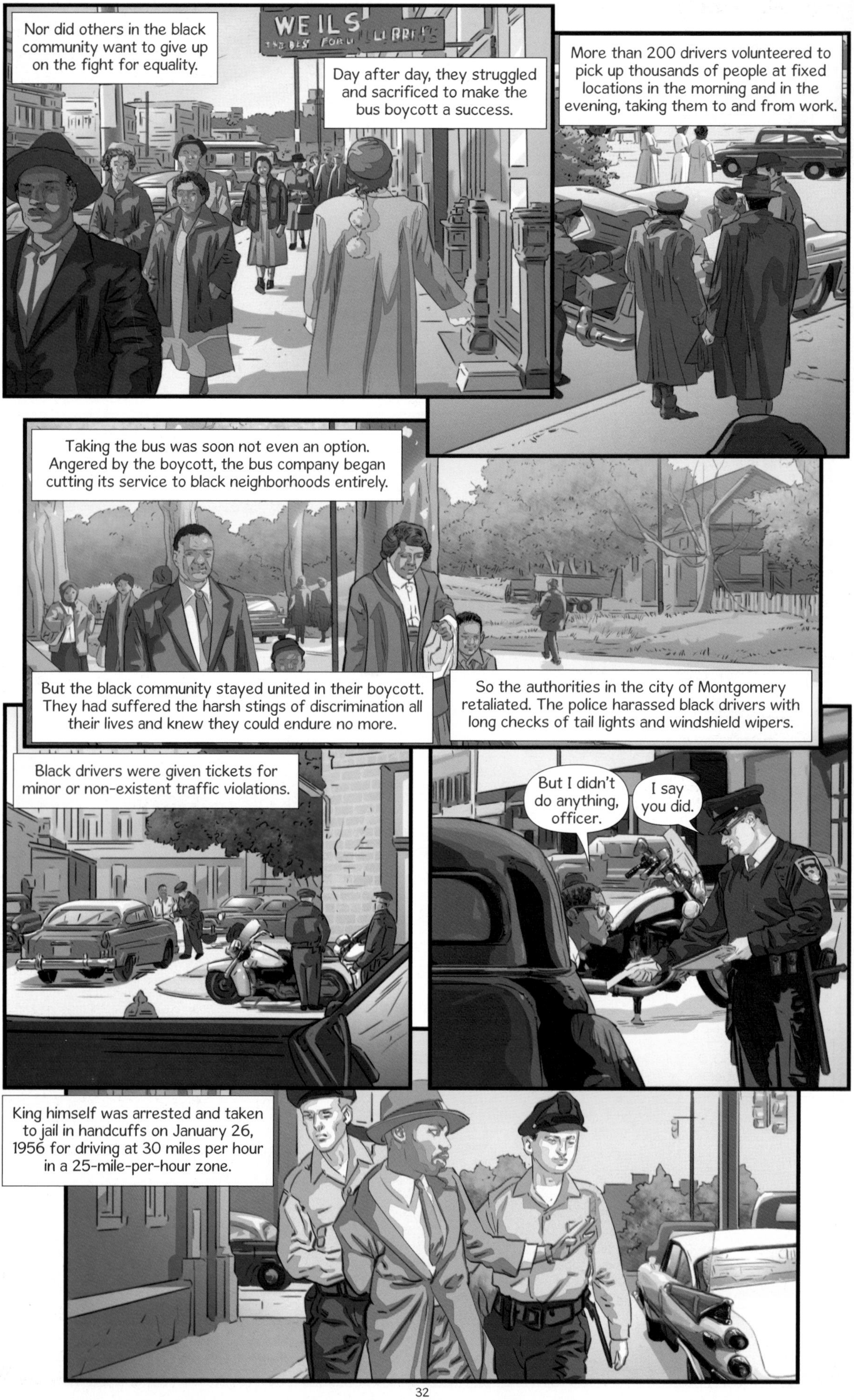

Nor did others in the black community want to give up on the fight for equality.
WEILS
Day after day, they struggled and sacrificed to make the bus boycott a success.
More than 200 drivers volunteered to pick up thousands of people at fixed locations in the morning and in the evening, taking them to and from work.
Taking the bus was soon not even an option. Angered by the boycott, the bus company began cutting its service to black neighborhoods entirely.
But the black community stayed united in their boycott. They had suffered the harsh stings of discrimination all their lives and knew they could endure no more.
So the authorities in the city of Montgomery retaliated. The police harassed black drivers with long checks of tail lights and windshield wipers.
Black drivers were given tickets for minor or non-existent traffic violations.
But I didn't do anything, officer.
I say you did.
King himself was arrested and taken to jail in handcuffs on January 26, 1956 for driving at 30 miles per hour in a 25-mile-per-hour zone.

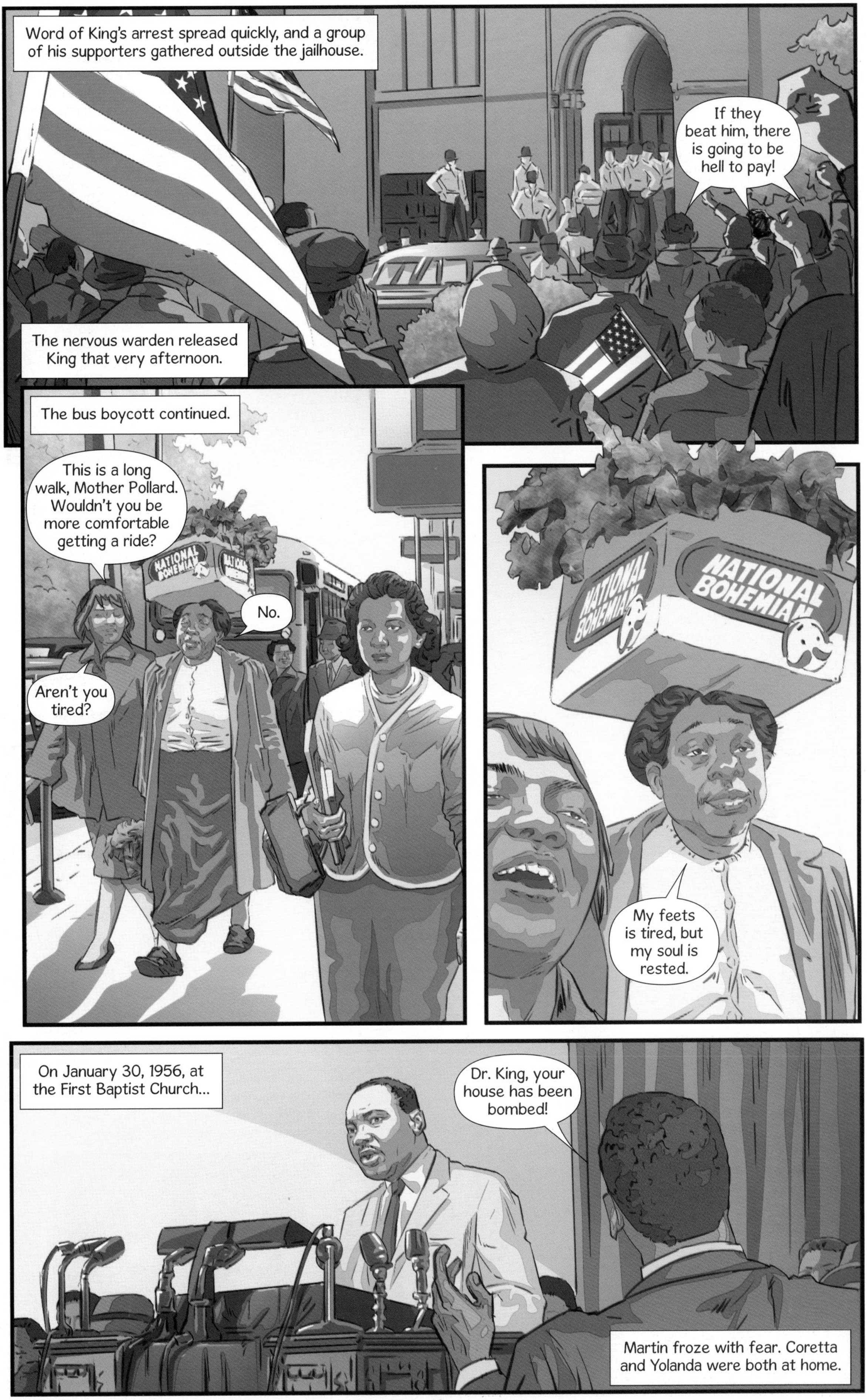
Word of King's arrest spread quickly, and a group of his supporters gathered outside the jailhouse.
If they beat him, there is going to be hell to pay!
The nervous warden released King that very afternoon.
The bus boycott continued.
This is a long walk, Mother Pollard. Wouldn't you be more comfortable getting a ride?
NATIONAL BOHEMIAN
No.
Aren't you tired?
NATIONAL BOHEMIAN
My feets is tired, but my soul is rested.
On January 30, 1956, at the First Baptist Church...
Dr. King, your house has been bombed!
Martin froze with fear. Coretta and Yolanda were both at home.

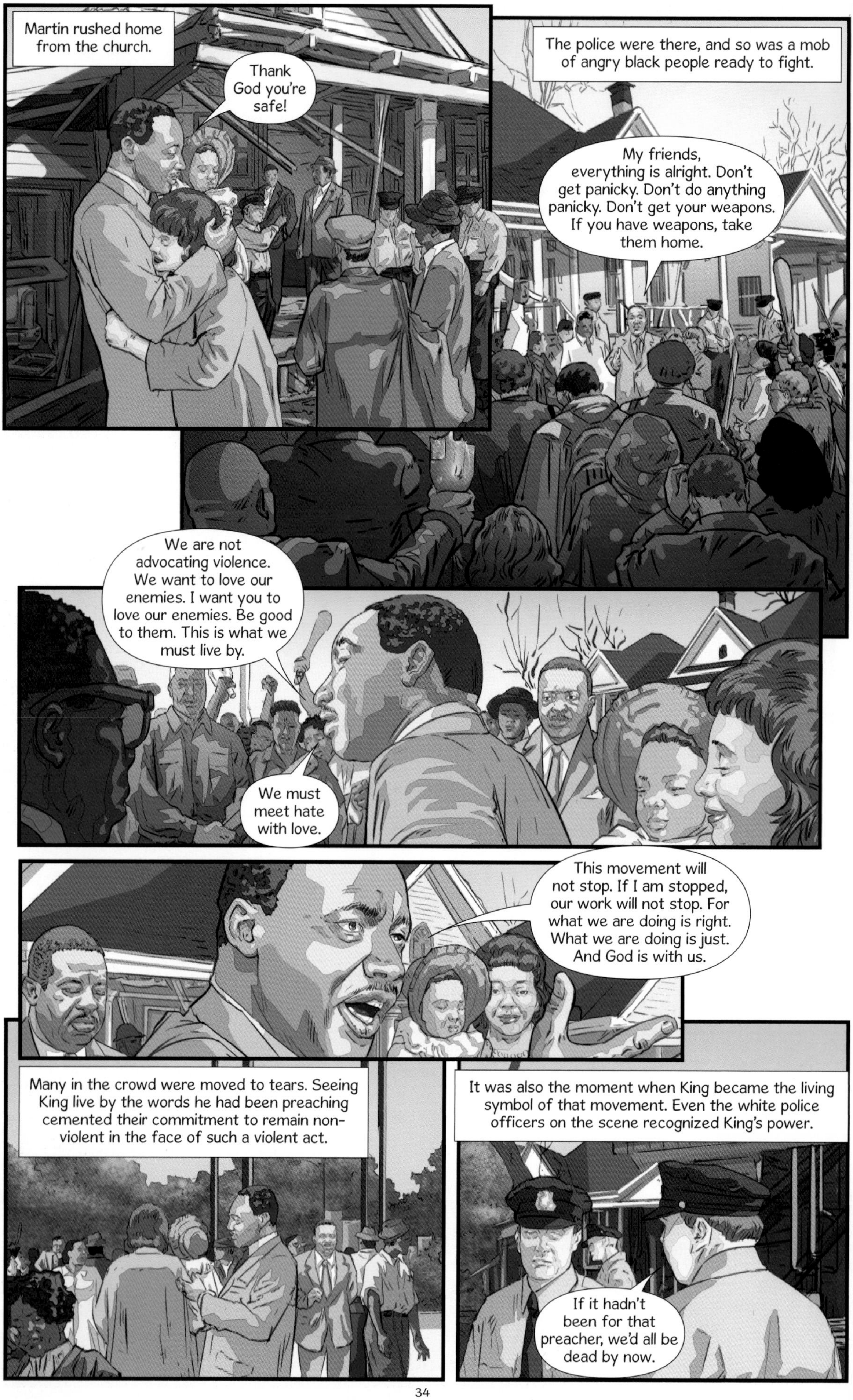
Martin rushed home from the church.
Thank God you're safe!
The police were there, and so was a mob of angry black people ready to fight.
My friends, everything is alright. Don't get panicky. Don't do anything panicky. Don't get your weapons. If you have weapons, take them home.
We are not advocating violence. We want to love our enemies. I want you to love our enemies. Be good to them. This is what we must live by.
We must meet hate with love.
This movement will not stop. If I am stopped, our work will not stop. For what we are doing is right. What we are doing is just. And God is with us.
Many in the crowd were moved to tears. Seeing King live by the words he had been preaching cemented their commitment to remain non-violent in the face of such a violent act.
It was also the moment when King became the living symbol of that movement. Even the white police officers on the scene recognized King's power.
If it hadn't been for that preacher, we'd all be dead by now.

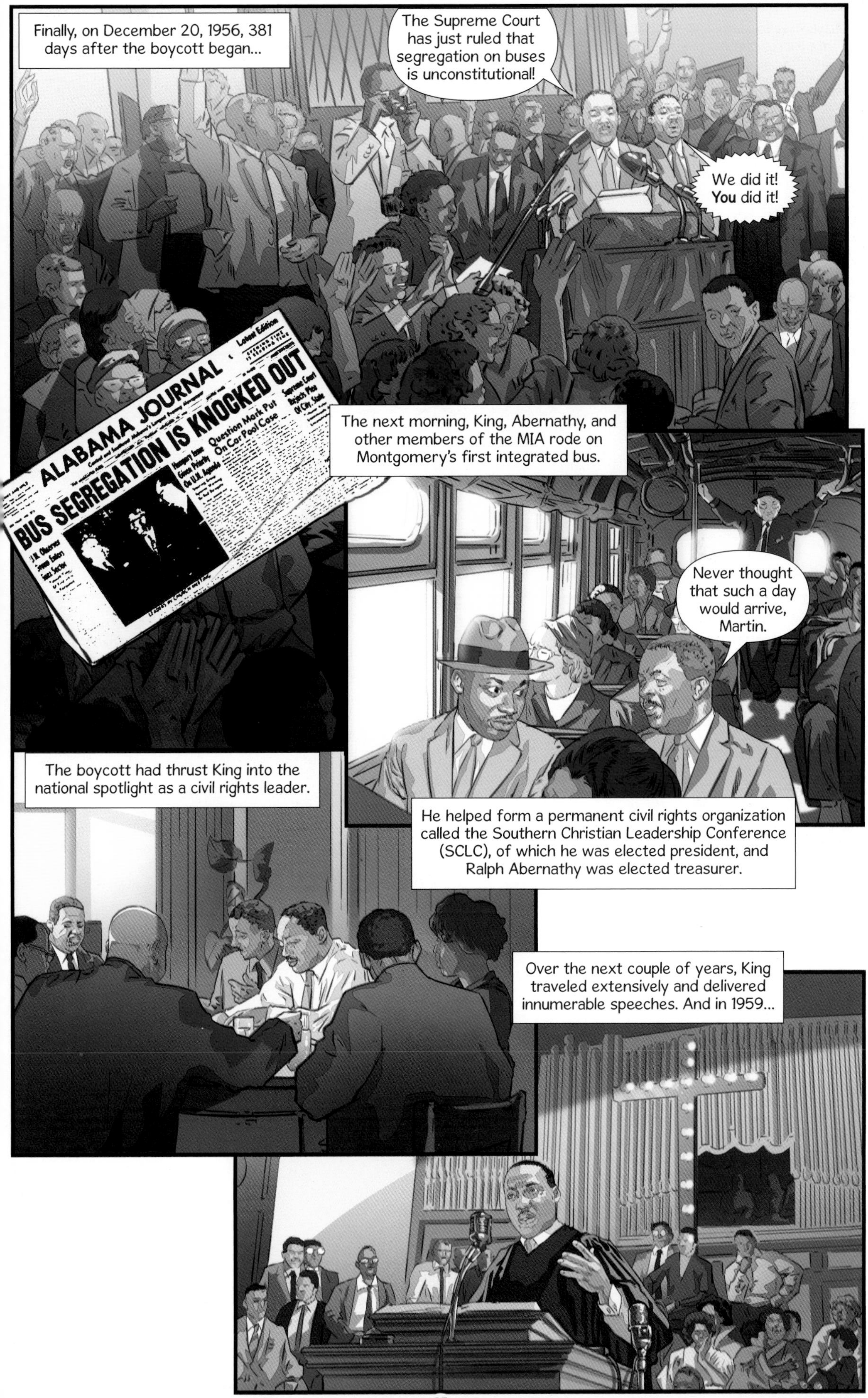

Finally, on December 20, 1956, 381 days after the boycott began...
The Supreme Court has just ruled that segregation on buses is unconstitutional!
We did it! **You** did it!
ALABAMA JOURNAL
Latest Edition
BUS SEGREGATION IS KNOCKED OUT
Question Mark Put On Car Pool Case
The next morning, King, Abernathy, and other members of the MIA rode on Montgomery's first integrated bus.
Never thought that such a day would arrive, Martin.
The boycott had thrust King into the national spotlight as a civil rights leader.
He helped form a permanent civil rights organization called the Southern Christian Leadership Conference (SCLC), of which he was elected president, and Ralph Abernathy was elected treasurer.
Over the next couple of years, King traveled extensively and delivered innumerable speeches. And in 1959...

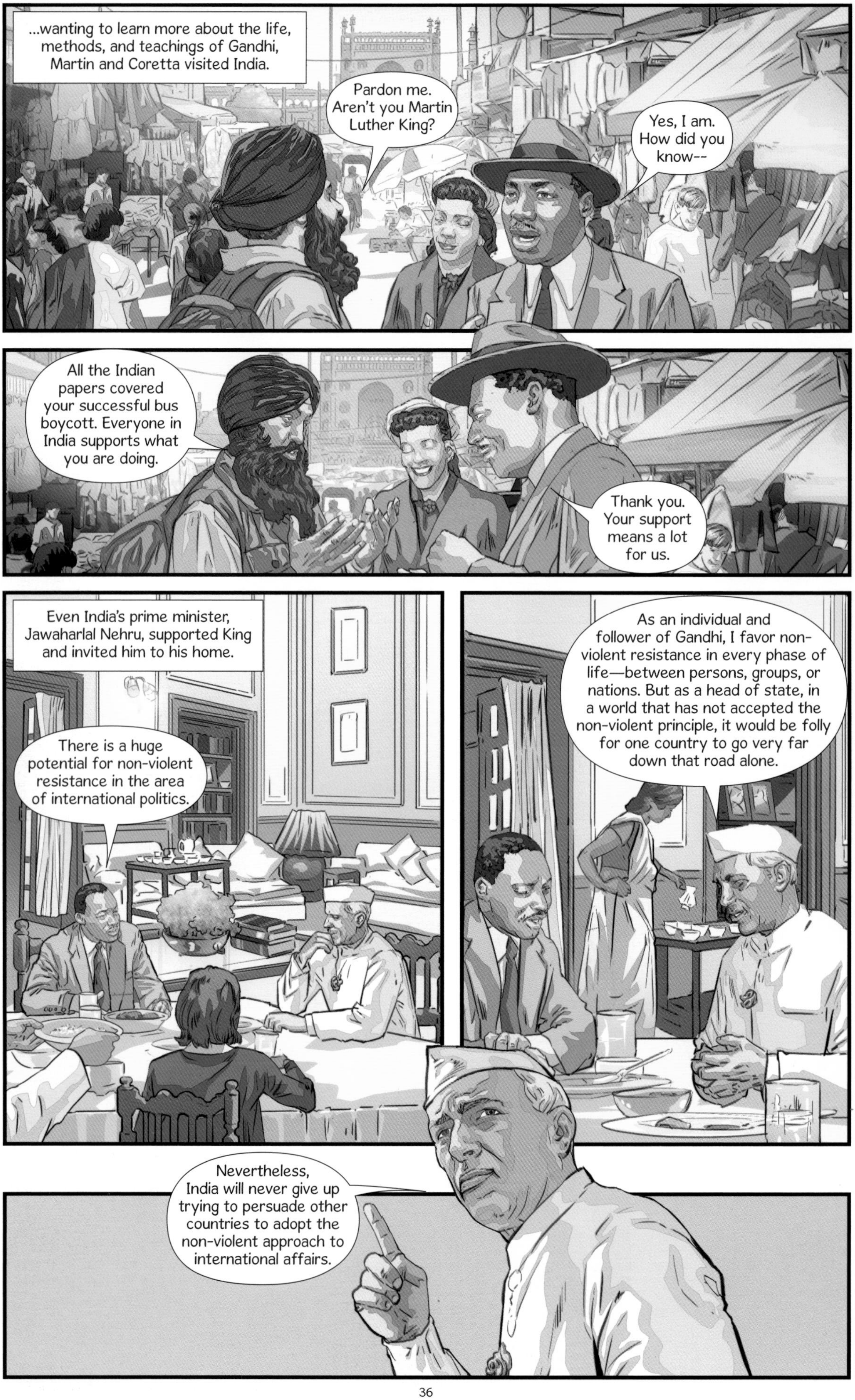
...wanting to learn more about the life, methods, and teachings of Gandhi, Martin and Coretta visited India.
Pardon me. Aren't you Martin Luther King?
Yes, I am. How did you know--
All the Indian papers covered your successful bus boycott. Everyone in India supports what you are doing.
Thank you. Your support means a lot for us.
Even India's prime minister, Jawaharlal Nehru, supported King and invited him to his home.
There is a huge potential for non-violent resistance in the area of international politics.
As an individual and follower of Gandhi, I favor non-violent resistance in every phase of life—between persons, groups, or nations. But as a head of state, in a world that has not accepted the non-violent principle, it would be folly for one country to go very far down that road alone.
Nevertheless, India will never give up trying to persuade other countries to adopt the non-violent approach to international affairs.

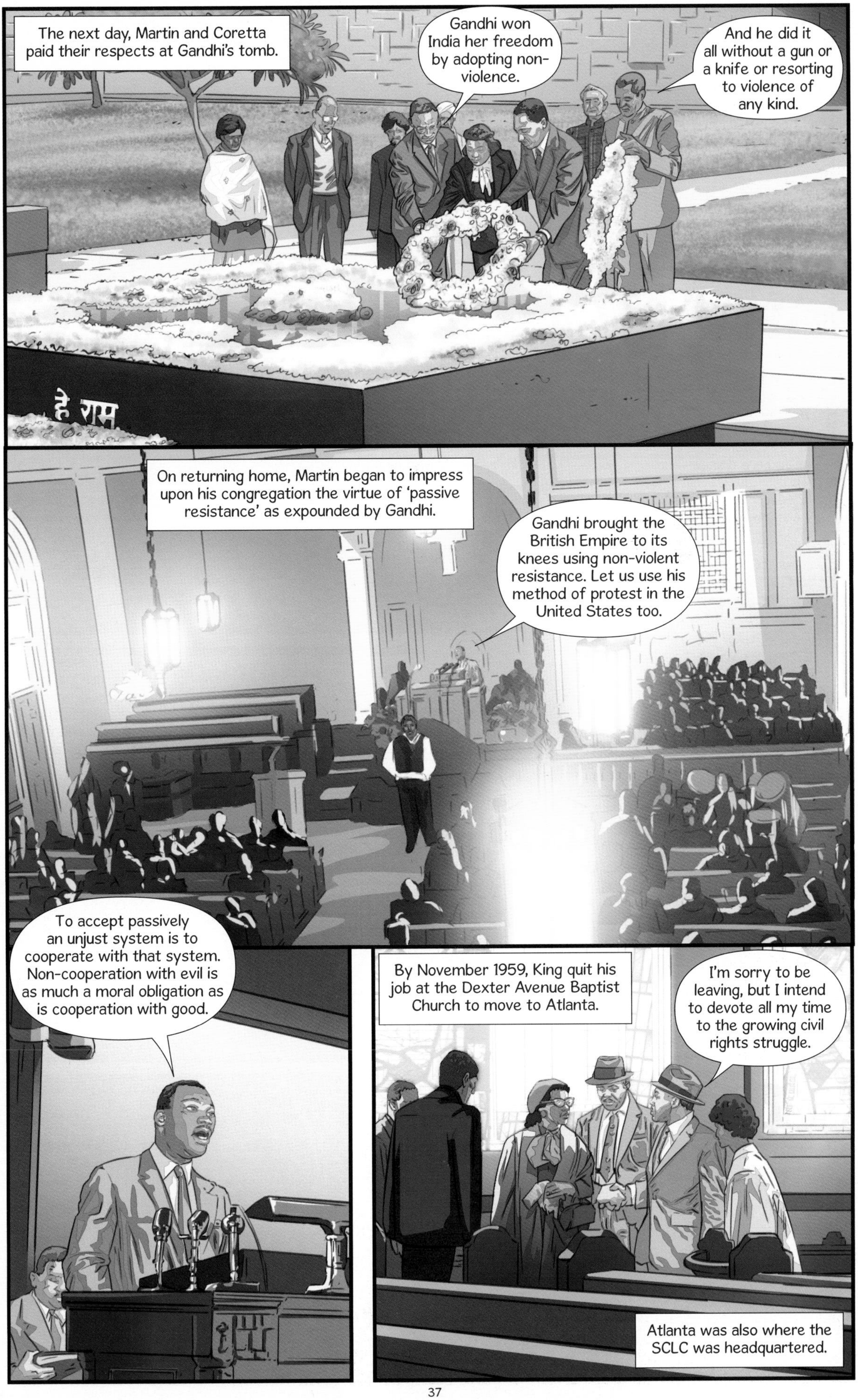
The next day, Martin and Coretta paid their respects at Gandhi's tomb.
Gandhi won India her freedom by adopting non-violence.
And he did it all without a gun or a knife or resorting to violence of any kind.
हे राम
On returning home, Martin began to impress upon his congregation the virtue of 'passive resistance' as expounded by Gandhi.
Gandhi brought the British Empire to its knees using non-violent resistance. Let us use his method of protest in the United States too.
To accept passively an unjust system is to cooperate with that system. Non-cooperation with evil is as much a moral obligation as is cooperation with good.
By November 1959, King quit his job at the Dexter Avenue Baptist Church to move to Atlanta.
I'm sorry to be leaving, but I intend to devote all my time to the growing civil rights struggle.
Atlanta was also where the SCLC was headquartered.

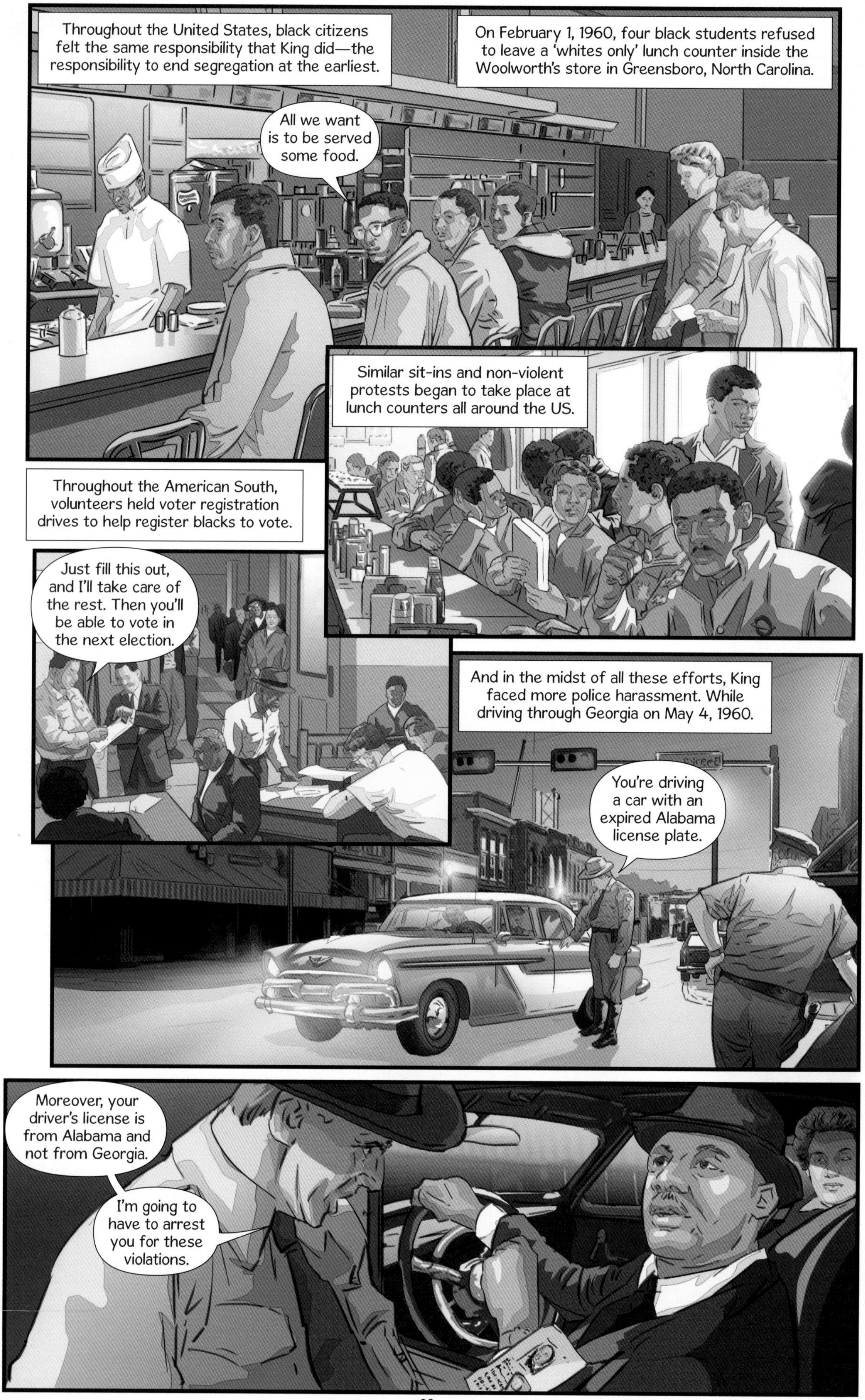
Throughout the United States, black citizens felt the same responsibility that King did—the responsibility to end segregation at the earliest.
On February 1, 1960, four black students refused to leave a 'whites only' lunch counter inside the Woolworth's store in Greensboro, North Carolina.
All we want is to be served some food.
Similar sit-ins and non-violent protests began to take place at lunch counters all around the US.
Throughout the American South, volunteers held voter registration drives to help register blacks to vote.
Just fill this out, and I'll take care of the rest. Then you'll be able to vote in the next election.
And in the midst of all these efforts, King faced more police harassment. While driving through Georgia on May 4, 1960.
You're driving a car with an expired Alabama license plate.
Moreover, your driver's license is from Alabama and not from Georgia.
I'm going to have to arrest you for these violations.

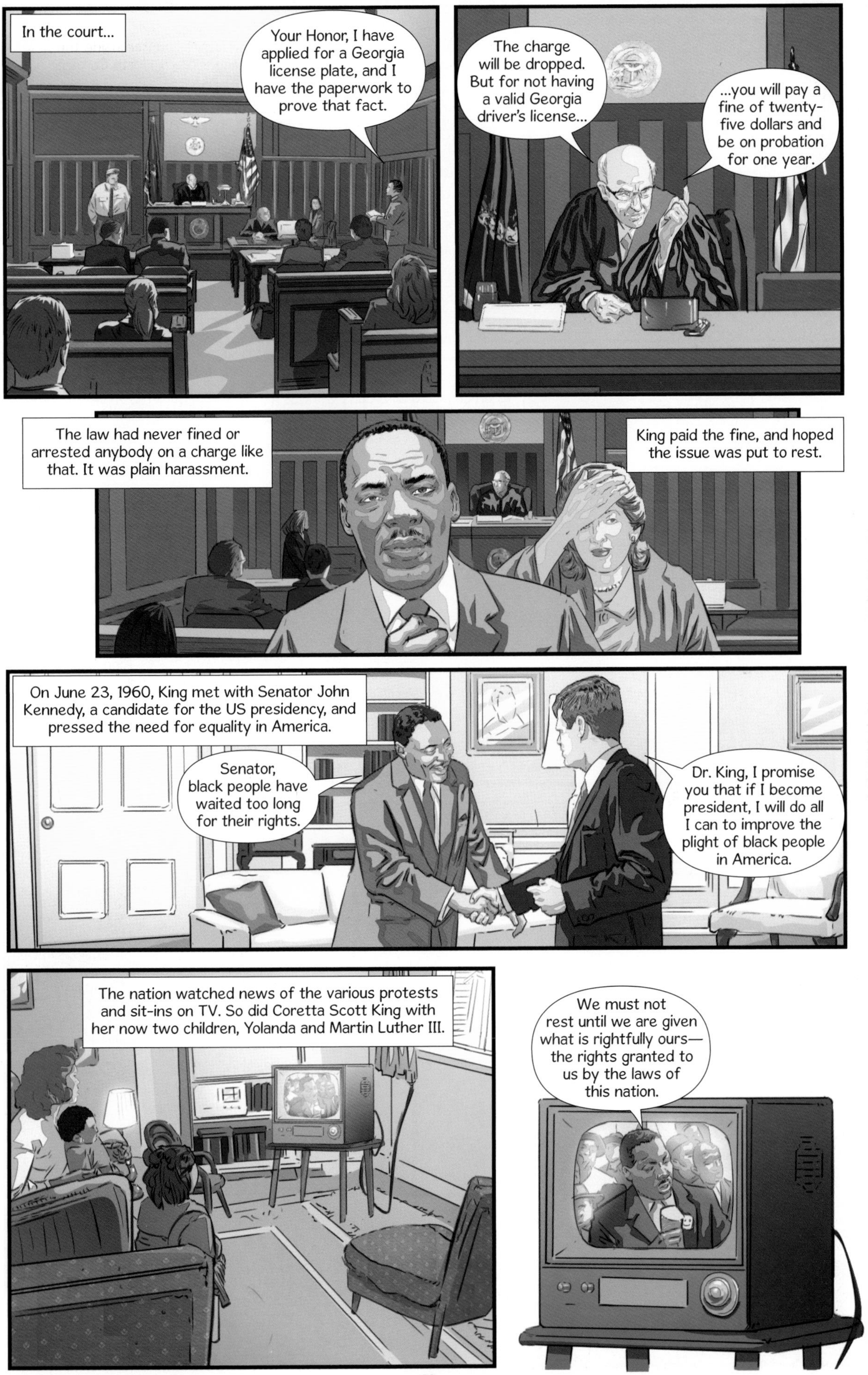
In the court...
Your Honor, I have applied for a Georgia license plate, and I have the paperwork to prove that fact.
The charge will be dropped. But for not having a valid Georgia driver's license...
...you will pay a fine of twenty-five dollars and be on probation for one year.
The law had never fined or arrested anybody on a charge like that. It was plain harassment.
King paid the fine, and hoped the issue was put to rest.
On June 23, 1960, King met with Senator John Kennedy, a candidate for the US presidency, and pressed the need for equality in America.
Senator, black people have waited too long for their rights.
Dr. King, I promise you that if I become president, I will do all I can to improve the plight of black people in America.
The nation watched news of the various protests and sit-ins on TV. So did Coretta Scott King with her now two children, Yolanda and Martin Luther III.
We must not rest until we are given what is rightfully ours—the rights granted to us by the laws of this nation.

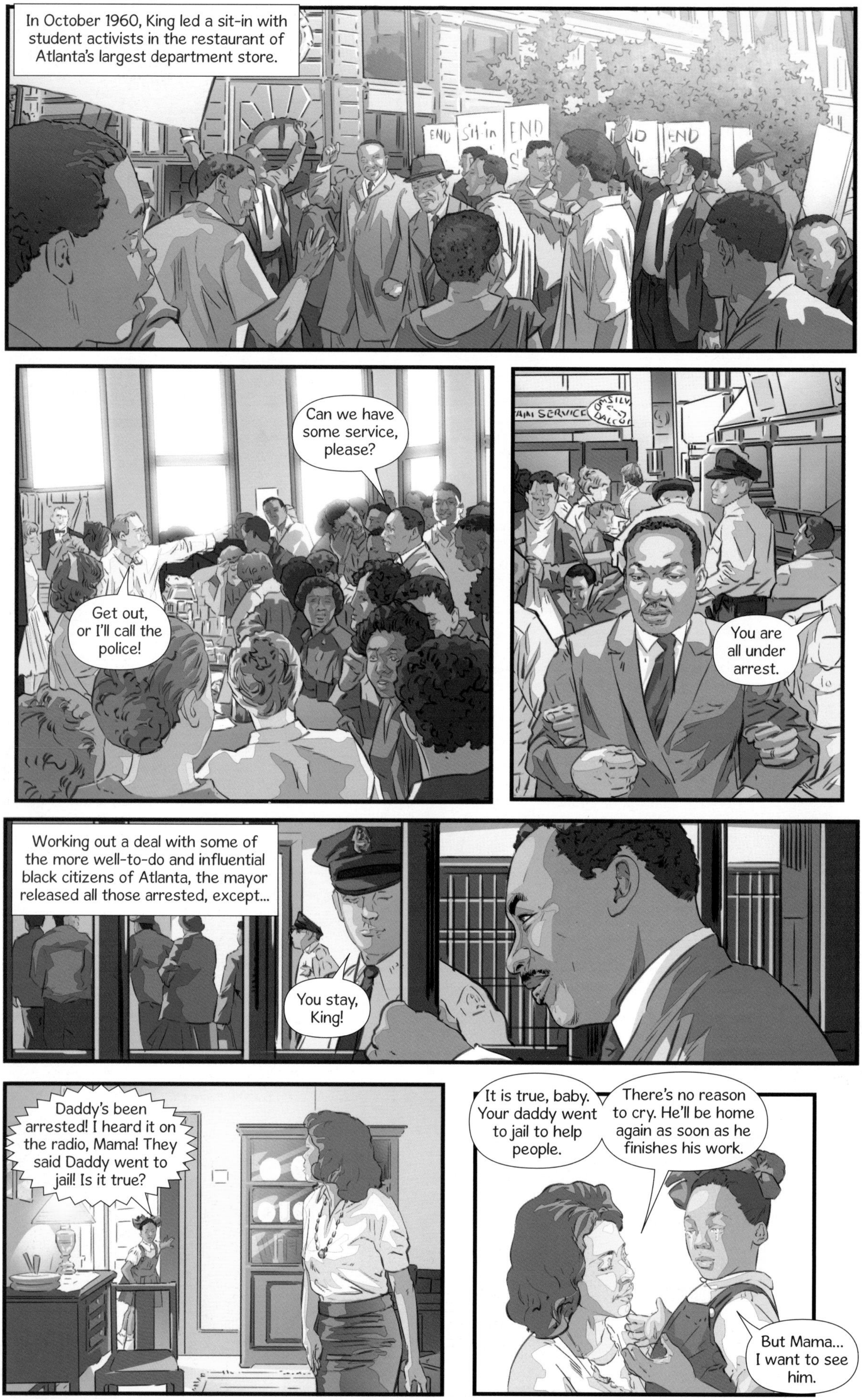
In October 1960, King led a sit-in with student activists in the restaurant of Atlanta's largest department store.
END
Sit-in
END
END
END
Can we have some service, please?
Get out, or I'll call the police!
You are all under arrest.
Working out a deal with some of the more well-to-do and influential black citizens of Atlanta, the mayor released all those arrested, except...
You stay, King!
Daddy's been arrested! I heard it on the radio, Mama! They said Daddy went to jail! Is it true?
It is true, baby. Your daddy went to jail to help people.
There's no reason to cry. He'll be home again as soon as he finishes his work.
But Mama... I want to see him.

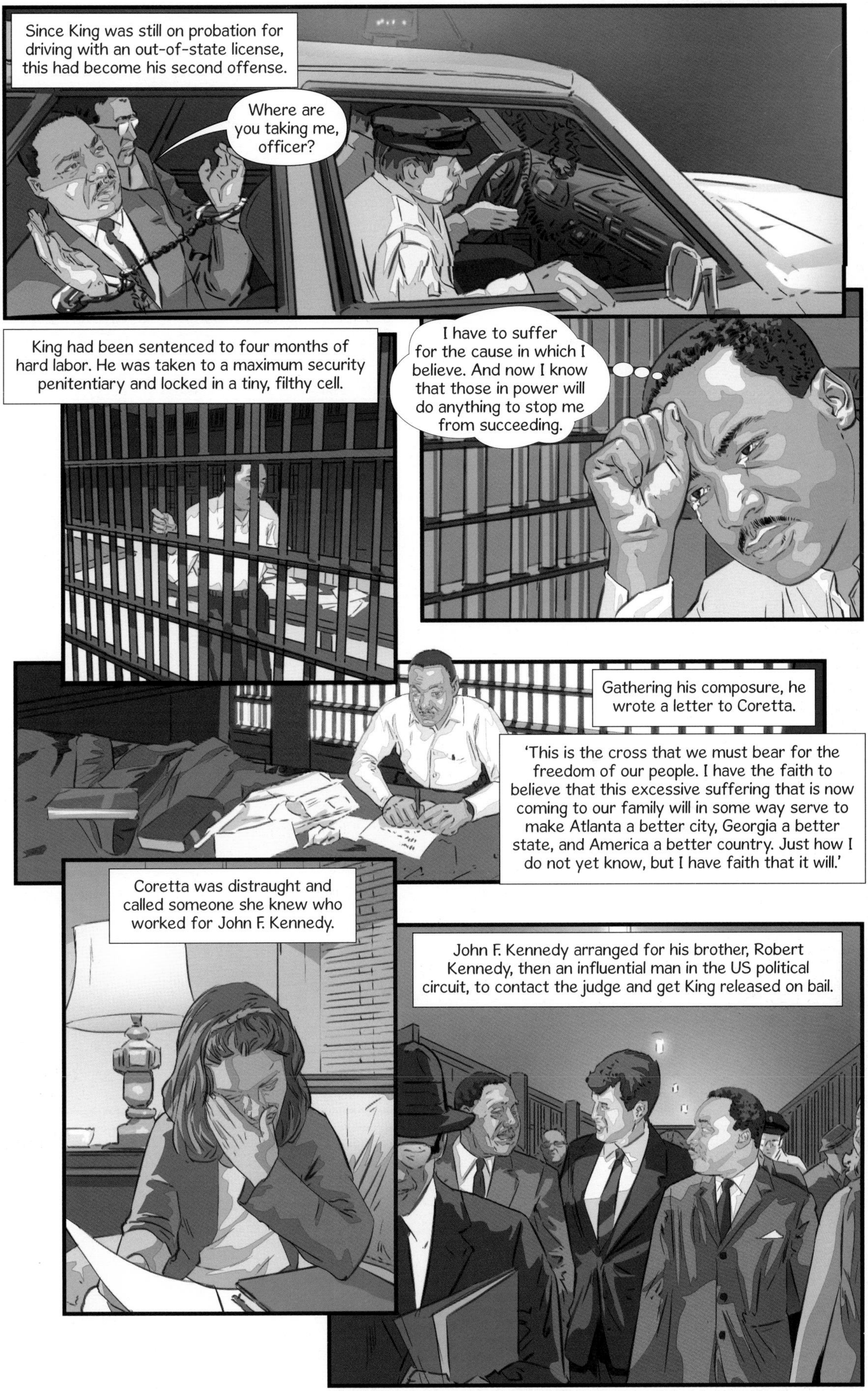

Since King was still on probation for driving with an out-of-state license, this had become his second offense.
Where are you taking me, officer?
King had been sentenced to four months of hard labor. He was taken to a maximum security penitentiary and locked in a tiny, filthy cell.
I have to suffer for the cause in which I believe. And now I know that those in power will do anything to stop me from succeeding.
Gathering his composure, he wrote a letter to Coretta.
'This is the cross that we must bear for the freedom of our people. I have the faith to believe that this excessive suffering that is now coming to our family will in some way serve to make Atlanta a better city, Georgia a better state, and America a better country. Just how I do not yet know, but I have faith that it will.'
Coretta was distraught and called someone she knew who worked for John F. Kennedy.
John F. Kennedy arranged for his brother, Robert Kennedy, then an influential man in the US political circuit, to contact the judge and get King released on bail.

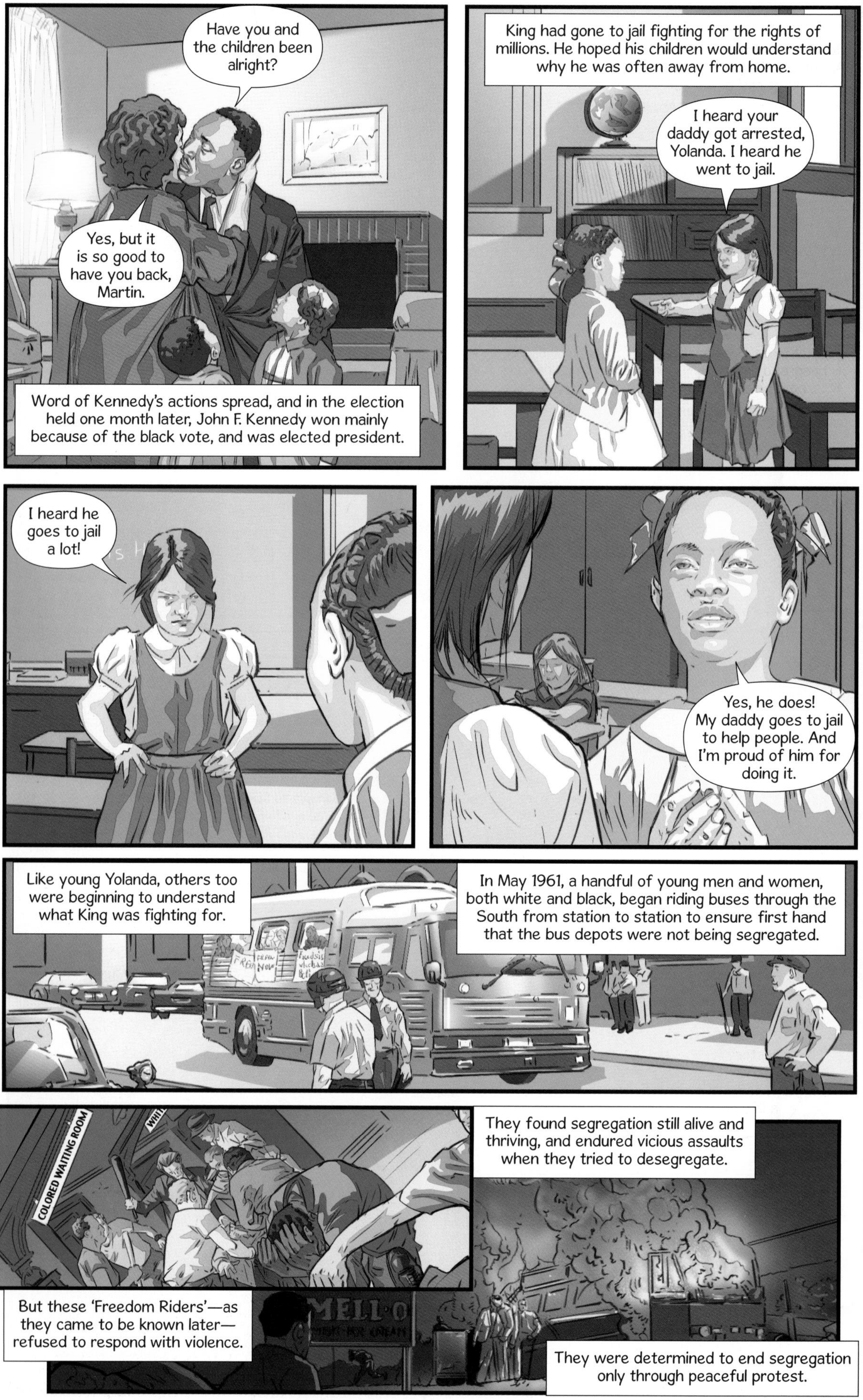

Have you and the children been alright?
Yes, but it is so good to have you back, Martin.
Word of Kennedy's actions spread, and in the election held one month later, John F. Kennedy won mainly because of the black vote, and was elected president.
King had gone to jail fighting for the rights of millions. He hoped his children would understand why he was often away from home.
I heard your daddy got arrested, Yolanda. I heard he went to jail.
I heard he goes to jail a lot!
Yes, he does! My daddy goes to jail to help people. And I'm proud of him for doing it.
Like young Yolanda, others too were beginning to understand what King was fighting for.
In May 1961, a handful of young men and women, both white and black, began riding buses through the South from station to station to ensure first hand that the bus depots were not being segregated.
COLORED WAITING ROOM
They found segregation still alive and thriving, and endured vicious assaults when they tried to desegregate.
But these 'Freedom Riders'—as they came to be known later—refused to respond with violence.
They were determined to end segregation only through peaceful protest.

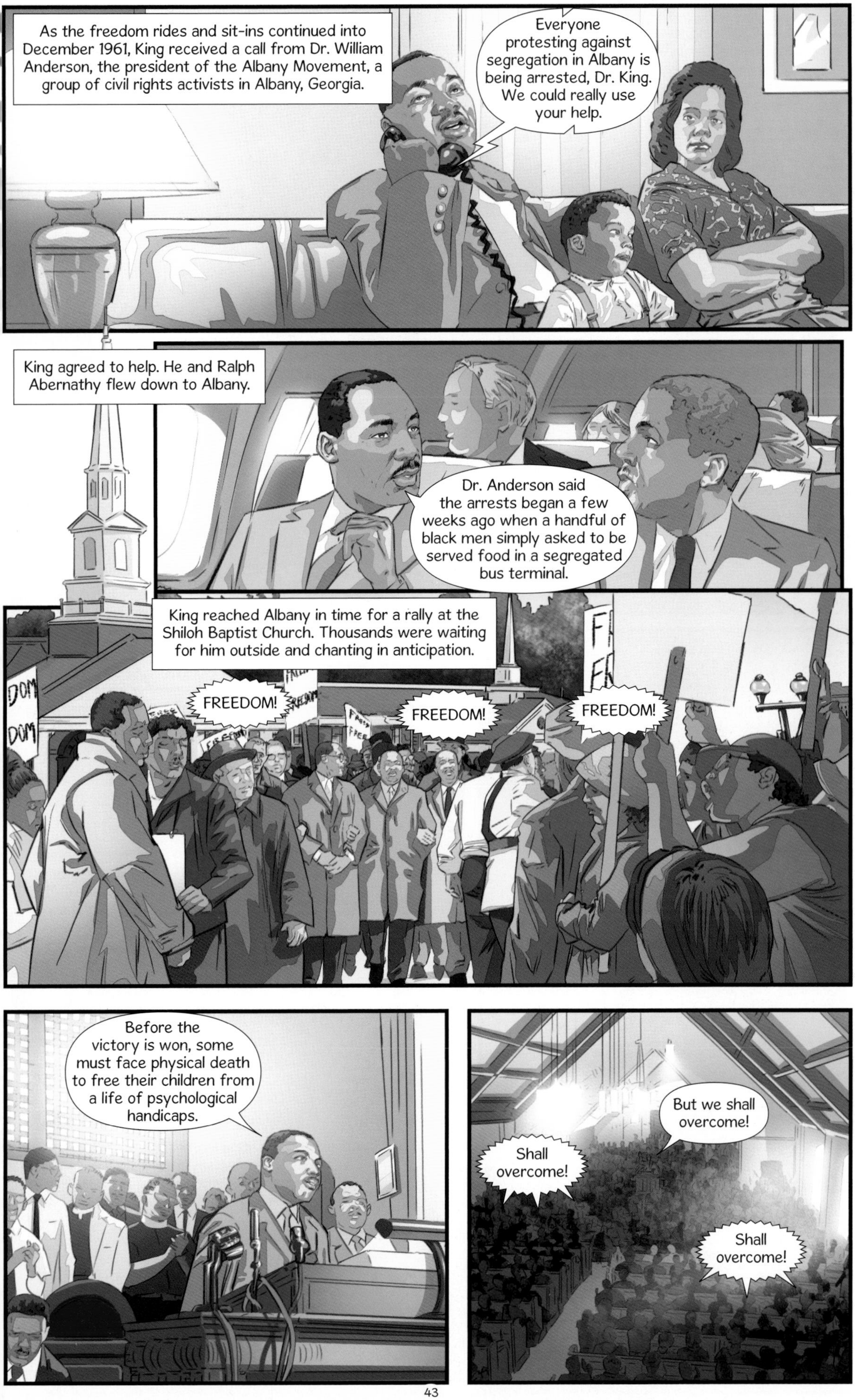
As the freedom rides and sit-ins continued into December 1961, King received a call from Dr. William Anderson, the president of the Albany Movement, a group of civil rights activists in Albany, Georgia.
Everyone protesting against segregation in Albany is being arrested, Dr. King. We could really use your help.
King agreed to help. He and Ralph Abernathy flew down to Albany.
Dr. Anderson said the arrests began a few weeks ago when a handful of black men simply asked to be served food in a segregated bus terminal.
King reached Albany in time for a rally at the Shiloh Baptist Church. Thousands were waiting for him outside and chanting in anticipation.
FREEDOM!
FREEDOM!
FREEDOM!
Before the victory is won, some must face physical death to free their children from a life of psychological handicaps.
But we shall overcome!
Shall overcome!
Shall overcome!

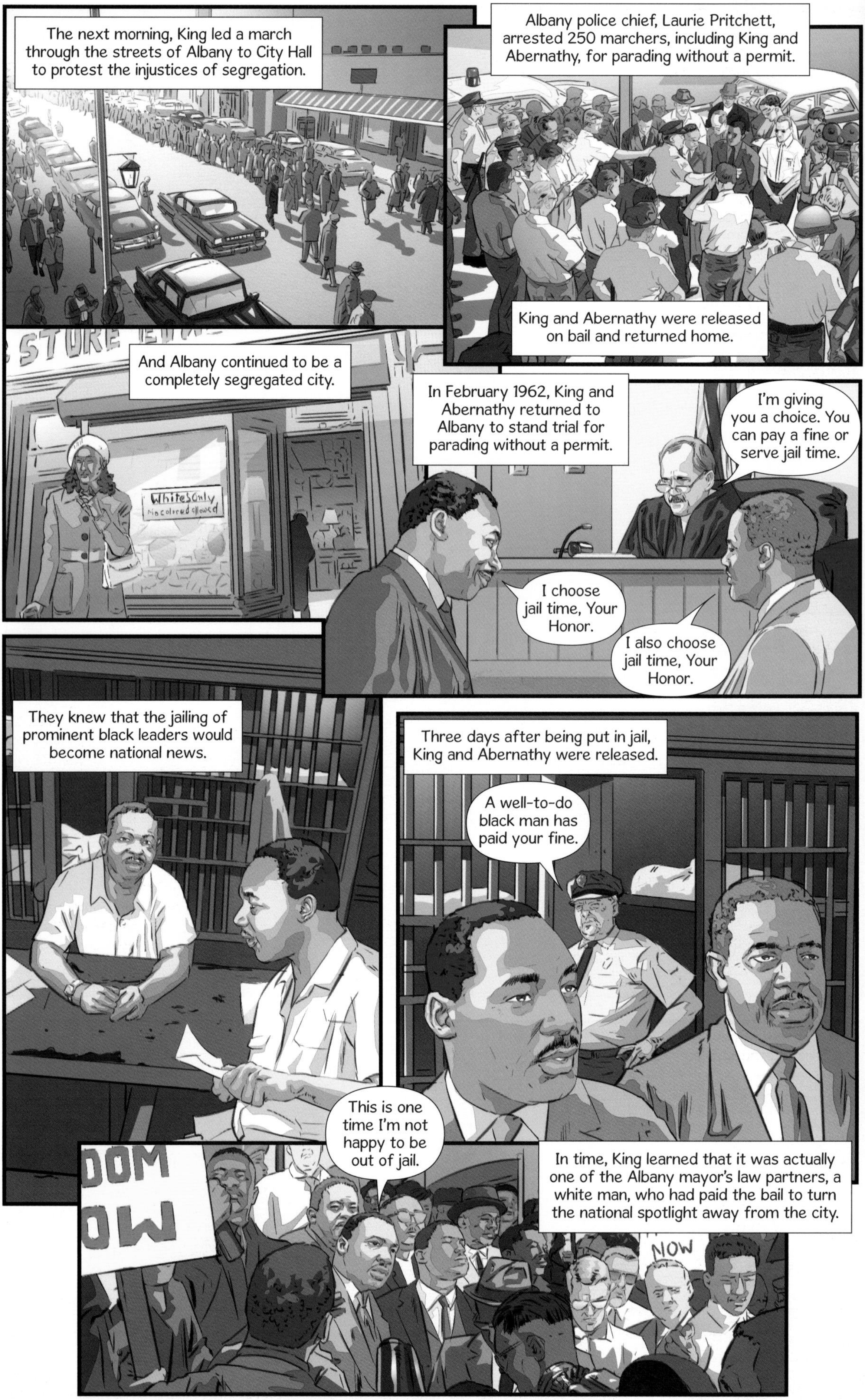

The next morning, King led a march through the streets of Albany to City Hall to protest the injustices of segregation.
Albany police chief, Laurie Pritchett, arrested 250 marchers, including King and Abernathy, for parading without a permit.
King and Abernathy were released on bail and returned home.
STORE
And Albany continued to be a completely segregated city.
Whites Only
No colored allowed
In February 1962, King and Abernathy returned to Albany to stand trial for parading without a permit.
I'm giving you a choice. You can pay a fine or serve jail time.
I choose jail time, Your Honor.
I also choose jail time, Your Honor.
They knew that the jailing of prominent black leaders would become national news.
Three days after being put in jail, King and Abernathy were released.
A well-to-do black man has paid your fine.
This is one time I'm not happy to be out of jail.
In time, King learned that it was actually one of the Albany mayor's law partners, a white man, who had paid the bail to turn the national spotlight away from the city.
DOM
OW
NOW

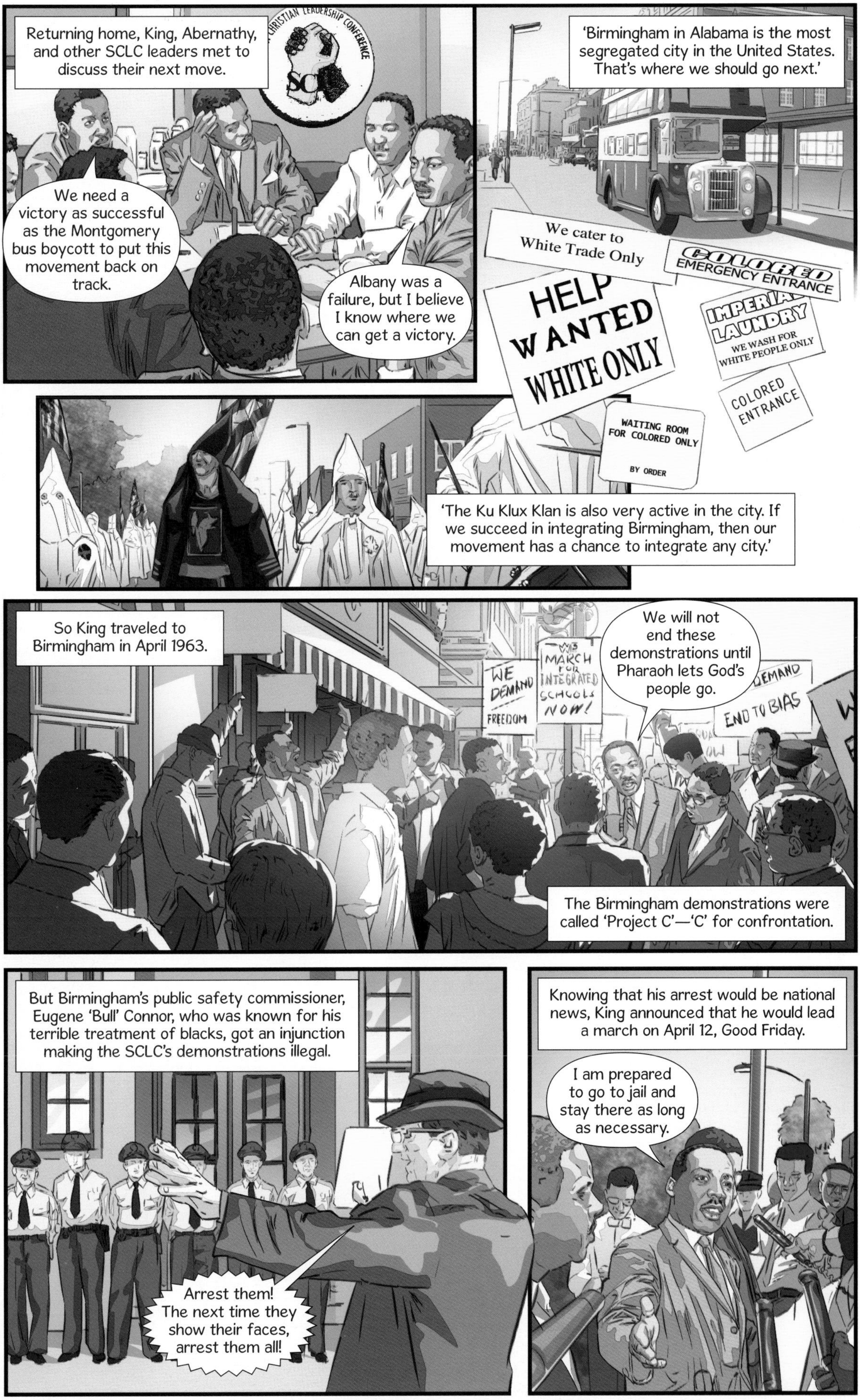
Returning home, King, Abernathy, and other SCLC leaders met to discuss their next move.
We need a victory as successful as the Montgomery bus boycott to put this movement back on track.
Albany was a failure, but I believe I know where we can get a victory.
'Birmingham in Alabama is the most segregated city in the United States. That's where we should go next.'
We cater to White Trade Only
COLORED EMERGENCY ENTRANCE
HELP WANTED WHITE ONLY
IMPERIAL LAUNDRY WE WASH FOR WHITE PEOPLE ONLY
COLORED ENTRANCE
WAITING ROOM FOR COLORED ONLY BY ORDER
'The Ku Klux Klan is also very active in the city. If we succeed in integrating Birmingham, then our movement has a chance to integrate any city.'
So King traveled to Birmingham in April 1963.
WE DEMAND FREEDOM
WE MARCH FOR INTEGRATED SCHOOLS NOW!
DEMAND
END TO BIAS
We will not end these demonstrations until Pharaoh lets God's people go.
The Birmingham demonstrations were called 'Project C'—'C' for confrontation.
But Birmingham's public safety commissioner, Eugene 'Bull' Connor, who was known for his terrible treatment of blacks, got an injunction making the SCLC's demonstrations illegal.
Arrest them! The next time they show their faces, arrest them all!
Knowing that his arrest would be national news, King announced that he would lead a march on April 12, Good Friday.
I am prepared to go to jail and stay there as long as necessary.

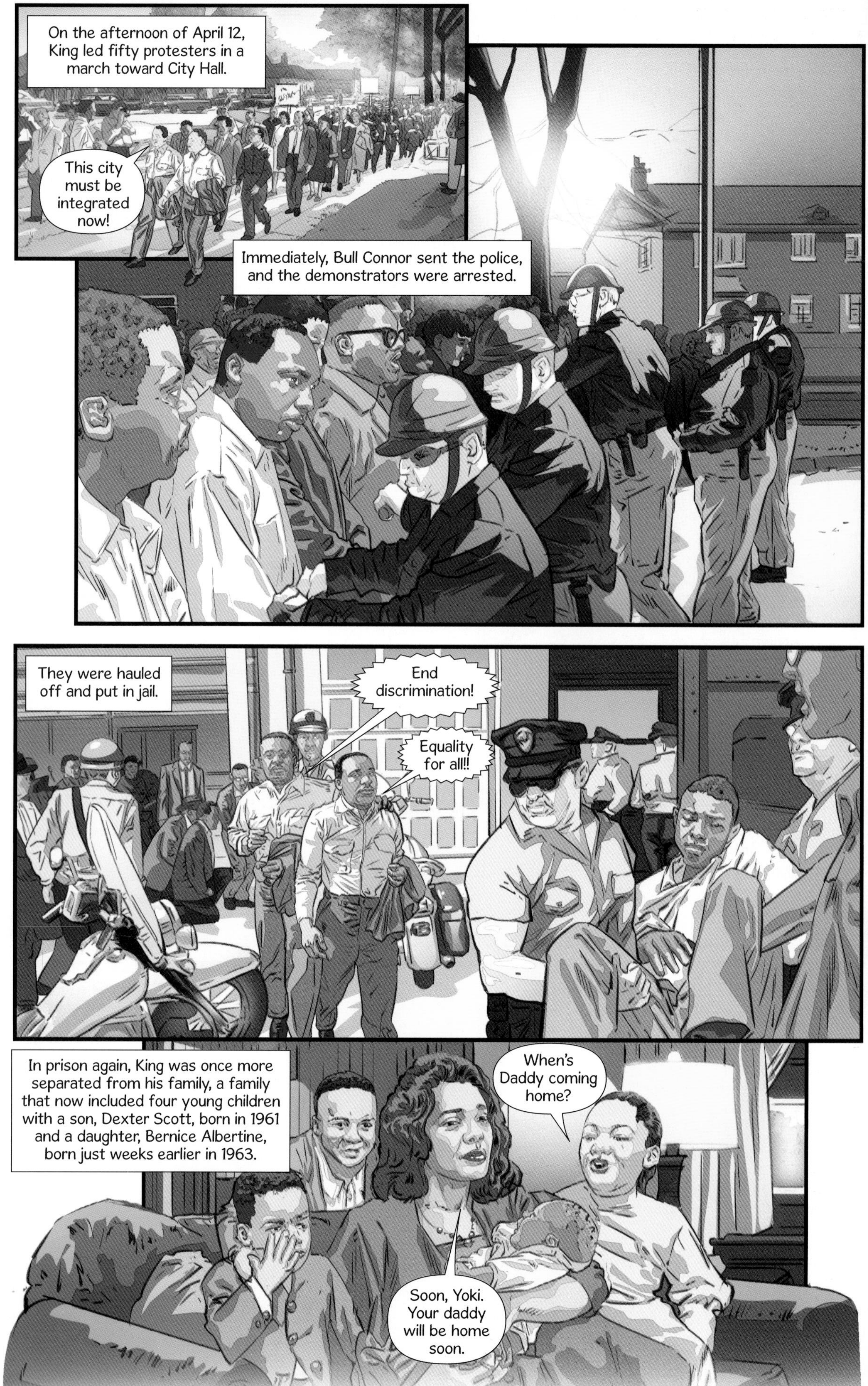
On the afternoon of April 12, King led fifty protesters in a march toward City Hall.
This city must be integrated now!
Immediately, Bull Connor sent the police, and the demonstrators were arrested.
They were hauled off and put in jail.
End discrimination!
Equality for all!!
In prison again, King was once more separated from his family, a family that now included four young children with a son, Dexter Scott, born in 1961 and a daughter, Bernice Albertine, born just weeks earlier in 1963.
When's Daddy coming home?
Soon, Yoki. Your daddy will be home soon.

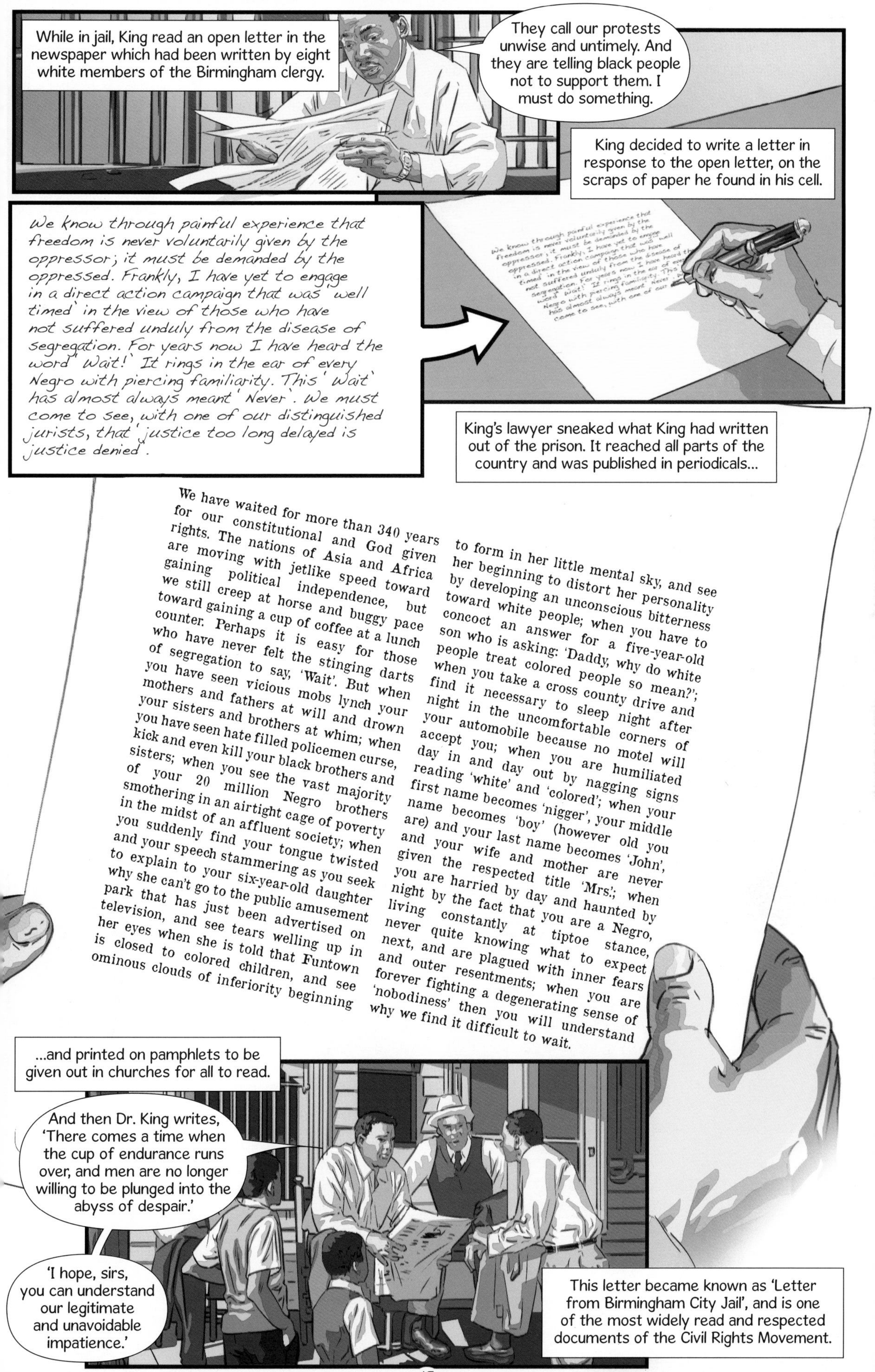

While in jail, King read an open letter in the newspaper which had been written by eight white members of the Birmingham clergy.
They call our protests unwise and untimely. And they are telling black people not to support them. I must do something.
King decided to write a letter in response to the open letter, on the scraps of paper he found in his cell.
We know through painful experience that freedom is never voluntarily given by the oppressor; it must be demanded by the oppressed. Frankly, I have yet to engage in a direct action campaign that was 'well timed' in the view of those who have not suffered unduly from the disease of segregation. For years now I have heard the word 'Wait!' It rings in the ear of every Negro with piercing familiarity. This 'Wait' has almost always meant 'Never'. We must come to see, with one of our distinguished jurists, that 'justice too long delayed is justice denied'.
King's lawyer sneaked what King had written out of the prison. It reached all parts of the country and was published in periodicals...
We have waited for more than 340 years for our constitutional and God given rights. The nations of Asia and Africa are moving with jetlike speed toward gaining political independence, but we still creep at horse and buggy pace toward gaining a cup of coffee at a lunch counter. Perhaps it is easy for those who have never felt the stinging darts of segregation to say, 'Wait'. But when you have seen vicious mobs lynch your mothers and fathers at will and drown your sisters and brothers at whim; when you have seen hate filled policemen curse, kick and even kill your black brothers and sisters; when you see the vast majority of your 20 million Negro brothers smothering in an airtight cage of poverty in the midst of an affluent society; when you suddenly find your tongue twisted and your speech stammering as you seek to explain to your six-year-old daughter why she can't go to the public amusement park that has just been advertised on television, and see tears welling up in her eyes when she is told that Funtown is closed to colored children, and see ominous clouds of inferiority beginning to form in her little mental sky, and see her beginning to distort her personality by developing an unconscious bitterness toward white people; when you have to concoct an answer for a five-year-old son who is asking: 'Daddy, why do white people treat colored people so mean?'; when you take a cross county drive and find it necessary to sleep night after night in the uncomfortable corners of your automobile because no motel will accept you; when you are humiliated day in and day out by nagging signs reading 'white' and 'colored'; when your first name becomes 'nigger', your middle name becomes 'boy' (however old you are) and your last name becomes 'John', and your wife and mother are never given the respected title 'Mrs.'; when you are harried by day and haunted by night by the fact that you are a Negro, living constantly at tiptoe stance, never quite knowing what to expect next, and are plagued with inner fears and outer resentments; when you are forever fighting a degenerating sense of 'nobodiness' then you will understand why we find it difficult to wait.
...and printed on pamphlets to be given out in churches for all to read.
And then Dr. King writes, 'There comes a time when the cup of endurance runs over, and men are no longer willing to be plunged into the abyss of despair.'
'I hope, sirs, you can understand our legitimate and unavoidable impatience.'
This letter became known as 'Letter from Birmingham City Jail', and is one of the most widely read and respected documents of the Civil Rights Movement.

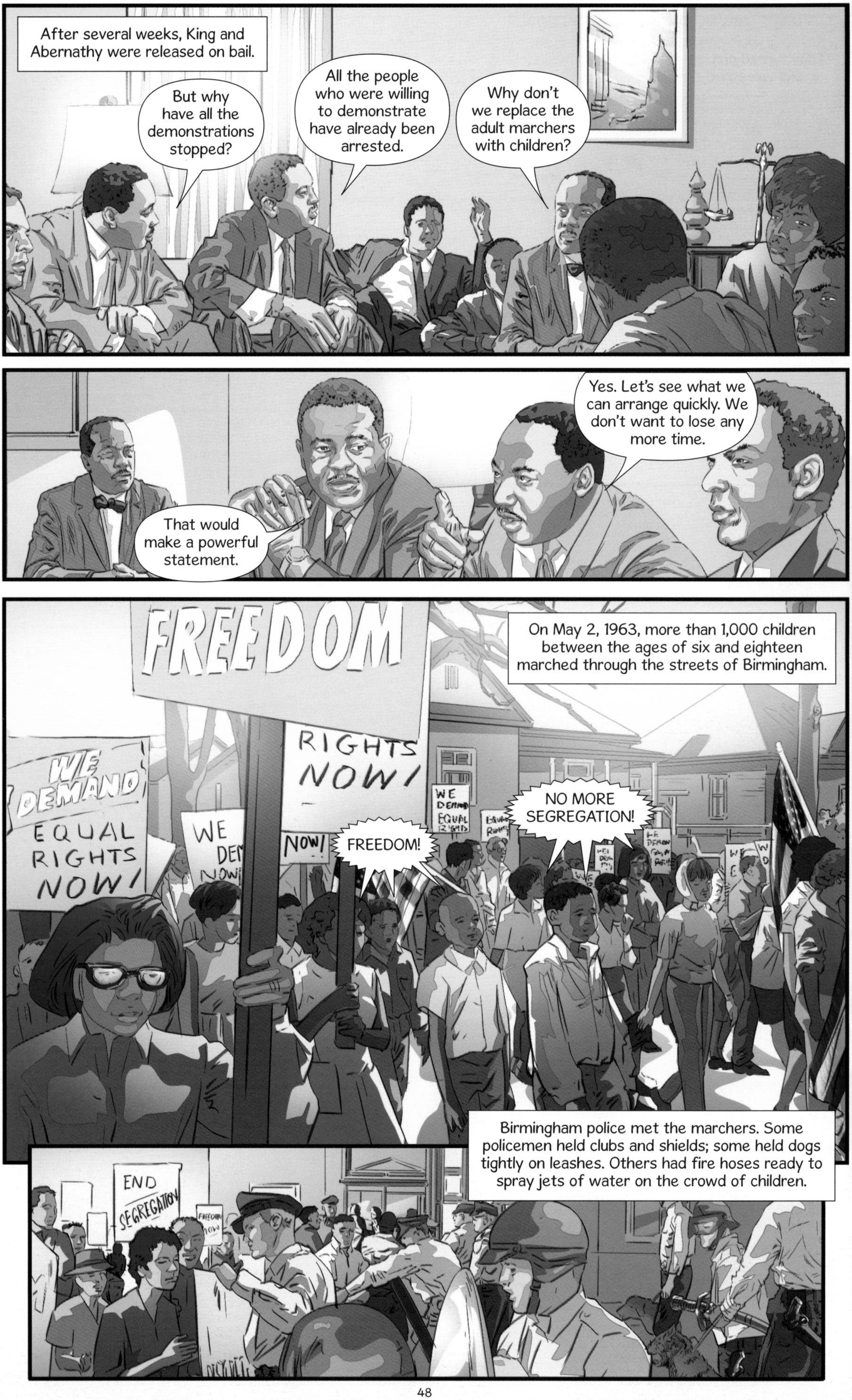
After several weeks, King and Abernathy were released on bail.
But why have all the demonstrations stopped?
All the people who were willing to demonstrate have already been arrested.
Why don't we replace the adult marchers with children?
That would make a powerful statement.
Yes. Let's see what we can arrange quickly. We don't want to lose any more time.
On May 2, 1963, more than 1,000 children between the ages of six and eighteen marched through the streets of Birmingham.
FREEDOM
RIGHTS NOW!
WE DEMAND EQUAL RIGHTS NOW!
NOW!
FREEDOM!
NO MORE SEGREGATION!
Birmingham police met the marchers. Some policemen held clubs and shields; some held dogs tightly on leashes. Others had fire hoses ready to spray jets of water on the crowd of children.
END SEGREGATION

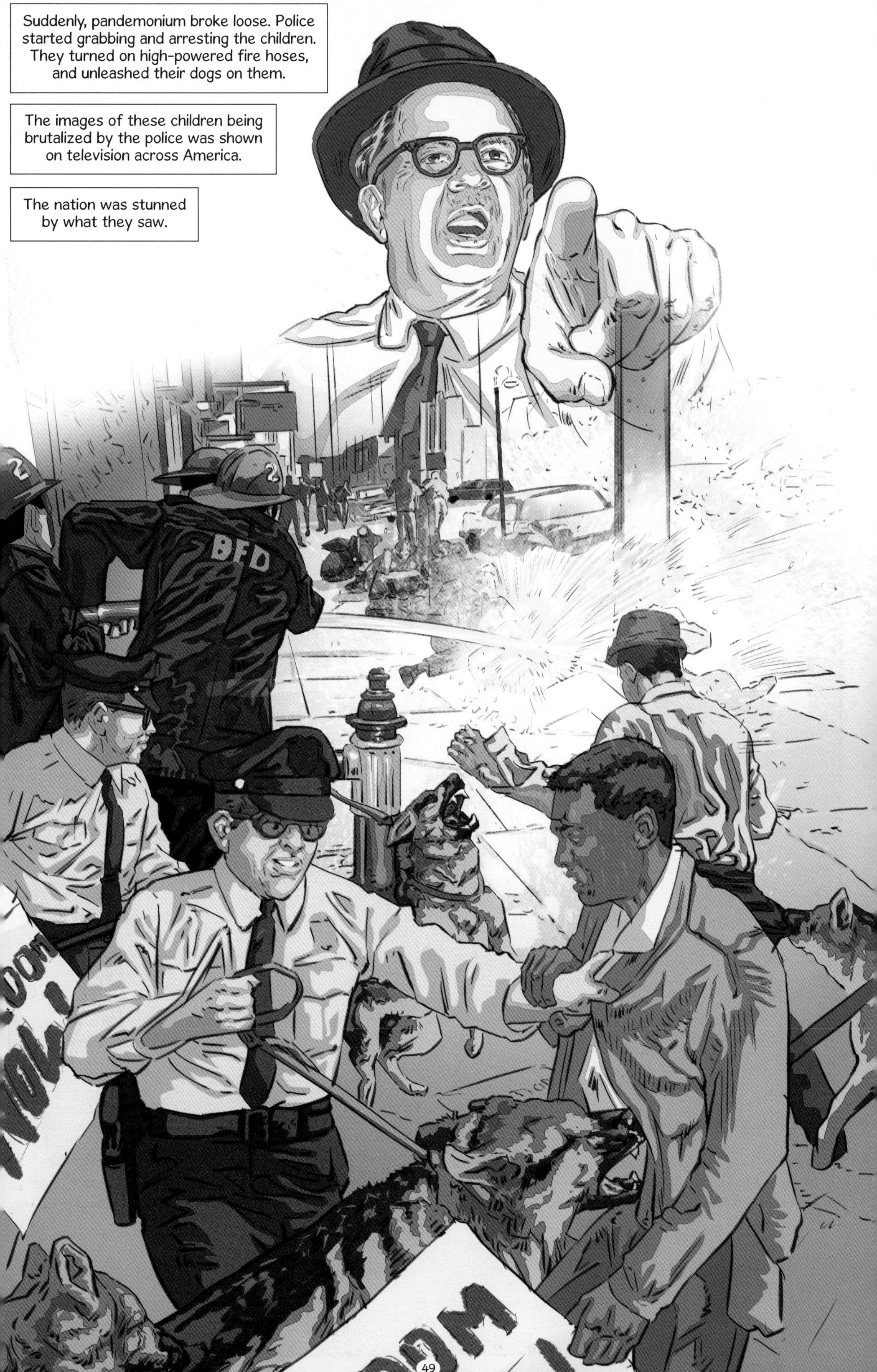
Suddenly, pandemonium broke loose. Police started grabbing and arresting the children. They turned on high-powered fire hoses, and unleashed their dogs on them.
The images of these children being brutalized by the police was shown on television across America.
The nation was stunned by what they saw.
BFD

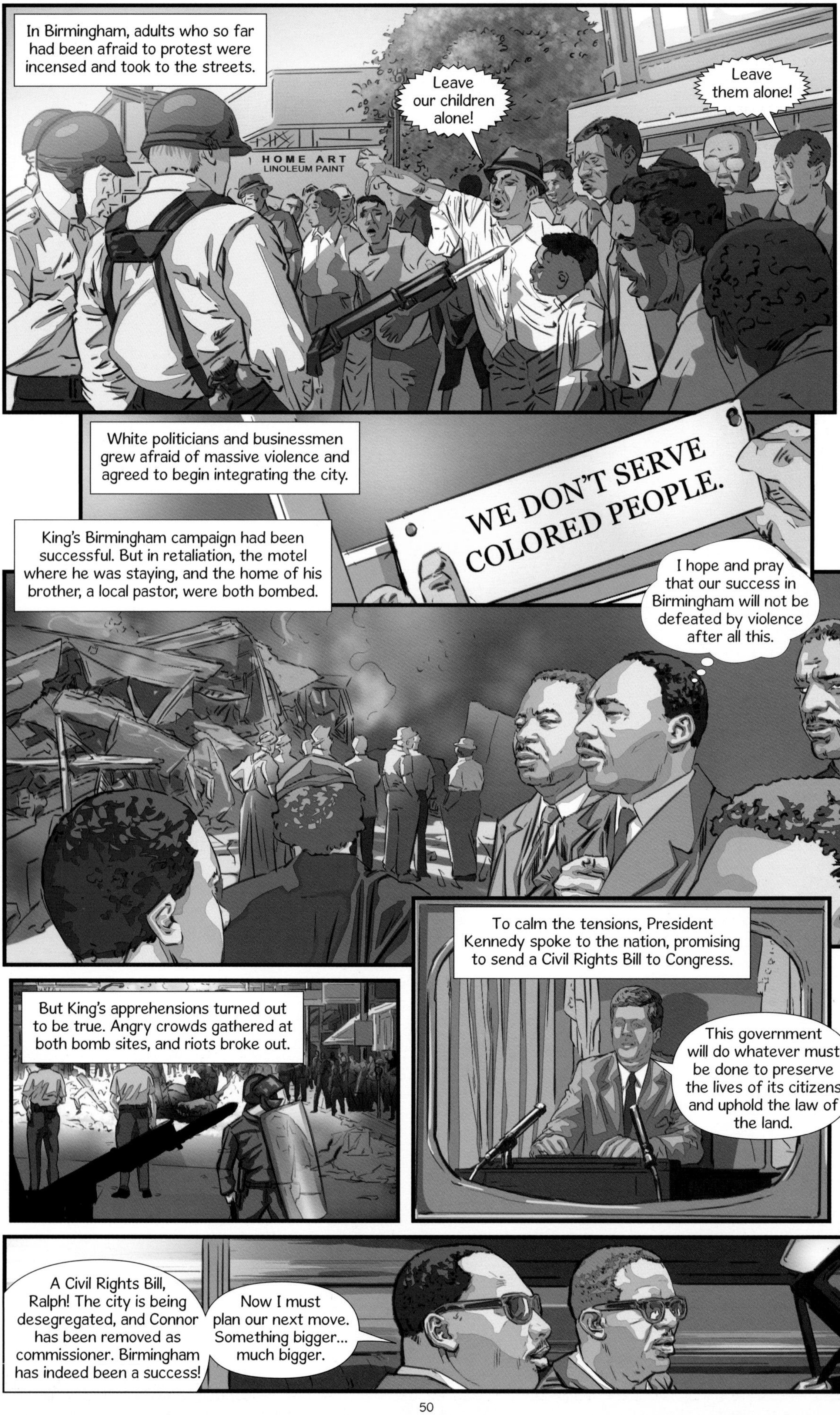
In Birmingham, adults who so far had been afraid to protest were incensed and took to the streets.
Leave our children alone!
Leave them alone!
HOME ART
LINOLEUM PAINT
White politicians and businessmen grew afraid of massive violence and agreed to begin integrating the city.
WE DON'T SERVE COLORED PEOPLE.
King's Birmingham campaign had been successful. But in retaliation, the motel where he was staying, and the home of his brother, a local pastor, were both bombed.
I hope and pray that our success in Birmingham will not be defeated by violence after all this.
But King's apprehensions turned out to be true. Angry crowds gathered at both bomb sites, and riots broke out.
To calm the tensions, President Kennedy spoke to the nation, promising to send a Civil Rights Bill to Congress.
This government will do whatever must be done to preserve the lives of its citizens and uphold the law of the land.
A Civil Rights Bill, Ralph! The city is being desegregated, and Connor has been removed as commissioner. Birmingham has indeed been a success!
Now I must plan our next move. Something bigger... much bigger.

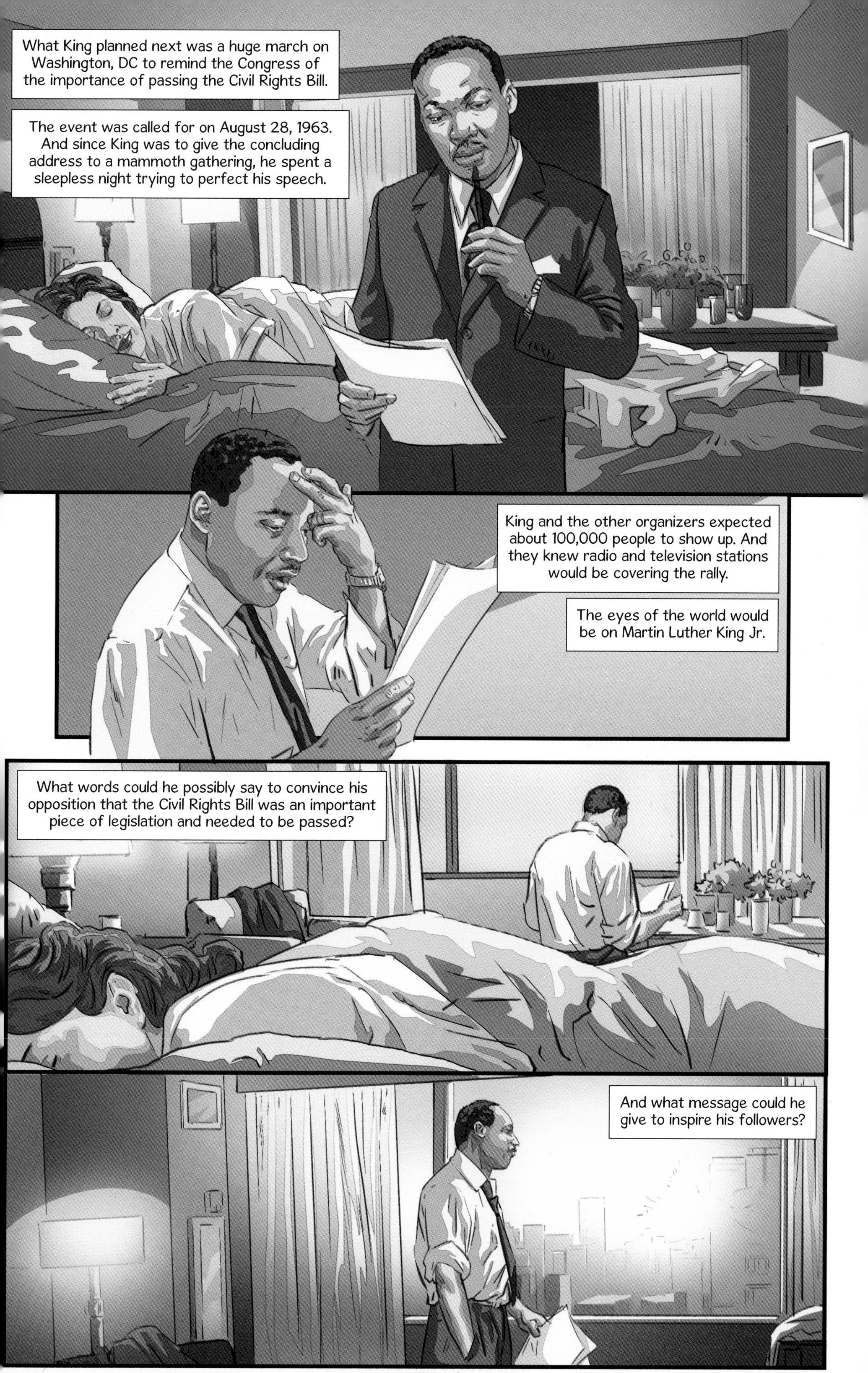
What King planned next was a huge march on Washington, DC to remind the Congress of the importance of passing the Civil Rights Bill.
The event was called for on August 28, 1963. And since King was to give the concluding address to a mammoth gathering, he spent a sleepless night trying to perfect his speech.
King and the other organizers expected about 100,000 people to show up. And they knew radio and television stations would be covering the rally.
The eyes of the world would be on Martin Luther King Jr.
What words could he possibly say to convince his opposition that the Civil Rights Bill was an important piece of legislation and needed to be passed?
And what message could he give to inspire his followers?

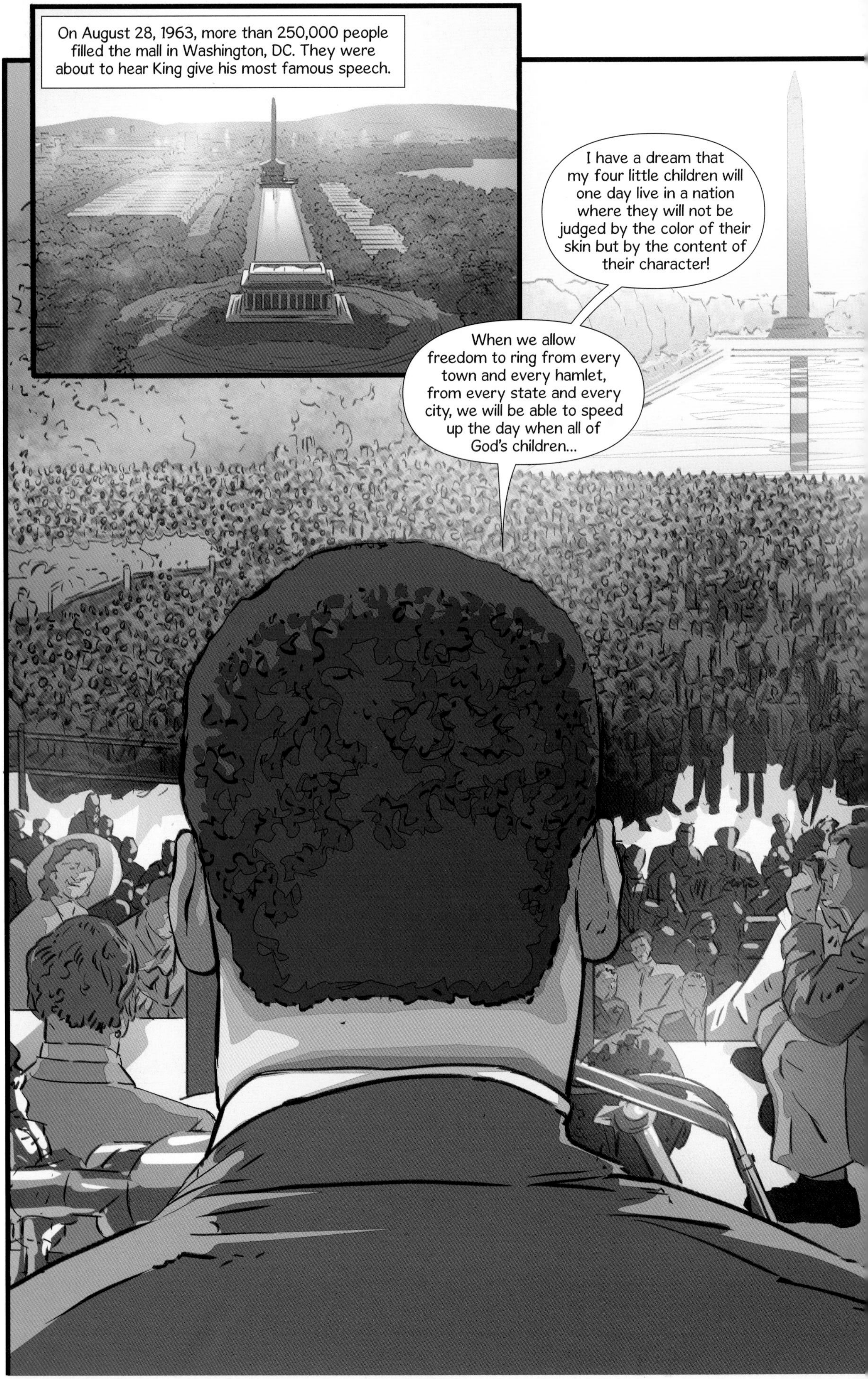
On August 28, 1963, more than 250,000 people filled the mall in Washington, DC. They were about to hear King give his most famous speech.
I have a dream that my four little children will one day live in a nation where they will not be judged by the color of their skin but by the content of their character!
When we allow freedom to ring from every town and every hamlet, from every state and every city, we will be able to speed up the day when all of God's children...

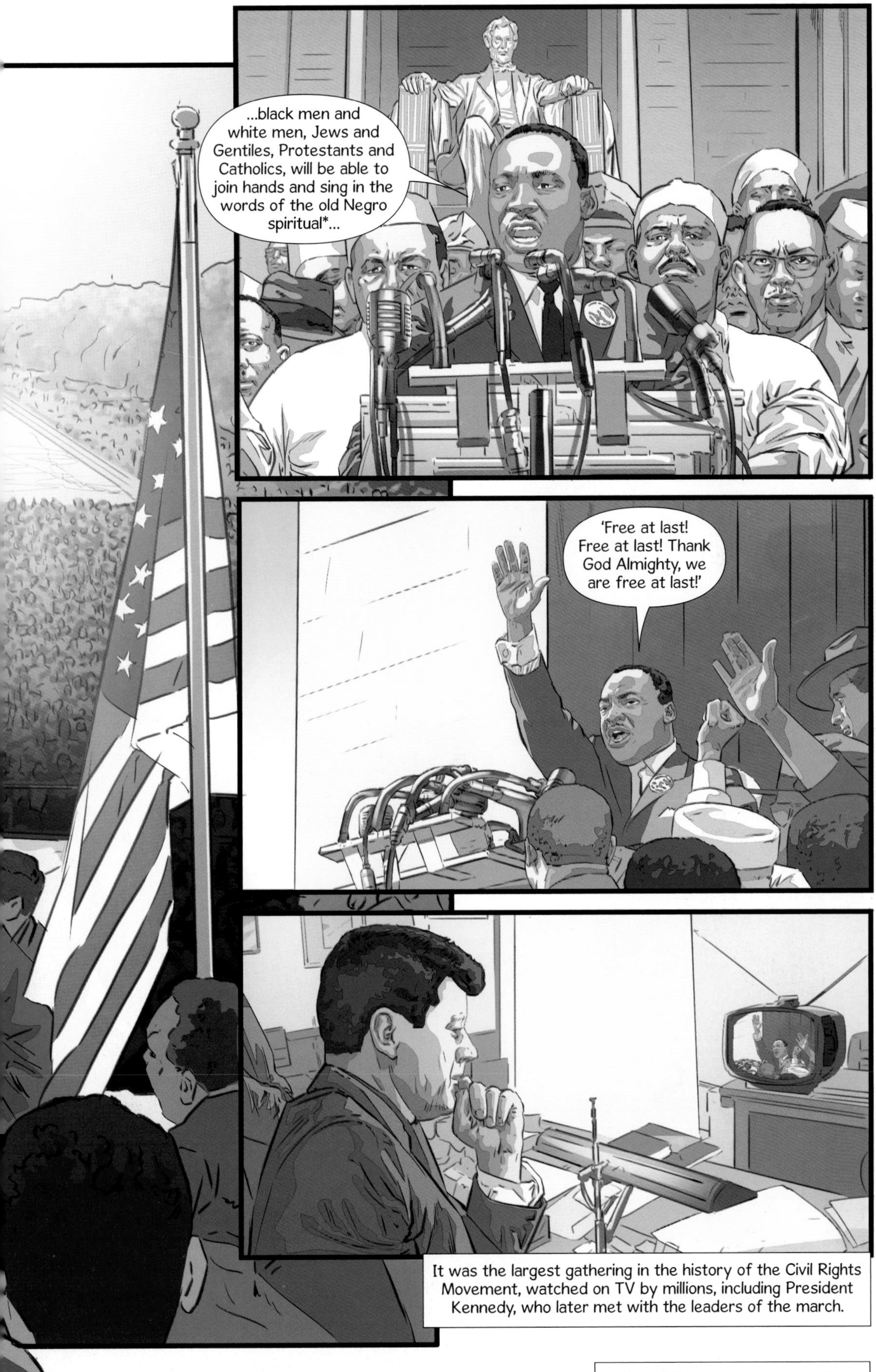
...black men and white men, Jews and Gentiles, Protestants and Catholics, will be able to join hands and sing in the words of the old Negro spiritual*...
'Free at last! Free at last! Thank God Almighty, we are free at last!'
It was the largest gathering in the history of the Civil Rights Movement, watched on TV by millions, including President Kennedy, who later met with the leaders of the march.

*A religious song composed by enslaved African people in America.

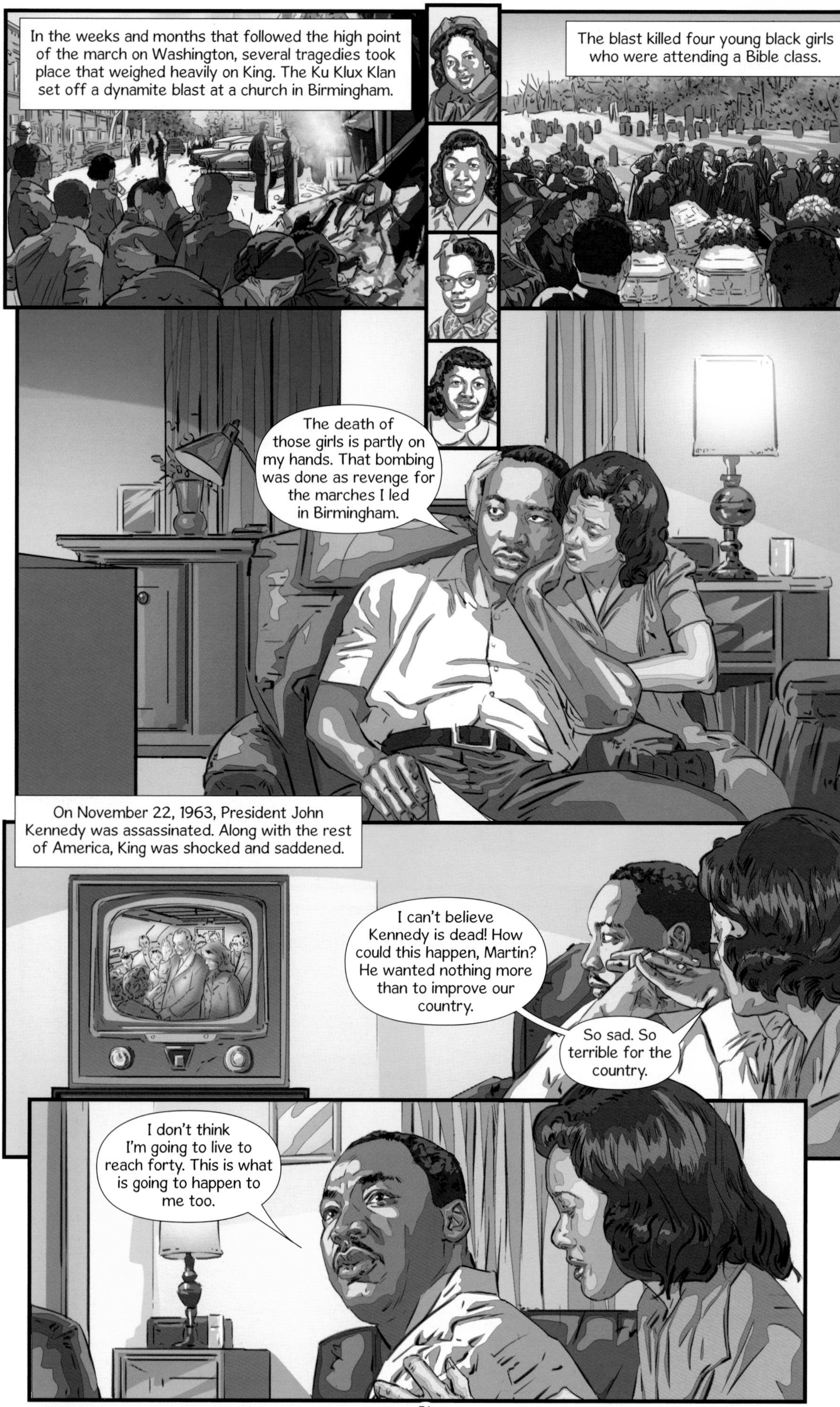
In the weeks and months that followed the high point of the march on Washington, several tragedies took place that weighed heavily on King. The Ku Klux Klan set off a dynamite blast at a church in Birmingham.
The blast killed four young black girls who were attending a Bible class.
The death of those girls is partly on my hands. That bombing was done as revenge for the marches I led in Birmingham.
On November 22, 1963, President John Kennedy was assassinated. Along with the rest of America, King was shocked and saddened.
I can't believe Kennedy is dead! How could this happen, Martin? He wanted nothing more than to improve our country.
So sad. So terrible for the country.
I don't think I'm going to live to reach forty. This is what is going to happen to me too.

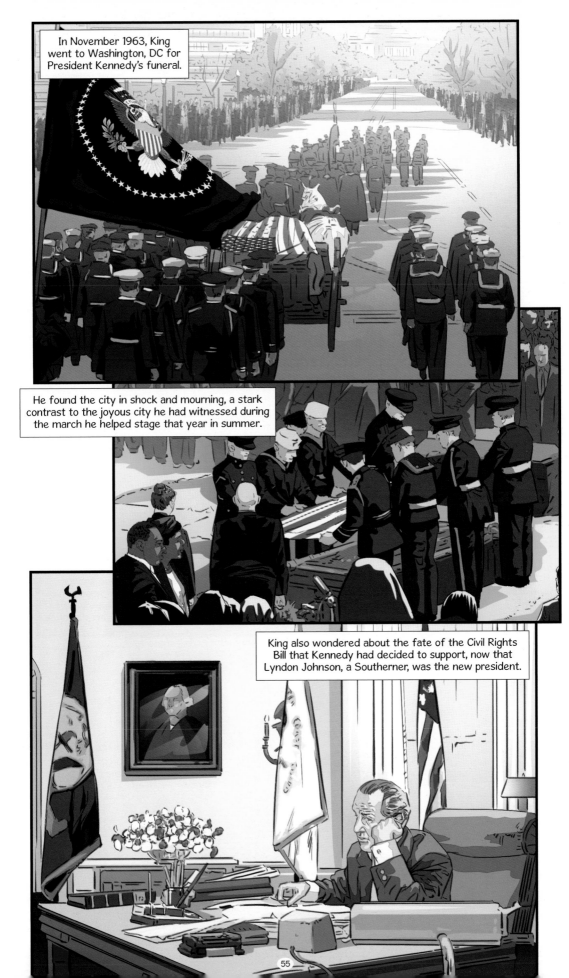

In November 1963, King went to Washington, DC for President Kennedy's funeral.

He found the city in shock and mourning, a stark contrast to the joyous city he had witnessed during the march he helped stage that year in summer.

King also wondered about the fate of the Civil Rights Bill that Kennedy had decided to support, now that Lyndon Johnson, a Southerner, was the new president.

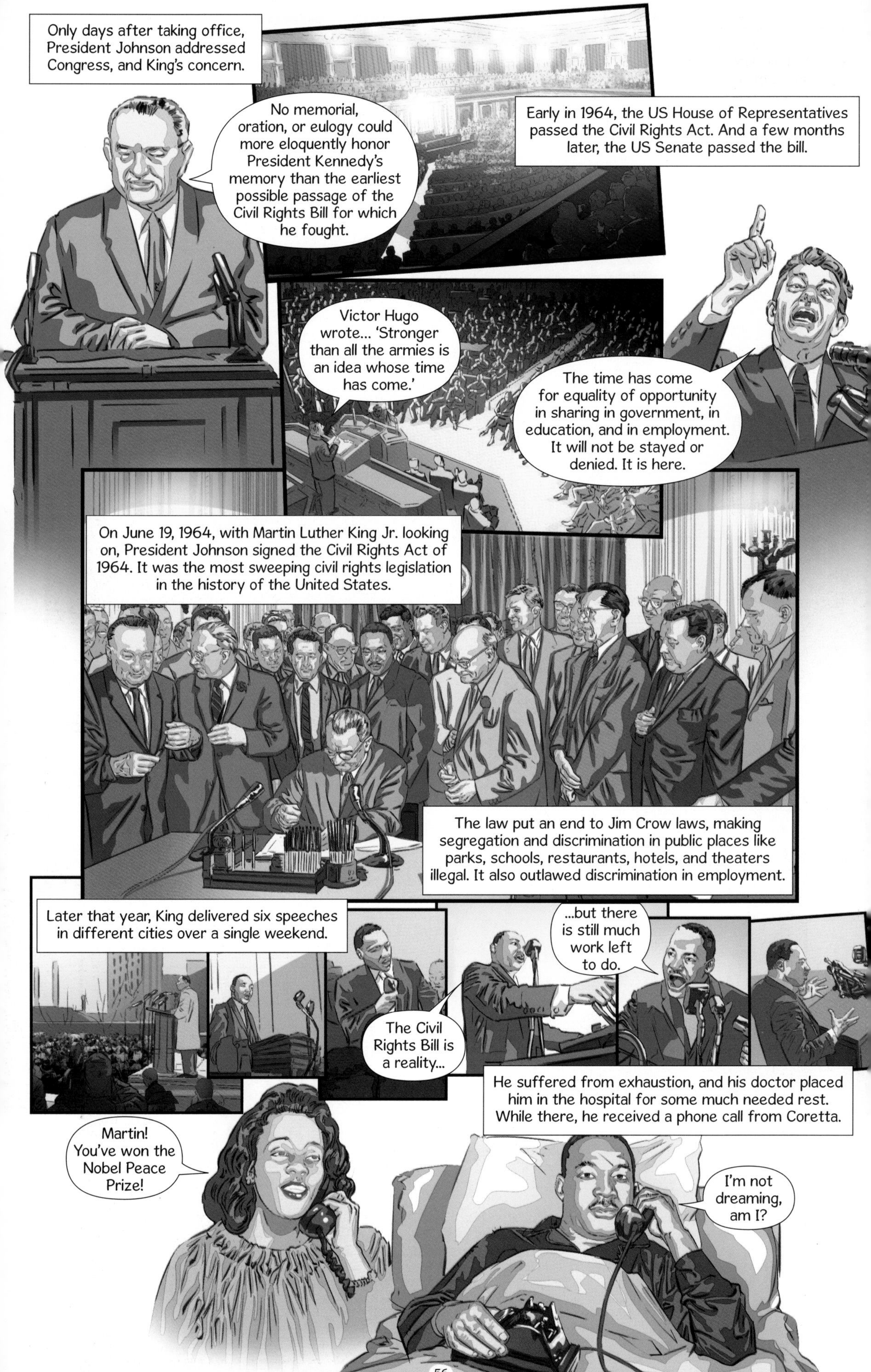
Only days after taking office, President Johnson addressed Congress, and King's concern.
No memorial, oration, or eulogy could more eloquently honor President Kennedy's memory than the earliest possible passage of the Civil Rights Bill for which he fought.
Early in 1964, the US House of Representatives passed the Civil Rights Act. And a few months later, the US Senate passed the bill.
Victor Hugo wrote... 'Stronger than all the armies is an idea whose time has come.'
The time has come for equality of opportunity in sharing in government, in education, and in employment. It will not be stayed or denied. It is here.
On June 19, 1964, with Martin Luther King Jr. looking on, President Johnson signed the Civil Rights Act of 1964. It was the most sweeping civil rights legislation in the history of the United States.
The law put an end to Jim Crow laws, making segregation and discrimination in public places like parks, schools, restaurants, hotels, and theaters illegal. It also outlawed discrimination in employment.
Later that year, King delivered six speeches in different cities over a single weekend.
The Civil Rights Bill is a reality...
...but there is still much work left to do.
He suffered from exhaustion, and his doctor placed him in the hospital for some much needed rest. While there, he received a phone call from Coretta.
Martin! You've won the Nobel Peace Prize!
I'm not dreaming, am I?

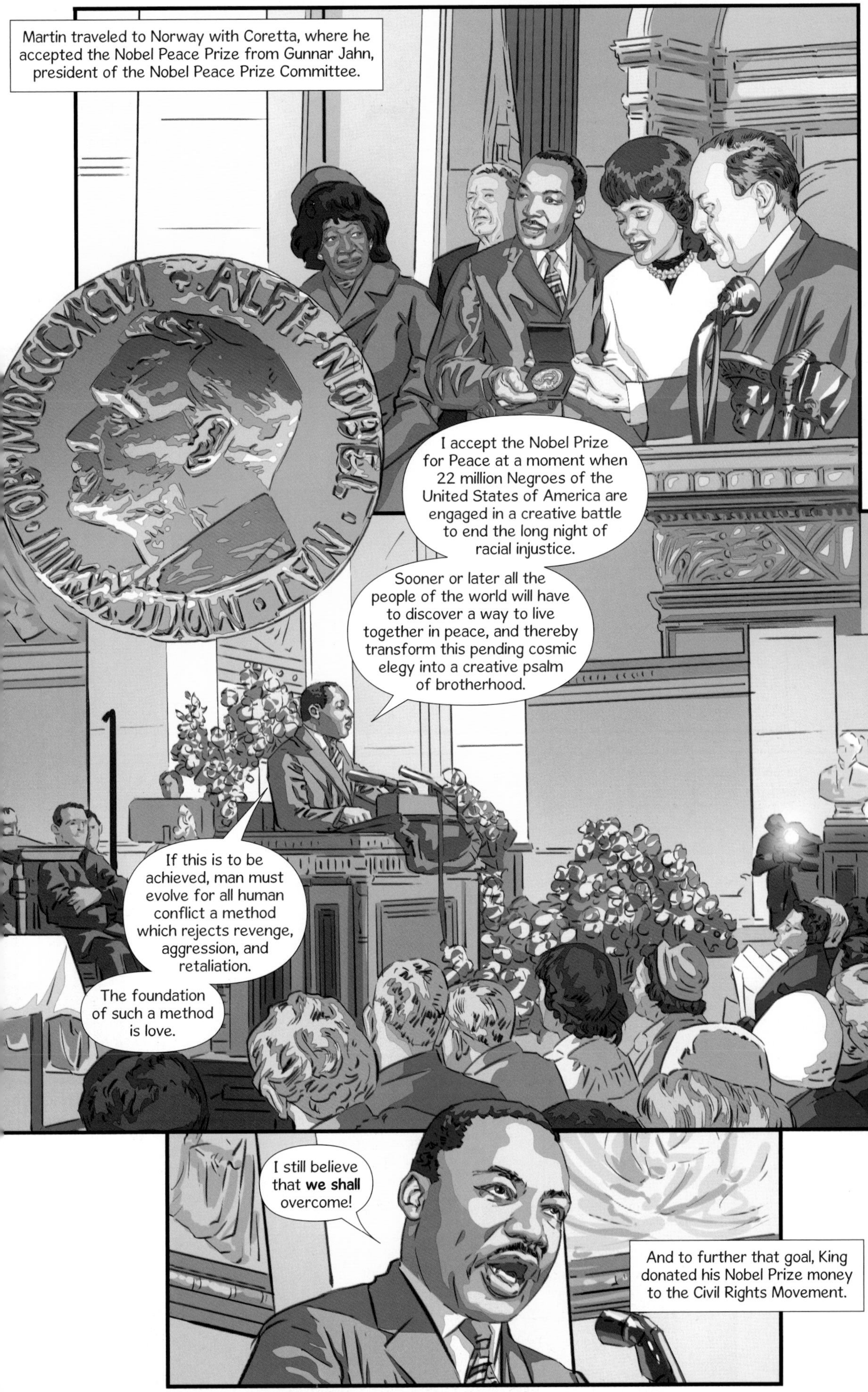
Martin traveled to Norway with Coretta, where he accepted the Nobel Peace Prize from Gunnar Jahn, president of the Nobel Peace Prize Committee.
I accept the Nobel Prize for Peace at a moment when 22 million Negroes of the United States of America are engaged in a creative battle to end the long night of racial injustice.
Sooner or later all the people of the world will have to discover a way to live together in peace, and thereby transform this pending cosmic elegy into a creative psalm of brotherhood.
If this is to be achieved, man must evolve for all human conflict a method which rejects revenge, aggression, and retaliation.
The foundation of such a method is love.
I still believe that **we shall** overcome!
And to further that goal, King donated his Nobel Prize money to the Civil Rights Movement.

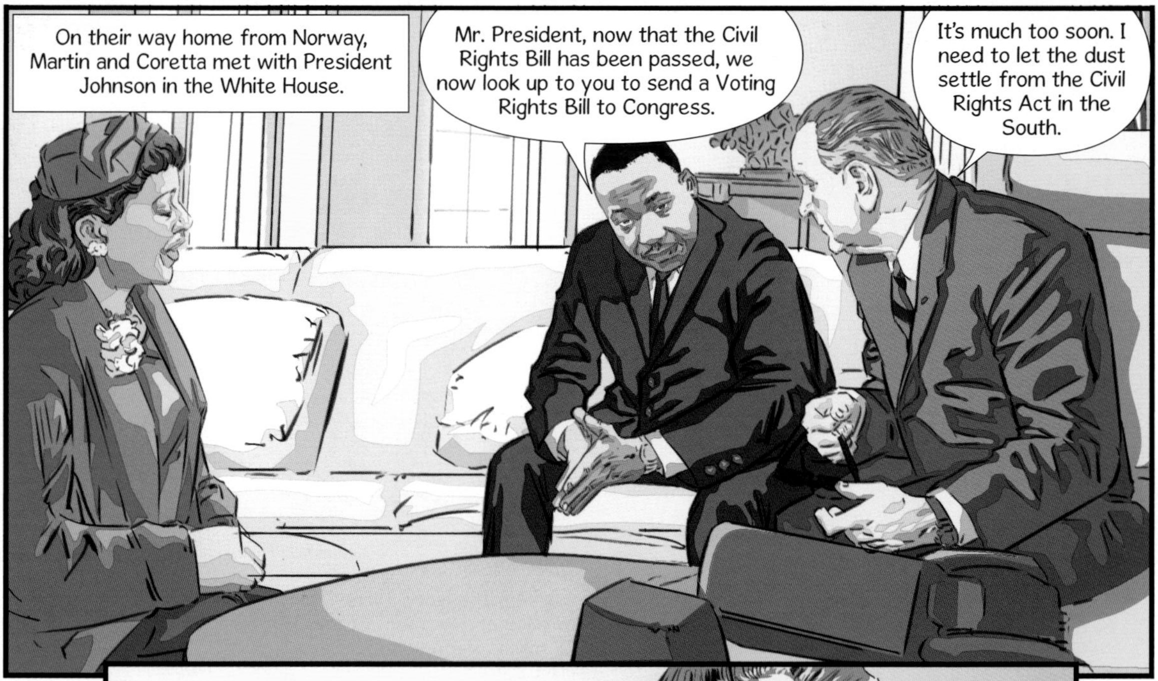
On their way home from Norway, Martin and Coretta met with President Johnson in the White House.
Mr. President, now that the Civil Rights Bill has been passed, we now look up to you to send a Voting Rights Bill to Congress.
It's much too soon. I need to let the dust settle from the Civil Rights Act in the South.

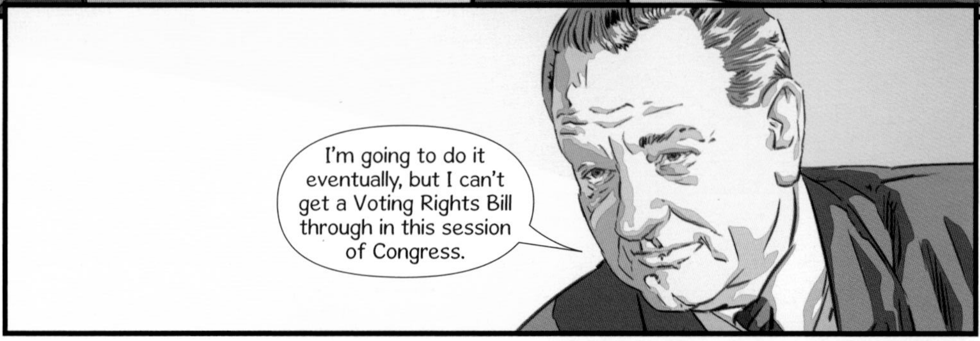
I'm going to do it eventually, but I can't get a Voting Rights Bill through in this session of Congress.

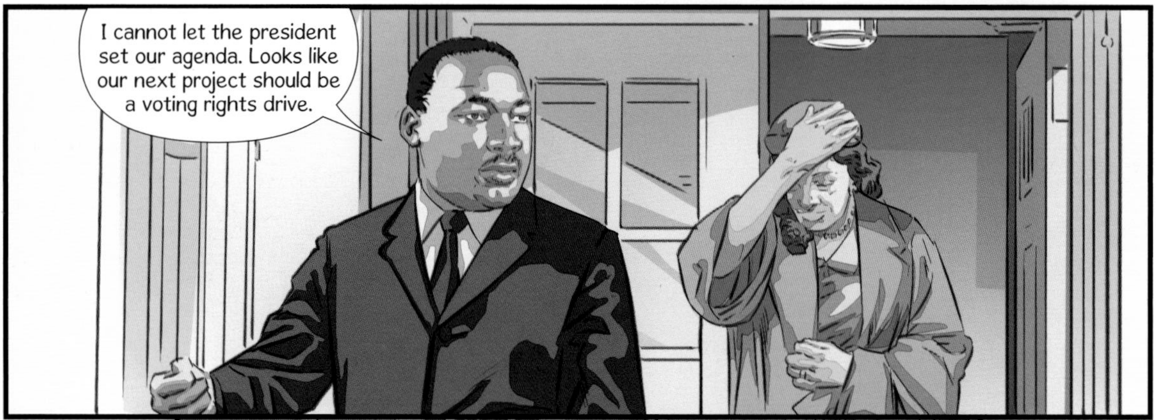
I cannot let the president set our agenda. Looks like our next project should be a voting rights drive.

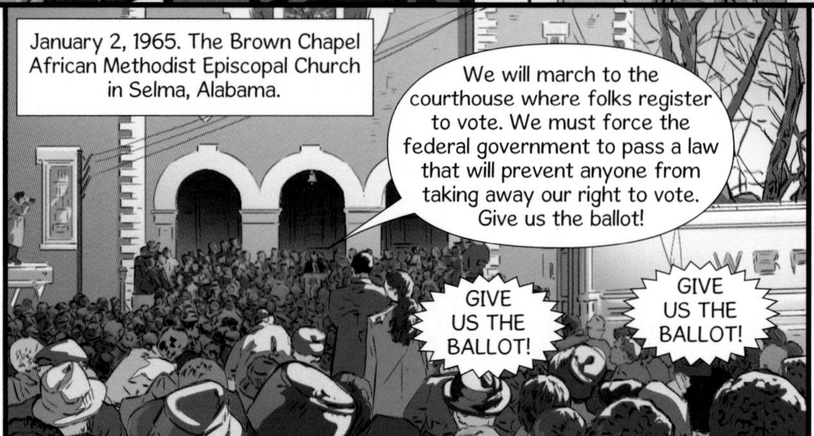
January 2, 1965. The Brown Chapel African Methodist Episcopal Church in Selma, Alabama.
We will march to the courthouse where folks register to vote. We must force the federal government to pass a law that will prevent anyone from taking away our right to vote. Give us the ballot!
GIVE US THE BALLOT!
GIVE US THE BALLOT!

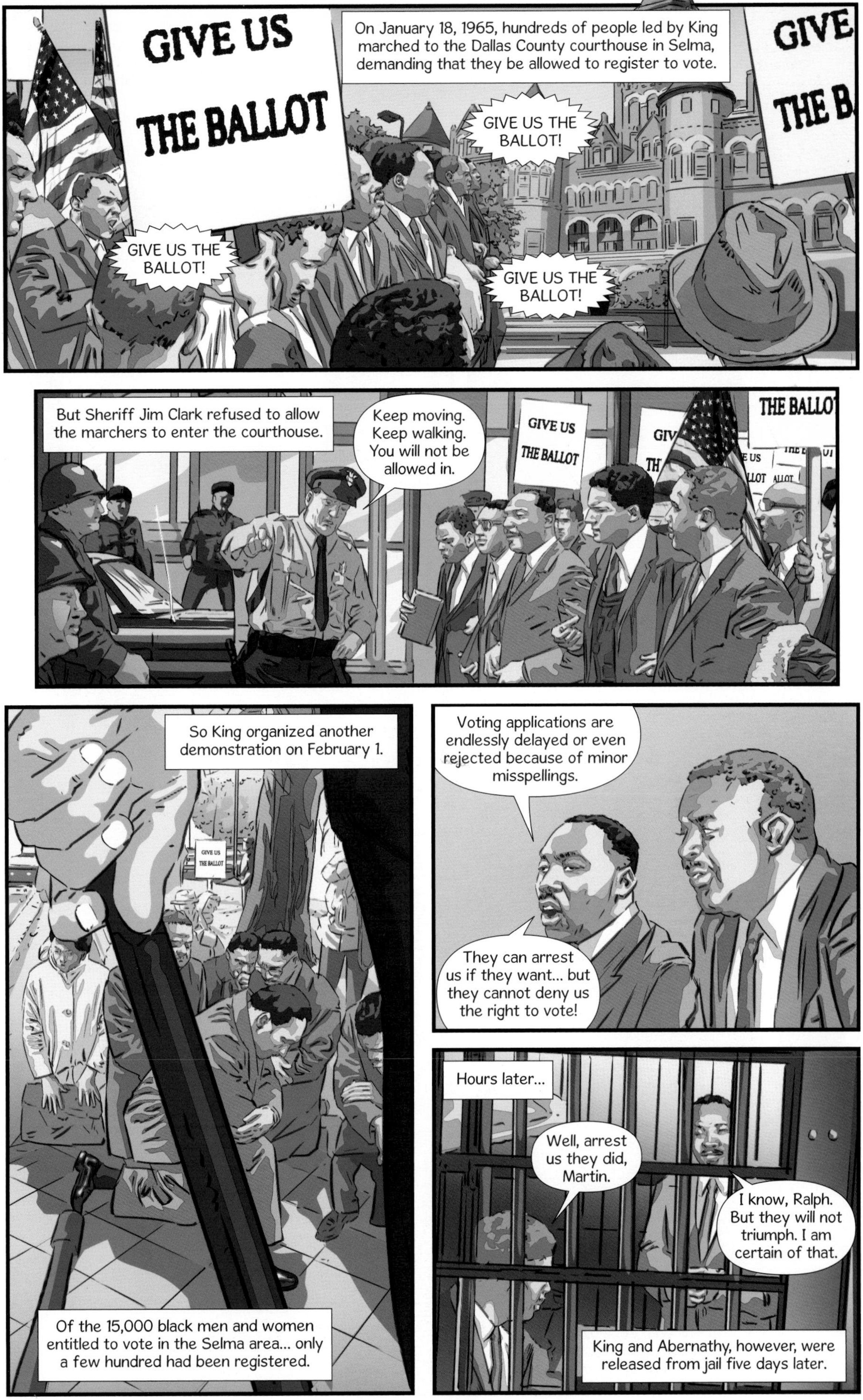
GIVE US THE BALLOT
On January 18, 1965, hundreds of people led by King marched to the Dallas County courthouse in Selma, demanding that they be allowed to register to vote.
GIVE US THE BALLOT!
GIVE US THE BALLOT!
GIVE US THE BALLOT!
But Sheriff Jim Clark refused to allow the marchers to enter the courthouse.
Keep moving. Keep walking. You will not be allowed in.
GIVE US THE BALLOT
So King organized another demonstration on February 1.
GIVE US THE BALLOT
Of the 15,000 black men and women entitled to vote in the Selma area... only a few hundred had been registered.
Voting applications are endlessly delayed or even rejected because of minor misspellings.
They can arrest us if they want... but they cannot deny us the right to vote!
Hours later...
Well, arrest us they did, Martin.
I know, Ralph. But they will not triumph. I am certain of that.
King and Abernathy, however, were released from jail five days later.

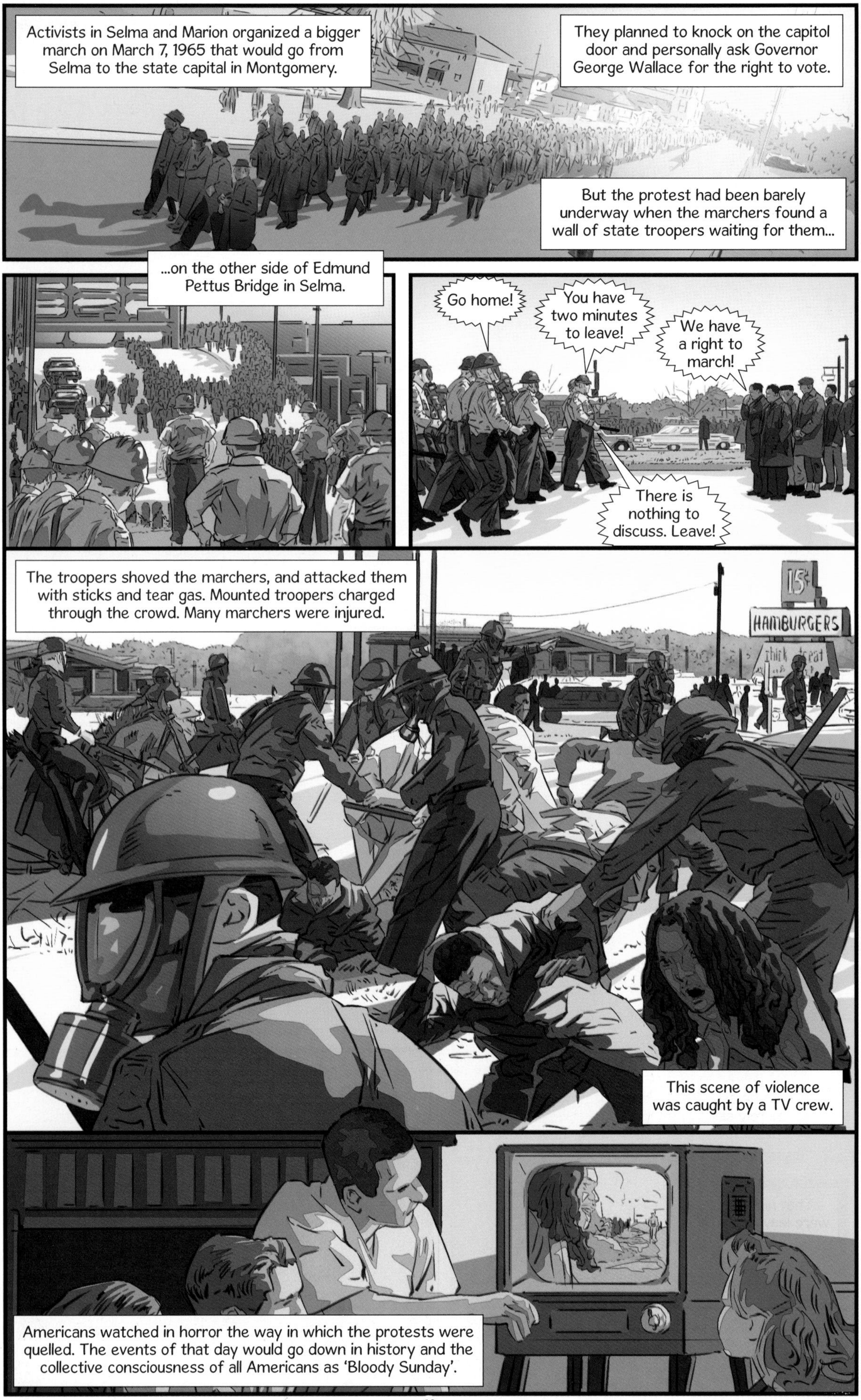

Activists in Selma and Marion organized a bigger march on March 7, 1965 that would go from Selma to the state capital in Montgomery.
They planned to knock on the capitol door and personally ask Governor George Wallace for the right to vote.
But the protest had been barely underway when the marchers found a wall of state troopers waiting for them...
...on the other side of Edmund Pettus Bridge in Selma.
Go home!
You have two minutes to leave!
We have a right to march!
There is nothing to discuss. Leave!
The troopers shoved the marchers, and attacked them with sticks and tear gas. Mounted troopers charged through the crowd. Many marchers were injured.
15¢
HAMBURGERS
This scene of violence was caught by a TV crew.
Americans watched in horror the way in which the protests were quelled. The events of that day would go down in history and the collective consciousness of all Americans as 'Bloody Sunday'.

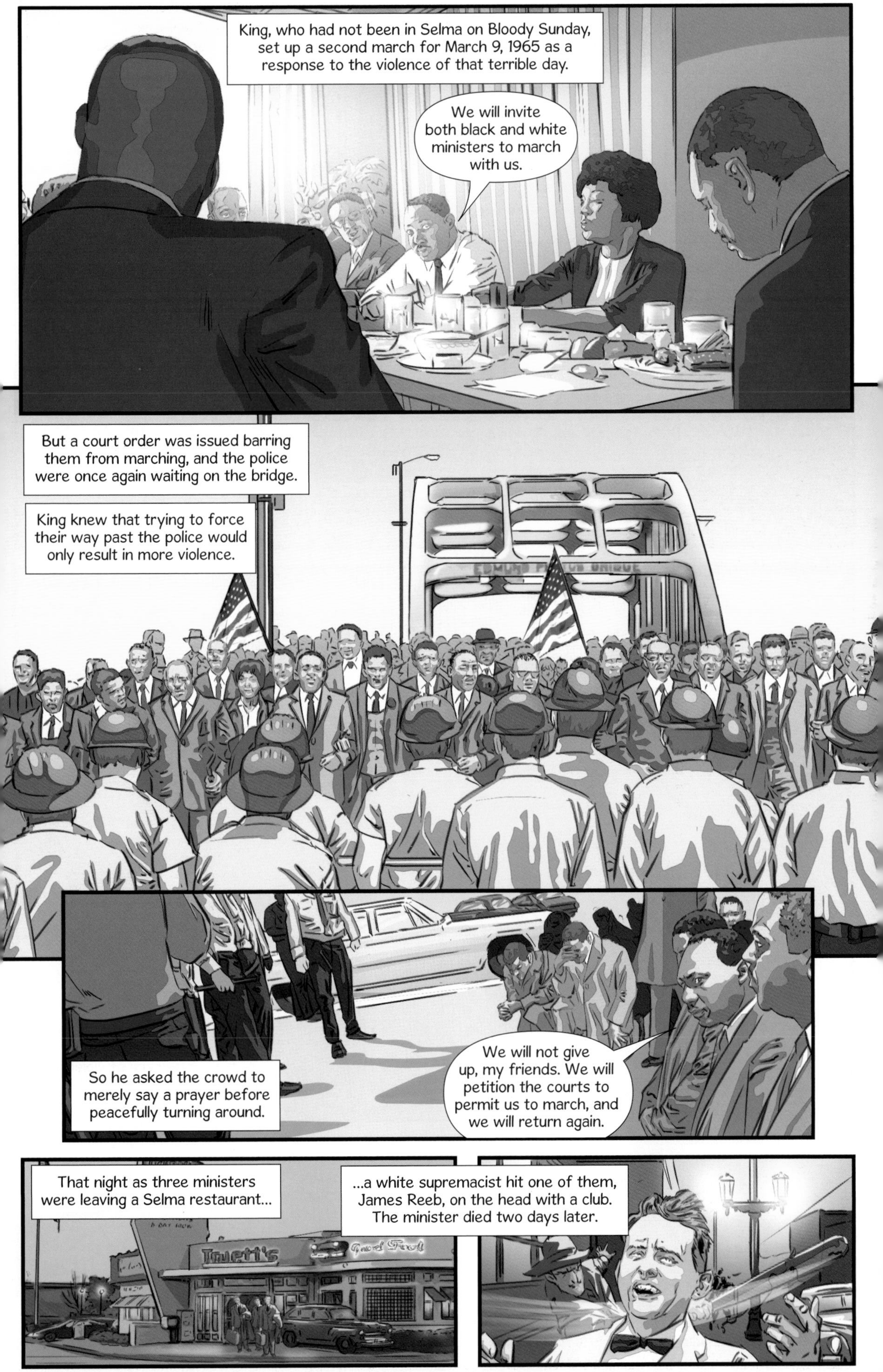
King, who had not been in Selma on Bloody Sunday, set up a second march for March 9, 1965 as a response to the violence of that terrible day.
We will invite both black and white ministers to march with us.
But a court order was issued barring them from marching, and the police were once again waiting on the bridge.
King knew that trying to force their way past the police would only result in more violence.
So he asked the crowd to merely say a prayer before peacefully turning around.
We will not give up, my friends. We will petition the courts to permit us to march, and we will return again.
That night as three ministers were leaving a Selma restaurant...
...a white supremacist hit one of them, James Reeb, on the head with a club. The minister died two days later.

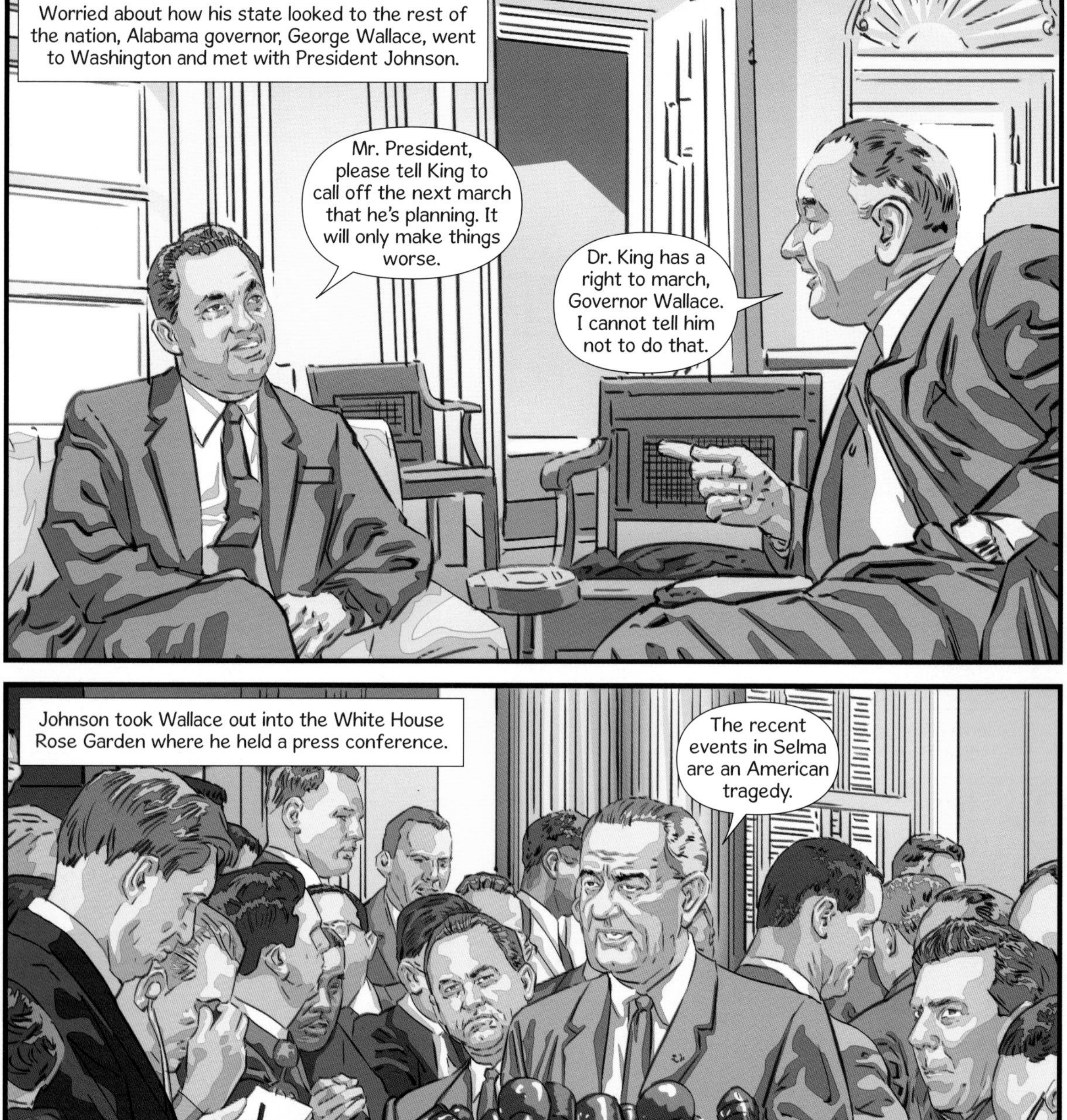
Worried about how his state looked to the rest of the nation, Alabama governor, George Wallace, went to Washington and met with President Johnson.
Mr. President, please tell King to call off the next march that he's planning. It will only make things worse.
Dr. King has a right to march, Governor Wallace. I cannot tell him not to do that.

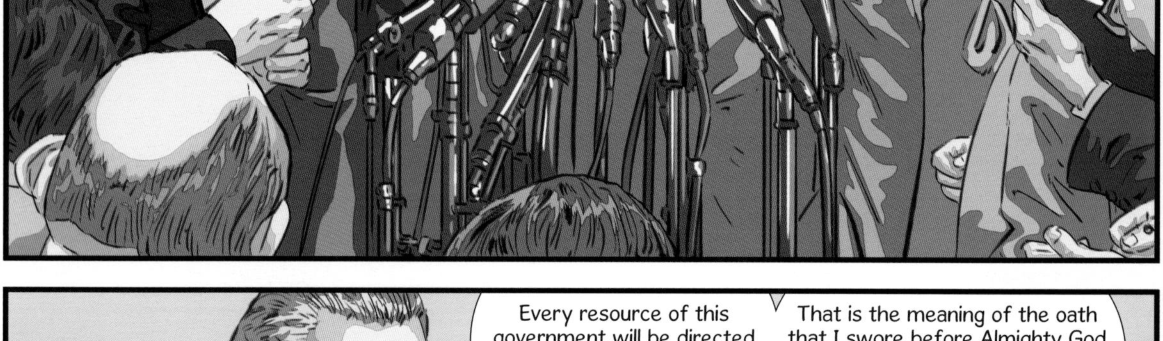
Johnson took Wallace out into the White House Rose Garden where he held a press conference.
The recent events in Selma are an American tragedy.

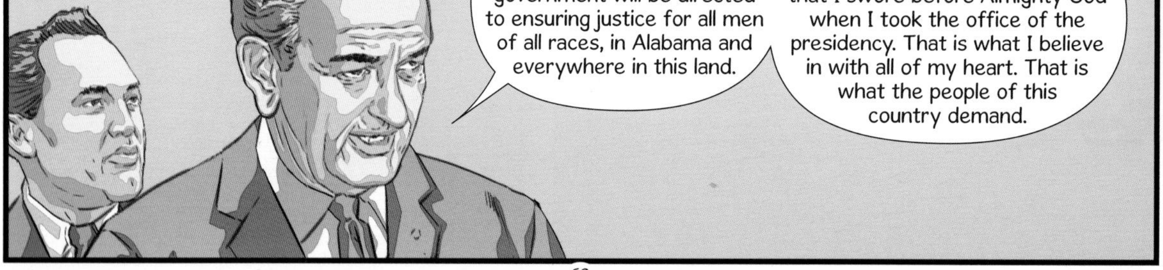
Every resource of this government will be directed to ensuring justice for all men of all races, in Alabama and everywhere in this land.
That is the meaning of the oath that I swore before Almighty God when I took the office of the presidency. That is what I believe in with all of my heart. That is what the people of this country demand.

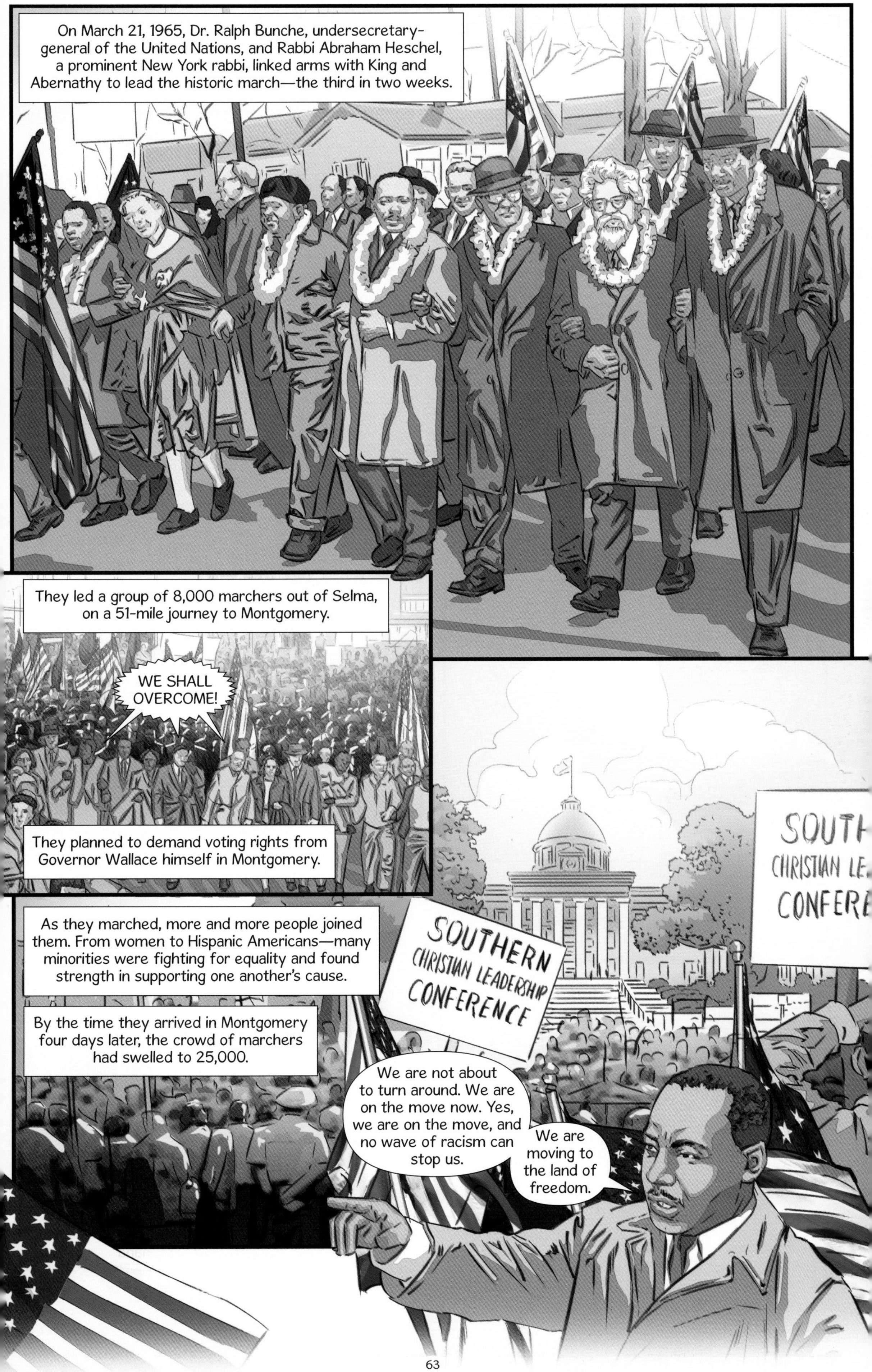
On March 21, 1965, Dr. Ralph Bunche, undersecretary-general of the United Nations, and Rabbi Abraham Heschel, a prominent New York rabbi, linked arms with King and Abernathy to lead the historic march—the third in two weeks.
They led a group of 8,000 marchers out of Selma, on a 51-mile journey to Montgomery.
WE SHALL OVERCOME!
They planned to demand voting rights from Governor Wallace himself in Montgomery.
SOUTH
CHRISTIAN LE
CONFERE
As they marched, more and more people joined them. From women to Hispanic Americans—many minorities were fighting for equality and found strength in supporting one another's cause.
SOUTHERN CHRISTIAN LEADERSHIP CONFERENCE
By the time they arrived in Montgomery four days later, the crowd of marchers had swelled to 25,000.
We are not about to turn around. We are on the move now. Yes, we are on the move, and no wave of racism can stop us.
We are moving to the land of freedom.

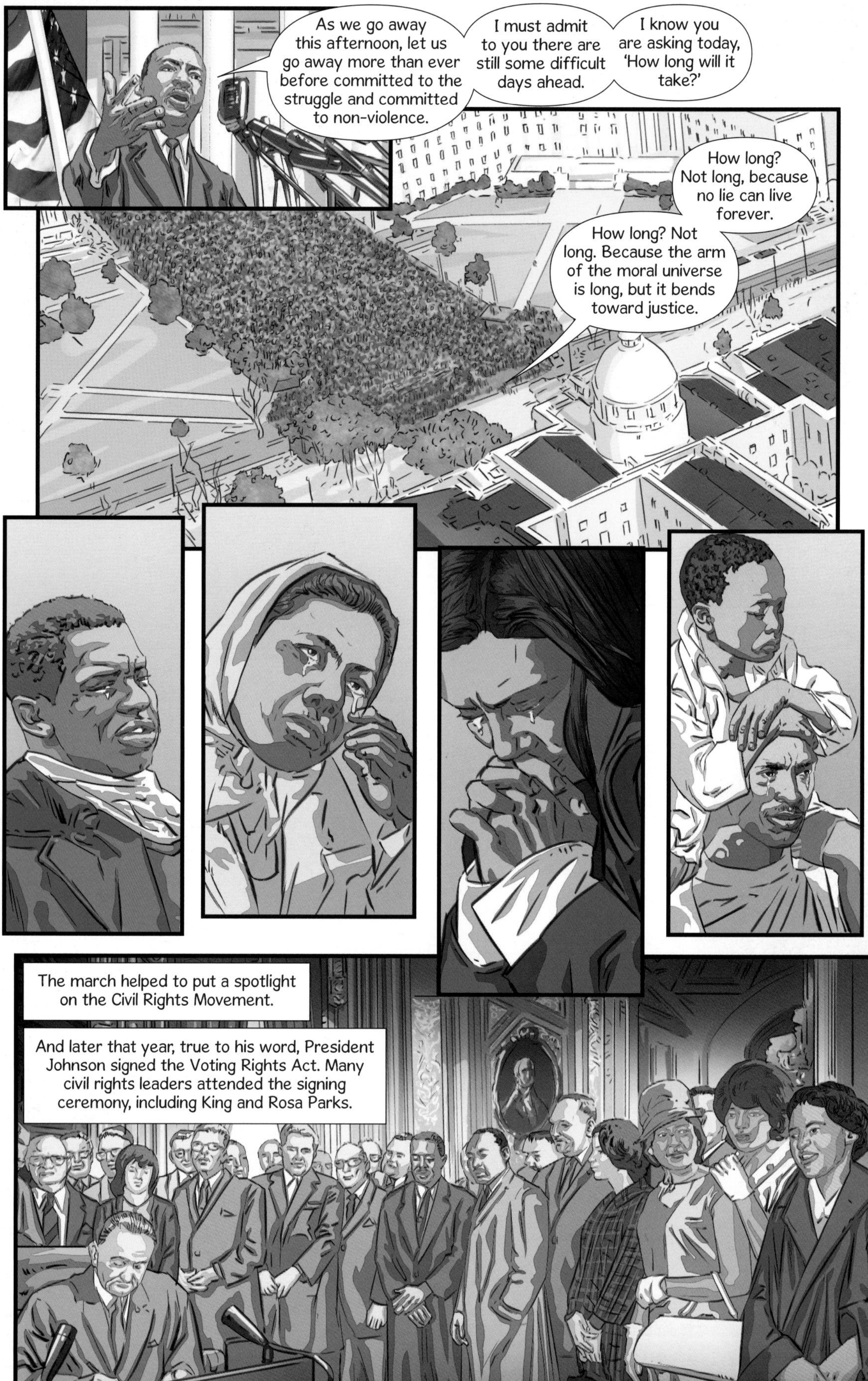
As we go away this afternoon, let us go away more than ever before committed to the struggle and committed to non-violence.
I must admit to you there are still some difficult days ahead.
I know you are asking today, 'How long will it take?'
How long? Not long, because no lie can live forever.
How long? Not long. Because the arm of the moral universe is long, but it bends toward justice.
The march helped to put a spotlight on the Civil Rights Movement.
And later that year, true to his word, President Johnson signed the Voting Rights Act. Many civil rights leaders attended the signing ceremony, including King and Rosa Parks.

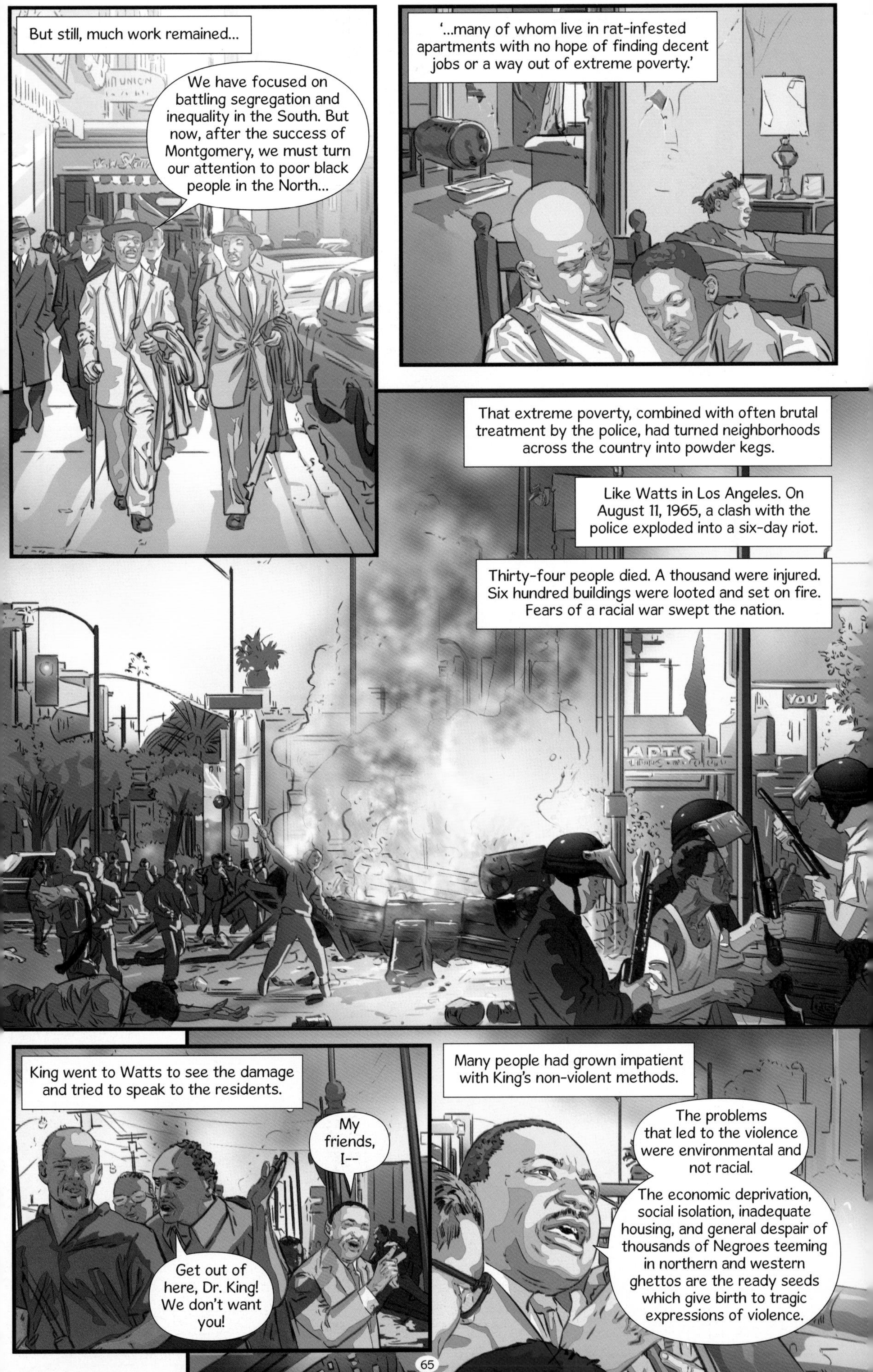
But still, much work remained...
UNION
We have focused on battling segregation and inequality in the South. But now, after the success of Montgomery, we must turn our attention to poor black people in the North...
'...many of whom live in rat-infested apartments with no hope of finding decent jobs or a way out of extreme poverty.'
That extreme poverty, combined with often brutal treatment by the police, had turned neighborhoods across the country into powder kegs.
Like Watts in Los Angeles. On August 11, 1965, a clash with the police exploded into a six-day riot.
Thirty-four people died. A thousand were injured. Six hundred buildings were looted and set on fire. Fears of a racial war swept the nation.
YOU
King went to Watts to see the damage and tried to speak to the residents.
My friends, I--
Get out of here, Dr. King! We don't want you!
Many people had grown impatient with King's non-violent methods.
The problems that led to the violence were environmental and not racial.
The economic deprivation, social isolation, inadequate housing, and general despair of thousands of Negroes teeming in northern and western ghettos are the ready seeds which give birth to tragic expressions of violence.

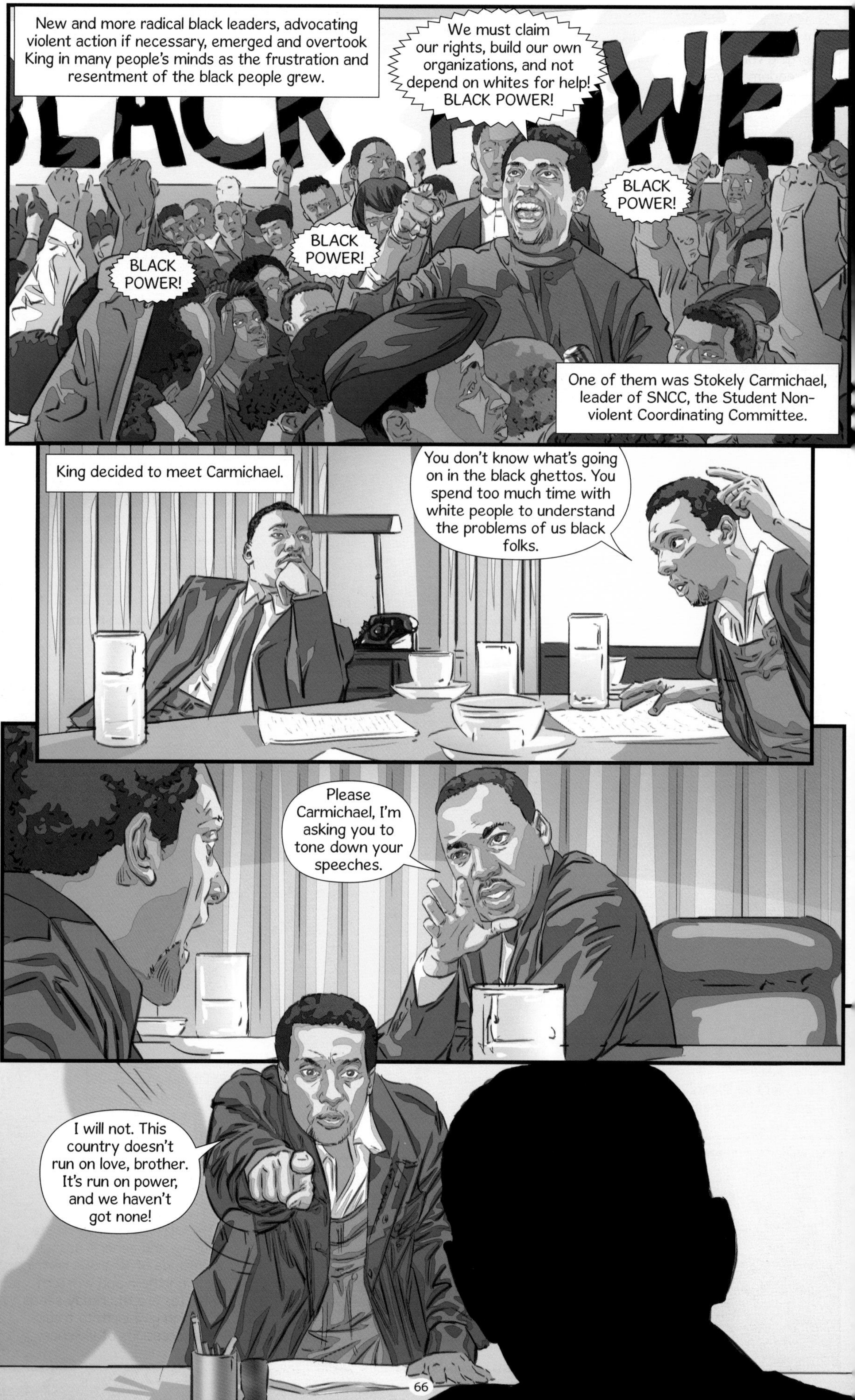
New and more radical black leaders, advocating violent action if necessary, emerged and overtook King in many people's minds as the frustration and resentment of the black people grew.
BLACK POWER
We must claim our rights, build our own organizations, and not depend on whites for help! BLACK POWER!
BLACK POWER!
BLACK POWER!
BLACK POWER!
One of them was Stokely Carmichael, leader of SNCC, the Student Non-violent Coordinating Committee.
King decided to meet Carmichael.
You don't know what's going on in the black ghettos. You spend too much time with white people to understand the problems of us black folks.
Please Carmichael, I'm asking you to tone down your speeches.
I will not. This country doesn't run on love, brother. It's run on power, and we haven't got none!

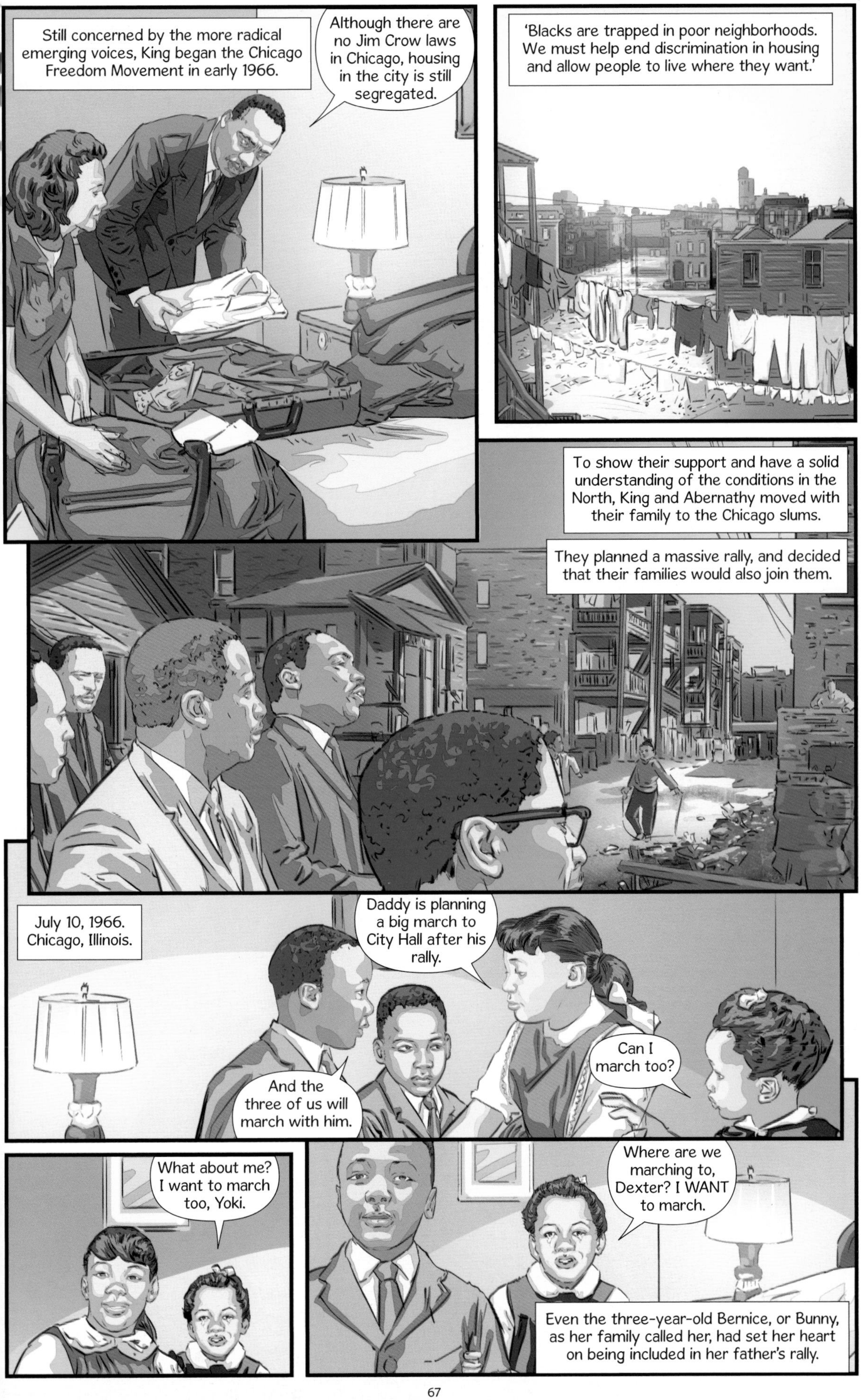
Still concerned by the more radical emerging voices, King began the Chicago Freedom Movement in early 1966.
Although there are no Jim Crow laws in Chicago, housing in the city is still segregated.
'Blacks are trapped in poor neighborhoods. We must help end discrimination in housing and allow people to live where they want.'
To show their support and have a solid understanding of the conditions in the North, King and Abernathy moved with their family to the Chicago slums.
They planned a massive rally, and decided that their families would also join them.
July 10, 1966. Chicago, Illinois.
Daddy is planning a big march to City Hall after his rally.
And the three of us will march with him.
Can I march too?
What about me? I want to march too, Yoki.
Where are we marching to, Dexter? I WANT to march.
Even the three-year-old Bernice, or Bunny, as her family called her, had set her heart on being included in her father's rally.

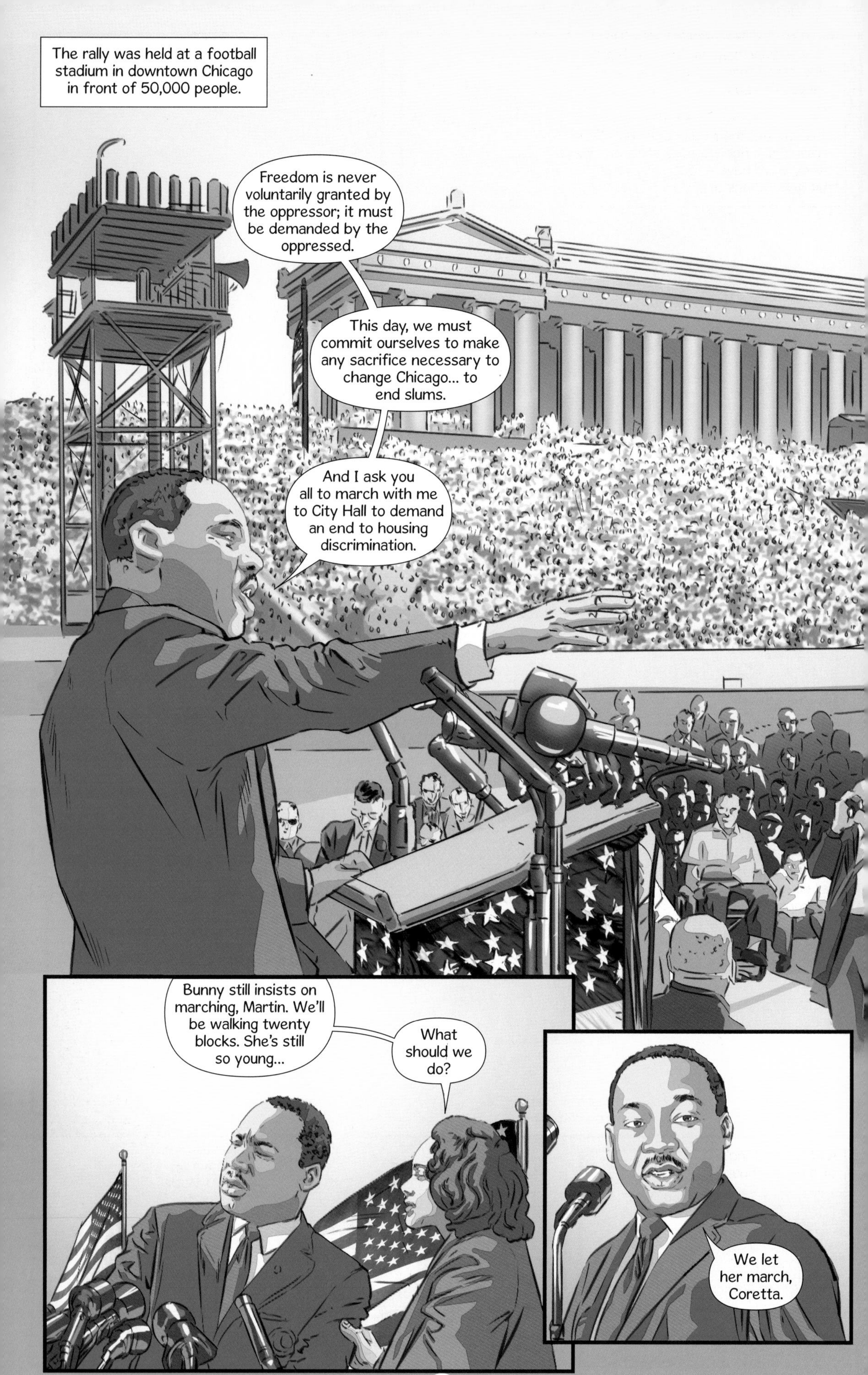
The rally was held at a football stadium in downtown Chicago in front of 50,000 people.
Freedom is never voluntarily granted by the oppressor; it must be demanded by the oppressed.
This day, we must commit ourselves to make any sacrifice necessary to change Chicago... to end slums.
And I ask you all to march with me to City Hall to demand an end to housing discrimination.
Bunny still insists on marching, Martin. We'll be walking twenty blocks. She's still so young...
What should we do?
We let her march, Coretta.

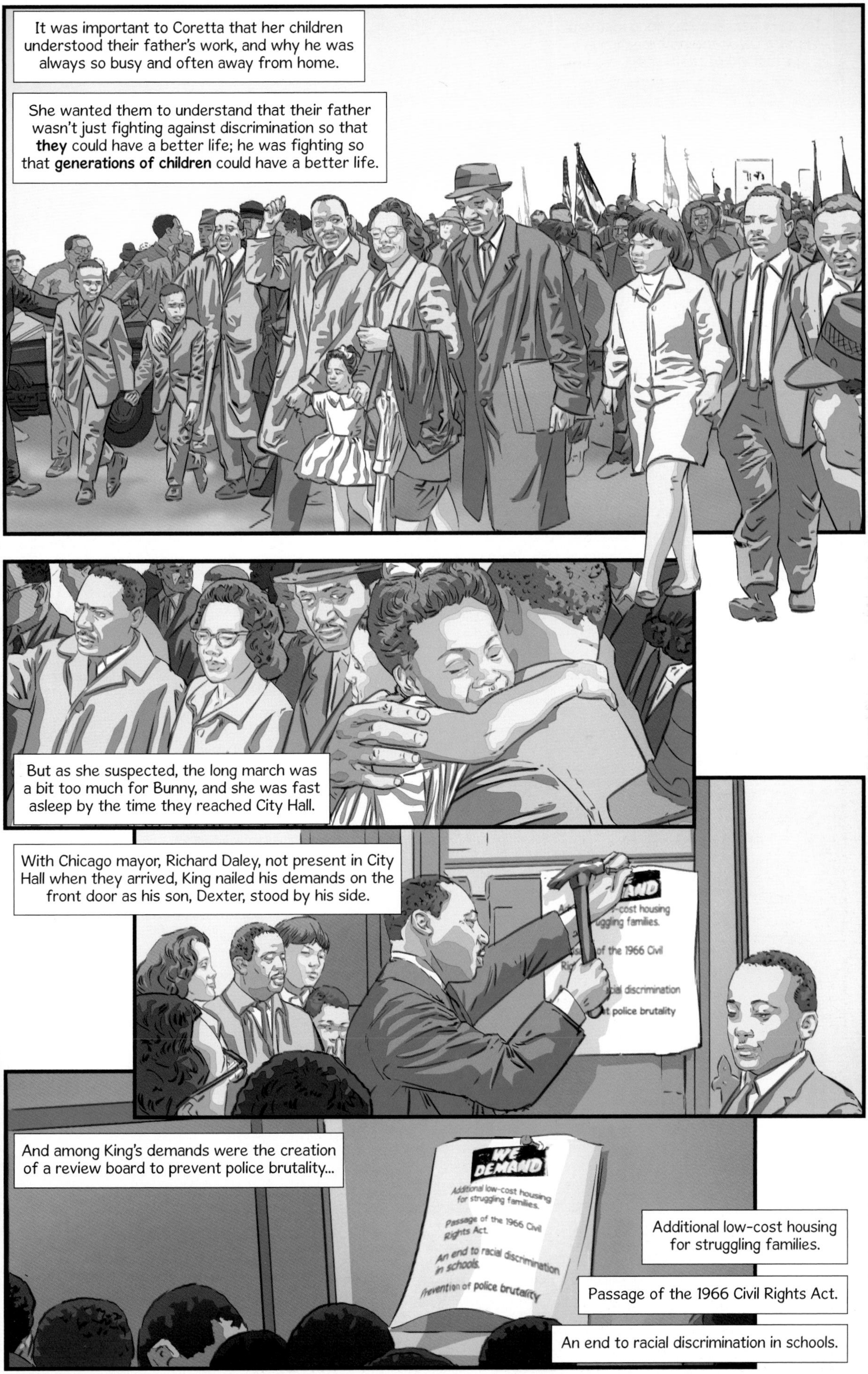

It was important to Coretta that her children understood their father's work, and why he was always so busy and often away from home.
She wanted them to understand that their father wasn't just fighting against discrimination so that **they** could have a better life; he was fighting so that **generations of children** could have a better life.
But as she suspected, the long march was a bit too much for Bunny, and she was fast asleep by the time they reached City Hall.
With Chicago mayor, Richard Daley, not present in City Hall when they arrived, King nailed his demands on the front door as his son, Dexter, stood by his side.
And among King's demands were the creation of a review board to prevent police brutality...
WE DEMAND
Additional low-cost housing for struggling families.
Passage of the 1966 Civil Rights Act.
An end to racial discrimination in schools.
Prevention of police brutality
Additional low-cost housing for struggling families.
Passage of the 1966 Civil Rights Act.
An end to racial discrimination in schools.

The very next morning, King met with Richard Daley, the first meeting in a series that would continue for months.

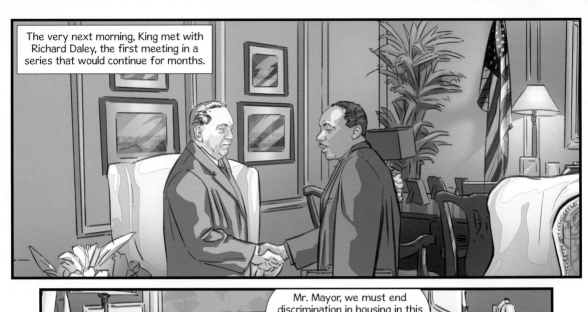

Mr. Mayor, we must end discrimination in housing in this city. Segregated housing only leads to an endless cycle of poverty and hopelessness.

I will do my best to address the housing problems here in Chicago.

But in reality, Daley offered nothing but empty promises. While the brutal violence faced by the peaceful protestors in the South had created a sense of urgency to end discrimination...

...the lack of brutality faced by protestors in the North gave many the belief that discrimination wasn't that urgent an issue there.

So when President Johnson sent his third Civil Rights Bill to Congress later that year to ban discrimination in housing throughout the US...

...the US Congress did not pass the bill into law, blaming extremists on both sides of the civil rights issue.

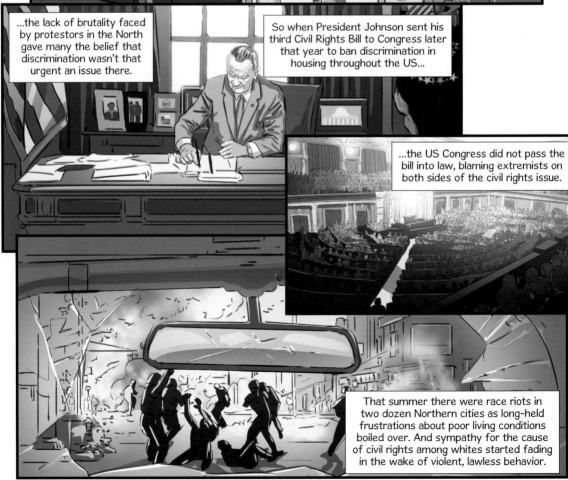

That summer there were race riots in two dozen Northern cities as long-held frustrations about poor living conditions boiled over. And sympathy for the cause of civil rights among whites started fading in the wake of violent, lawless behavior.

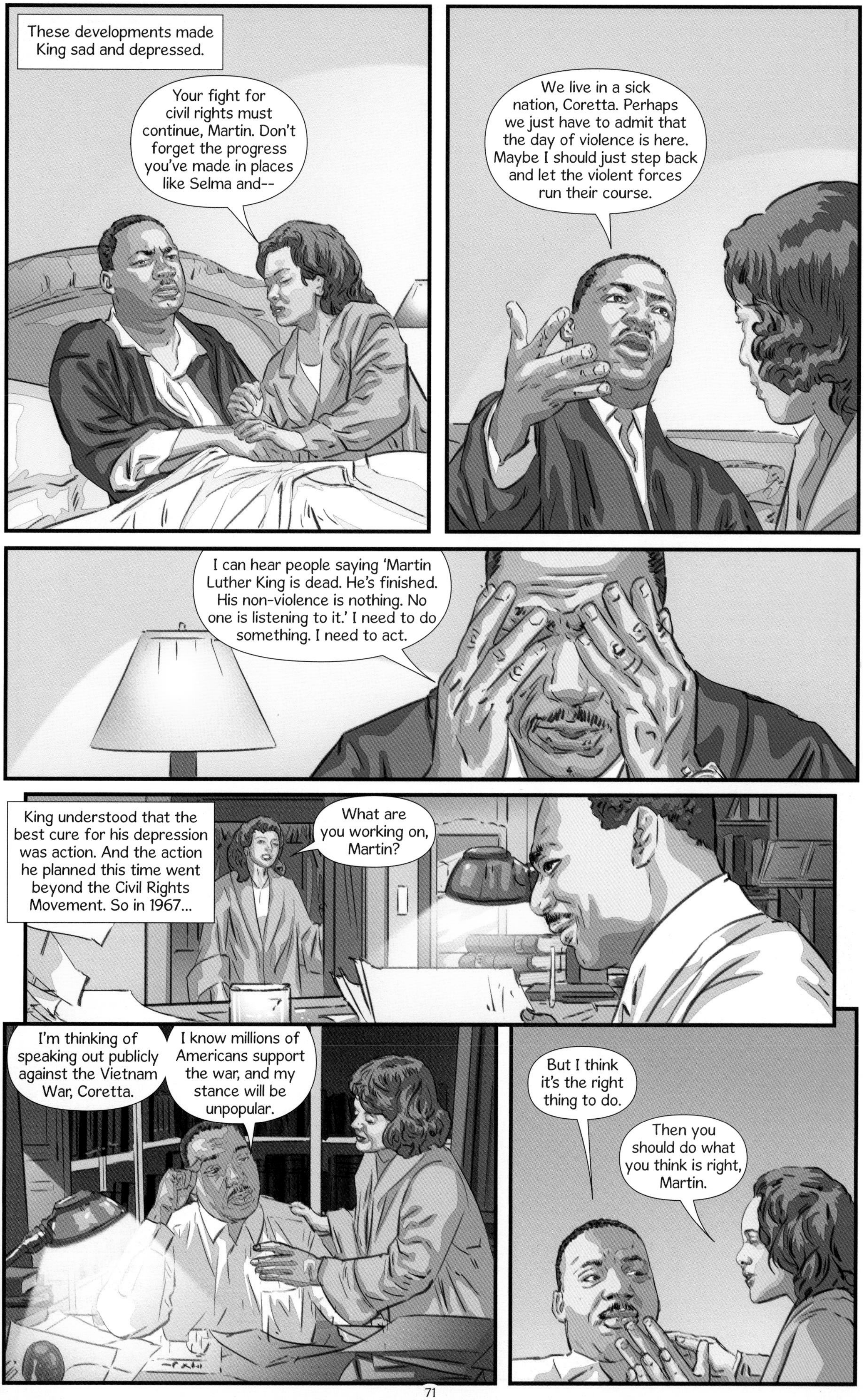

These developments made King sad and depressed.
Your fight for civil rights must continue, Martin. Don't forget the progress you've made in places like Selma and--
We live in a sick nation, Coretta. Perhaps we just have to admit that the day of violence is here. Maybe I should just step back and let the violent forces run their course.
I can hear people saying 'Martin Luther King is dead. He's finished. His non-violence is nothing. No one is listening to it.' I need to do something. I need to act.
King understood that the best cure for his depression was action. And the action he planned this time went beyond the Civil Rights Movement. So in 1967...
What are you working on, Martin?
I'm thinking of speaking out publicly against the Vietnam War, Coretta.
I know millions of Americans support the war, and my stance will be unpopular.
But I think it's the right thing to do.
Then you should do what you think is right, Martin.

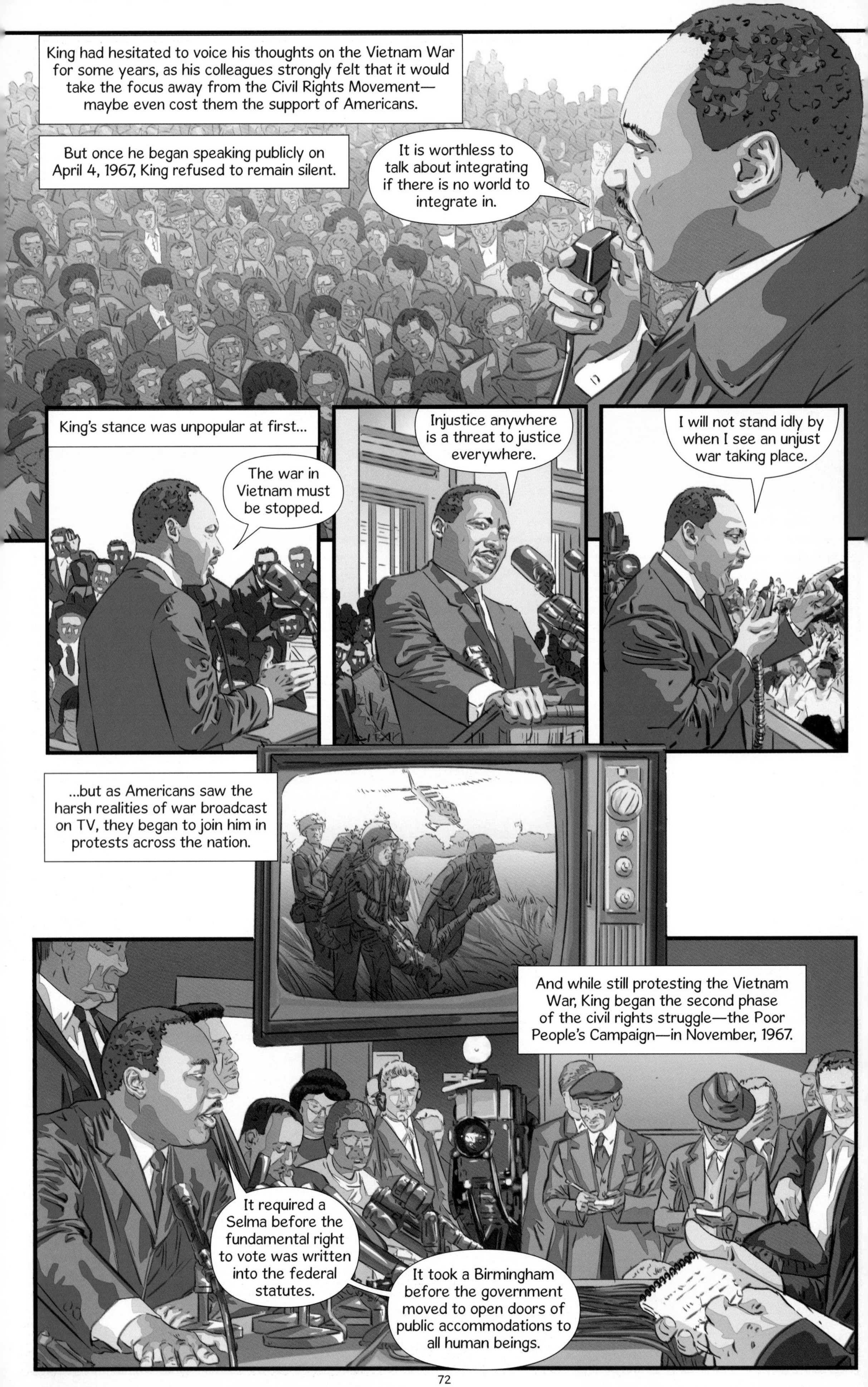
King had hesitated to voice his thoughts on the Vietnam War for some years, as his colleagues strongly felt that it would take the focus away from the Civil Rights Movement—maybe even cost them the support of Americans.
But once he began speaking publicly on April 4, 1967, King refused to remain silent.
It is worthless to talk about integrating if there is no world to integrate in.
King's stance was unpopular at first...
The war in Vietnam must be stopped.
Injustice anywhere is a threat to justice everywhere.
I will not stand idly by when I see an unjust war taking place.
...but as Americans saw the harsh realities of war broadcast on TV, they began to join him in protests across the nation.
And while still protesting the Vietnam War, King began the second phase of the civil rights struggle—the Poor People's Campaign—in November, 1967.
It required a Selma before the fundamental right to vote was written into the federal statutes.
It took a Birmingham before the government moved to open doors of public accommodations to all human beings.

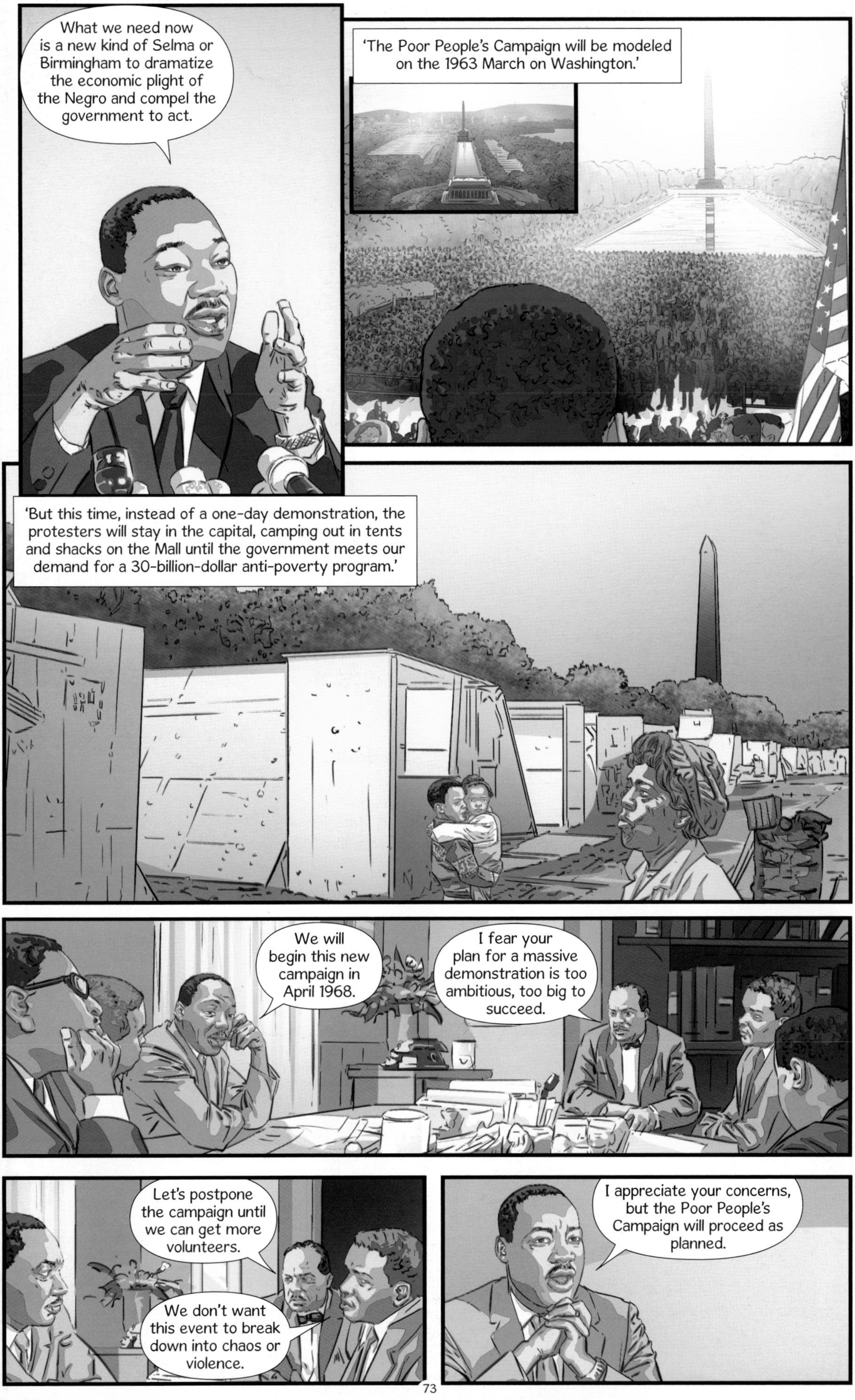
What we need now is a new kind of Selma or Birmingham to dramatize the economic plight of the Negro and compel the government to act.
'The Poor People's Campaign will be modeled on the 1963 March on Washington.'
'But this time, instead of a one-day demonstration, the protesters will stay in the capital, camping out in tents and shacks on the Mall until the government meets our demand for a 30-billion-dollar anti-poverty program.'
We will begin this new campaign in April 1968.
I fear your plan for a massive demonstration is too ambitious, too big to succeed.
Let's postpone the campaign until we can get more volunteers.
We don't want this event to break down into chaos or violence.
I appreciate your concerns, but the Poor People's Campaign will proceed as planned.

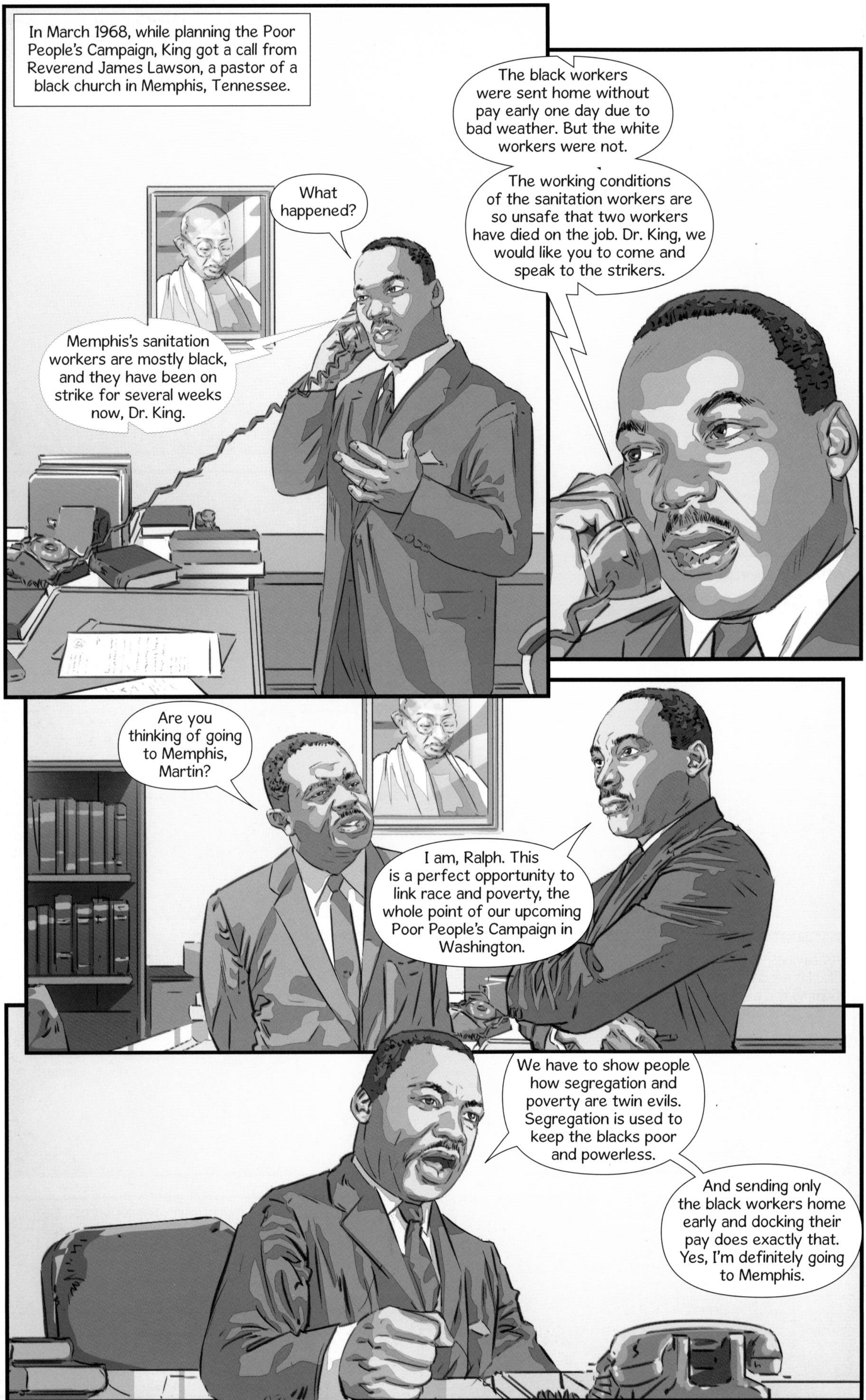
In March 1968, while planning the Poor People's Campaign, King got a call from Reverend James Lawson, a pastor of a black church in Memphis, Tennessee.
Memphis's sanitation workers are mostly black, and they have been on strike for several weeks now, Dr. King.
What happened?
The black workers were sent home without pay early one day due to bad weather. But the white workers were not.
The working conditions of the sanitation workers are so unsafe that two workers have died on the job. Dr. King, we would like you to come and speak to the strikers.
Are you thinking of going to Memphis, Martin?
I am, Ralph. This is a perfect opportunity to link race and poverty, the whole point of our upcoming Poor People's Campaign in Washington.
We have to show people how segregation and poverty are twin evils. Segregation is used to keep the blacks poor and powerless.
And sending only the black workers home early and docking their pay does exactly that. Yes, I'm definitely going to Memphis.

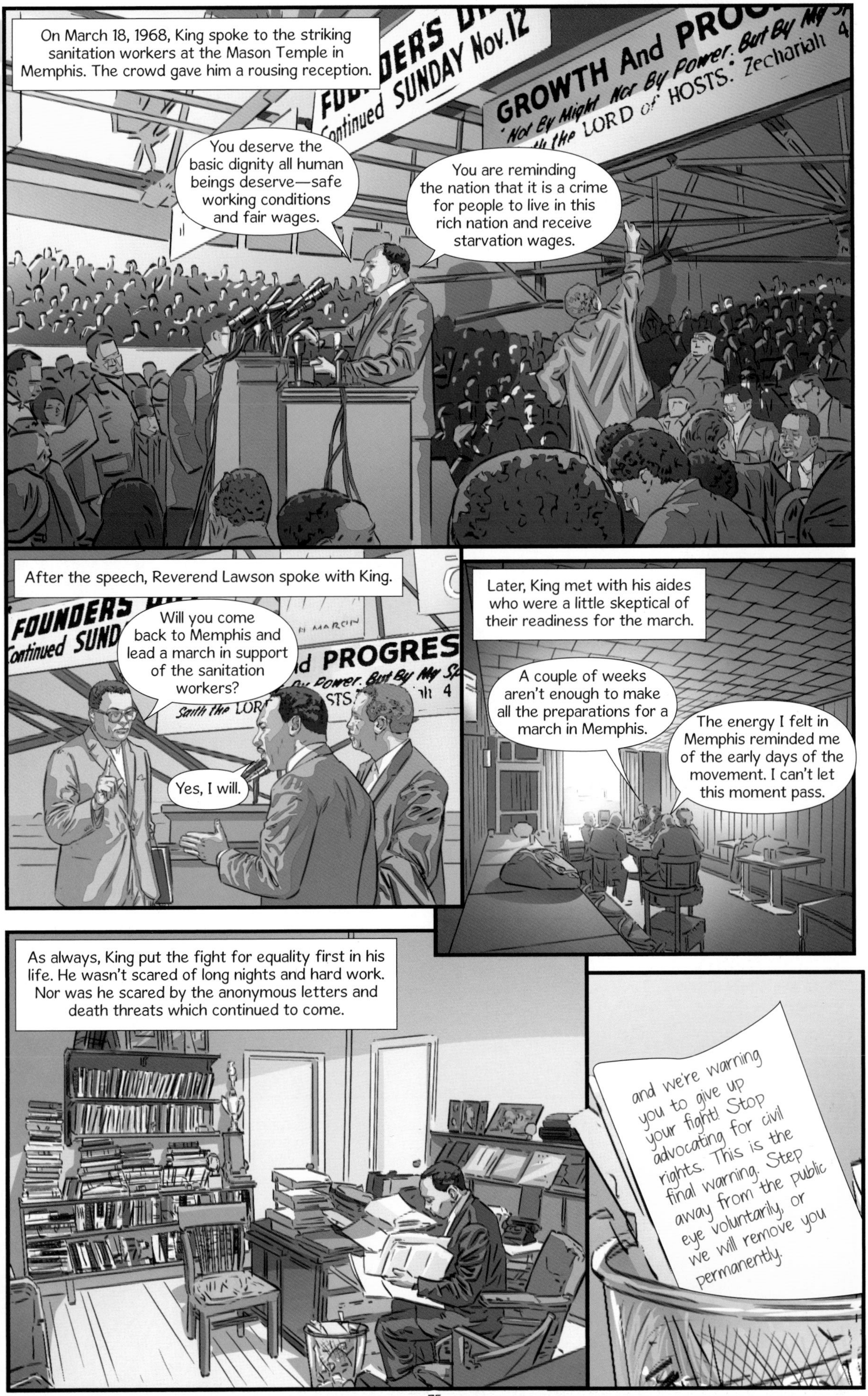
On March 18, 1968, King spoke to the striking sanitation workers at the Mason Temple in Memphis. The crowd gave him a rousing reception.
Continued SUNDAY Nov.12
You deserve the basic dignity all human beings deserve—safe working conditions and fair wages.
You are reminding the nation that it is a crime for people to live in this rich nation and receive starvation wages.
After the speech, Reverend Lawson spoke with King.
Will you come back to Memphis and lead a march in support of the sanitation workers?
Yes, I will.
Later, King met with his aides who were a little skeptical of their readiness for the march.
A couple of weeks aren't enough to make all the preparations for a march in Memphis.
The energy I felt in Memphis reminded me of the early days of the movement. I can't let this moment pass.
As always, King put the fight for equality first in his life. He wasn't scared of long nights and hard work. Nor was he scared by the anonymous letters and death threats which continued to come.
and we're warning you to give up your fight! Stop advocating for civil rights. This is the final warning. Step away from the public eye voluntarily, or we will remove you permanently.

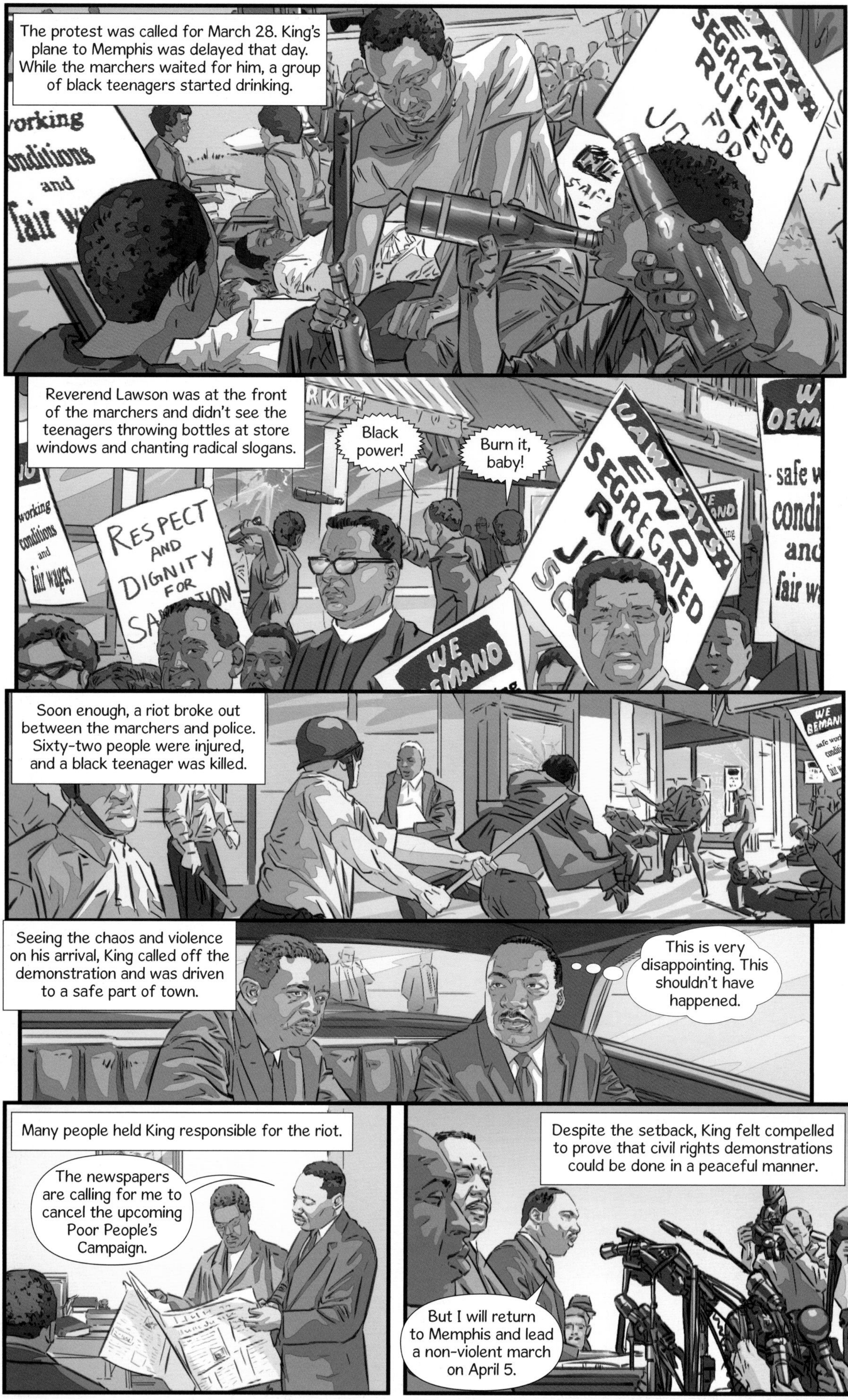
The protest was called for March 28. King's plane to Memphis was delayed that day. While the marchers waited for him, a group of black teenagers started drinking.
Reverend Lawson was at the front of the marchers and didn't see the teenagers throwing bottles at store windows and chanting radical slogans.
Black power!
Burn it, baby!
Soon enough, a riot broke out between the marchers and police. Sixty-two people were injured, and a black teenager was killed.
Seeing the chaos and violence on his arrival, King called off the demonstration and was driven to a safe part of town.
This is very disappointing. This shouldn't have happened.
Many people held King responsible for the riot.
The newspapers are calling for me to cancel the upcoming Poor People's Campaign.
Despite the setback, King felt compelled to prove that civil rights demonstrations could be done in a peaceful manner.
But I will return to Memphis and lead a non-violent march on April 5.

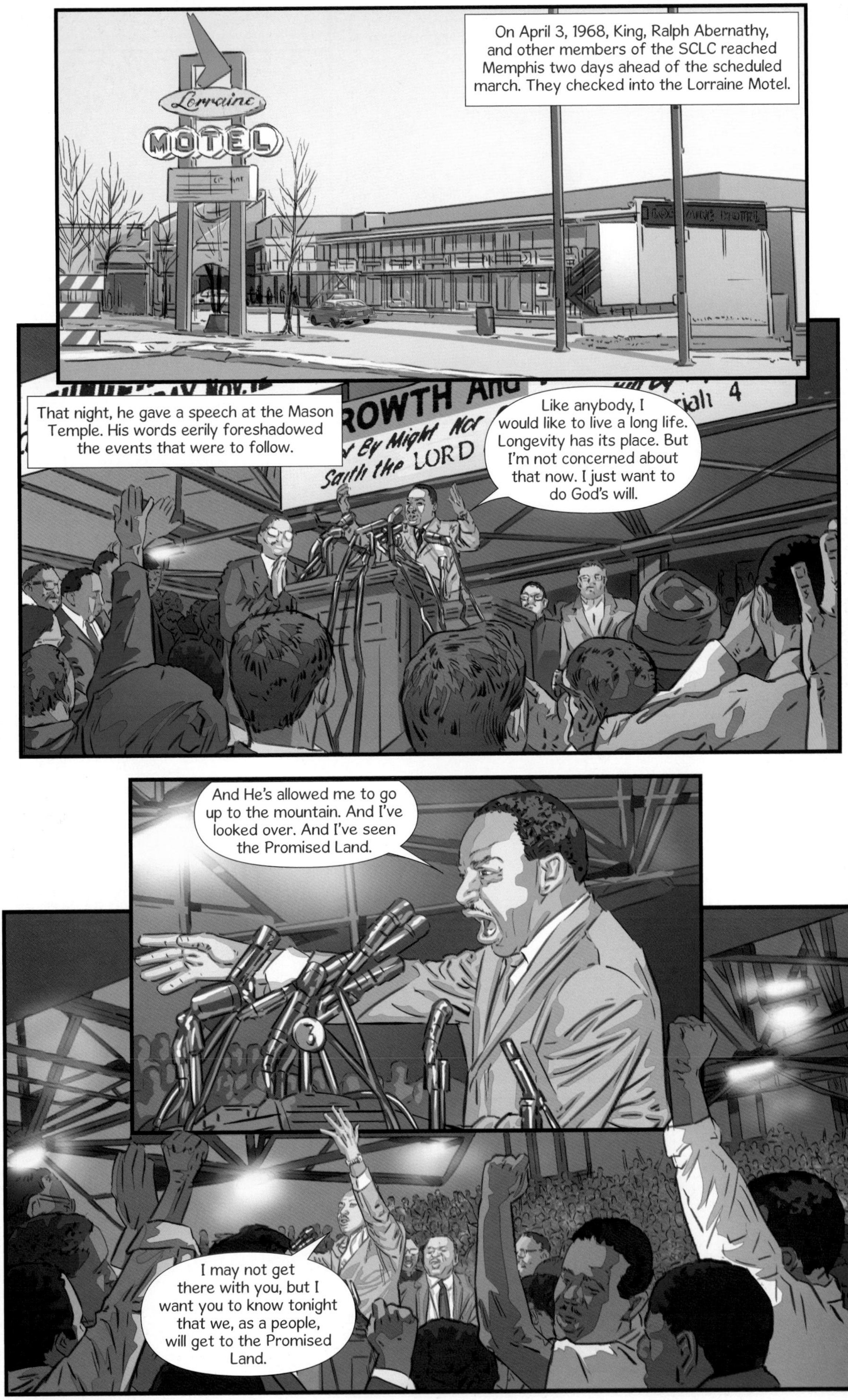
On April 3, 1968, King, Ralph Abernathy, and other members of the SCLC reached Memphis two days ahead of the scheduled march. They checked into the Lorraine Motel.
Lorraine
MOTEL
That night, he gave a speech at the Mason Temple. His words eerily foreshadowed the events that were to follow.
Saith the LORD
Like anybody, I would like to live a long life. Longevity has its place. But I'm not concerned about that now. I just want to do God's will.
And He's allowed me to go up to the mountain. And I've looked over. And I've seen the Promised Land.
I may not get there with you, but I want you to know tonight that we, as a people, will get to the Promised Land.

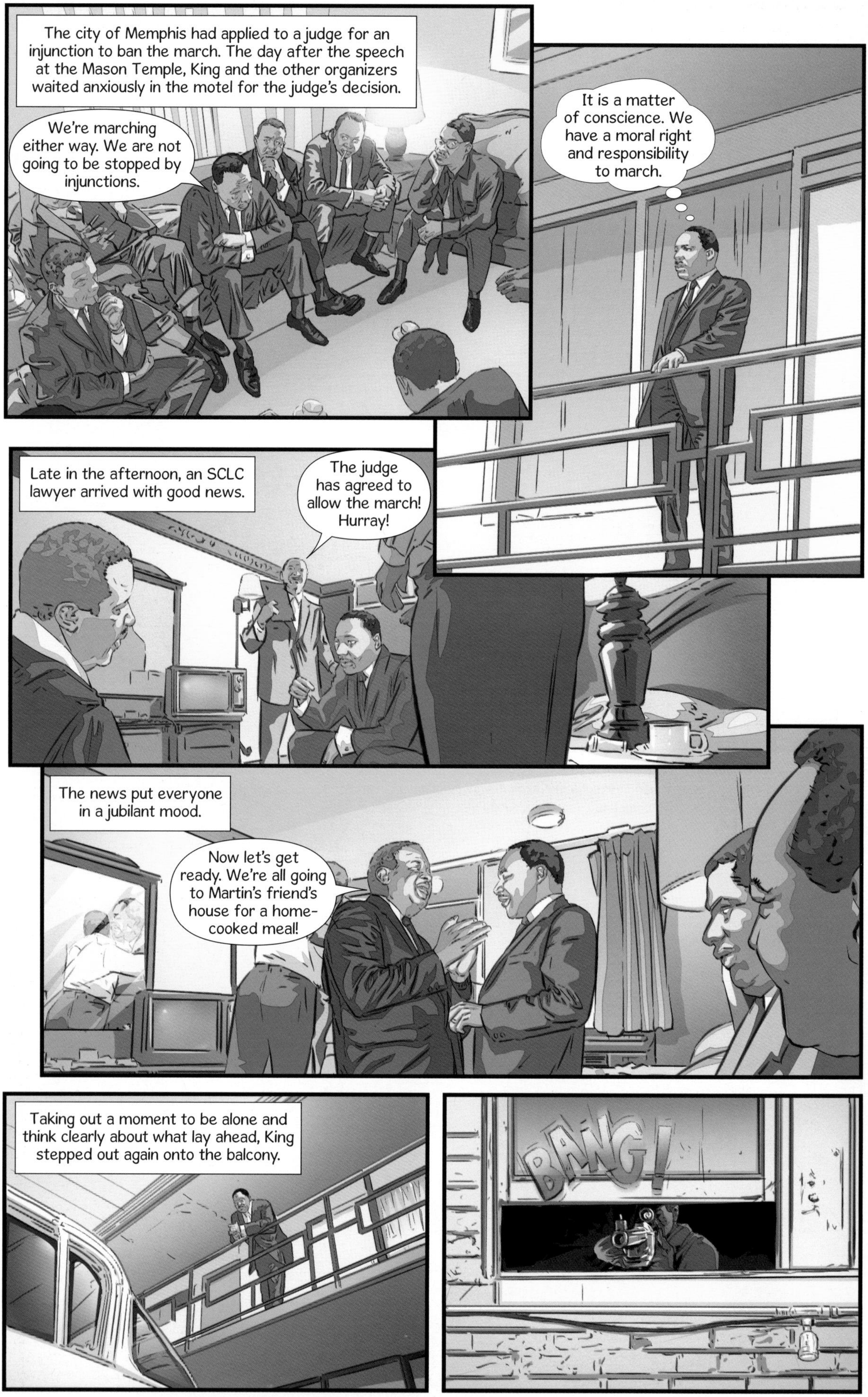

The city of Memphis had applied to a judge for an injunction to ban the march. The day after the speech at the Mason Temple, King and the other organizers waited anxiously in the motel for the judge's decision.
We're marching either way. We are not going to be stopped by injunctions.
It is a matter of conscience. We have a moral right and responsibility to march.
Late in the afternoon, an SCLC lawyer arrived with good news.
The judge has agreed to allow the march! Hurray!
The news put everyone in a jubilant mood.
Now let's get ready. We're all going to Martin's friend's house for a home-cooked meal!
Taking out a moment to be alone and think clearly about what lay ahead, King stepped out again onto the balcony.
BANG!

The single gunshot that rang out in that tranquil night found King.

MARTIN!

Martin... Martin, this is Ralph. Do you hear me? This is Ralph. DO YOU HEAR ME!

Abernathy received no reply.

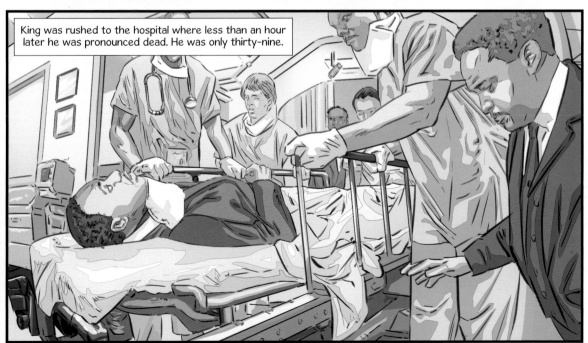

King was rushed to the hospital where less than an hour later he was pronounced dead. He was only thirty-nine.

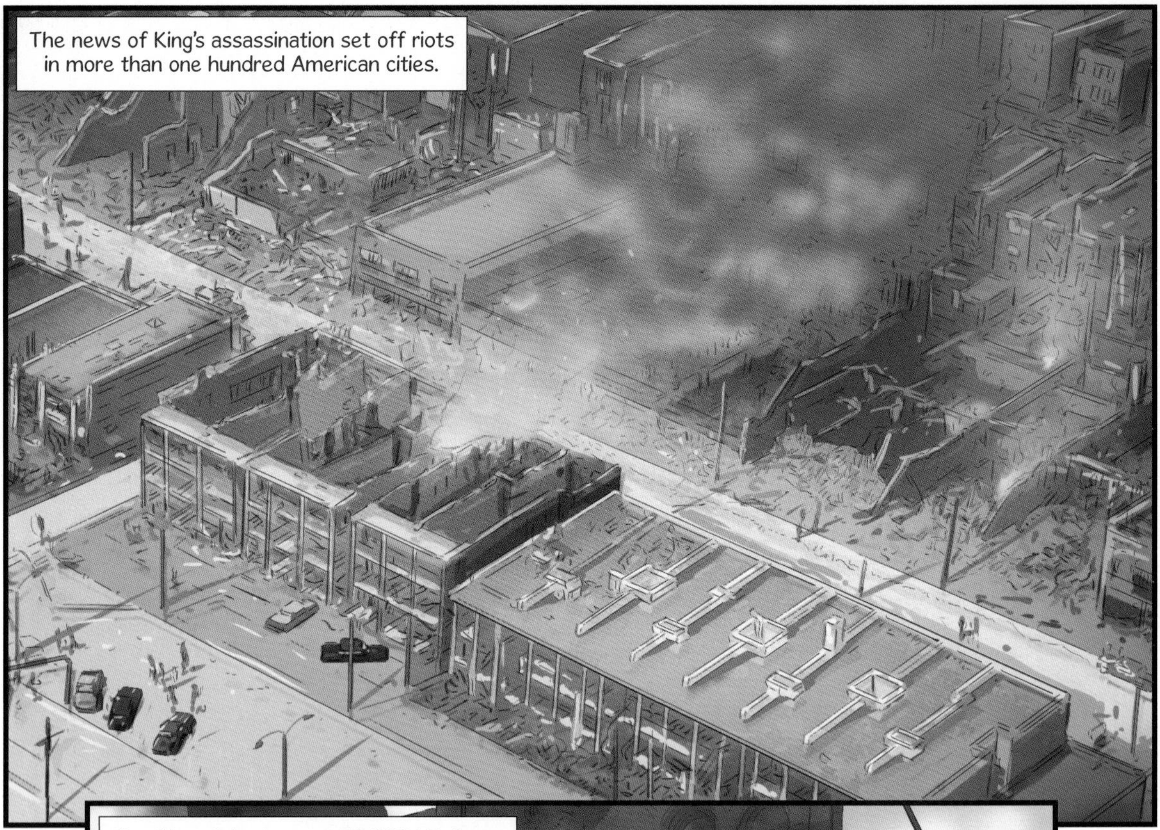
The news of King's assassination set off riots in more than one hundred American cities.

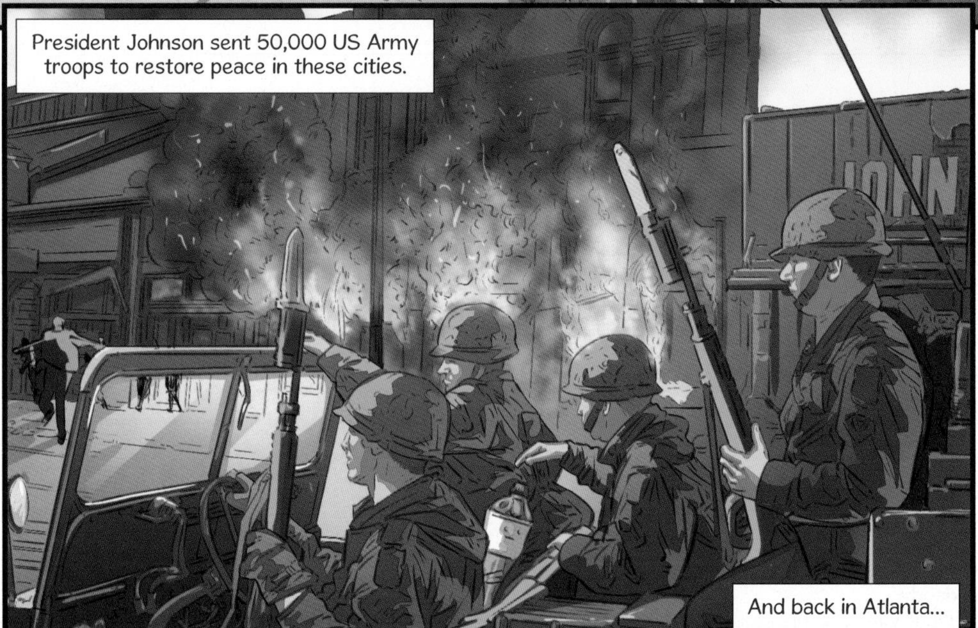
President Johnson sent 50,000 US Army troops to restore peace in these cities.
And back in Atlanta...

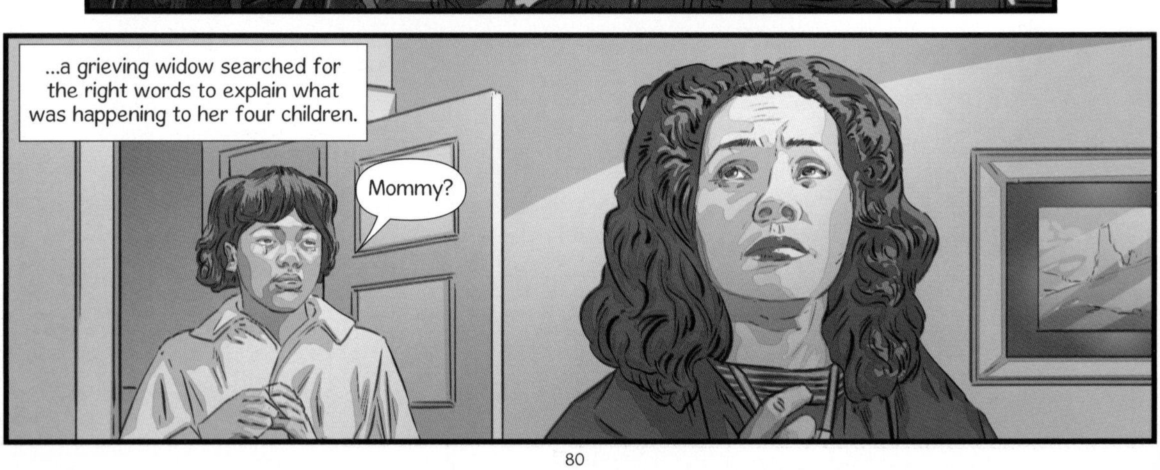
...a grieving widow searched for the right words to explain what was happening to her four children.
Mommy?

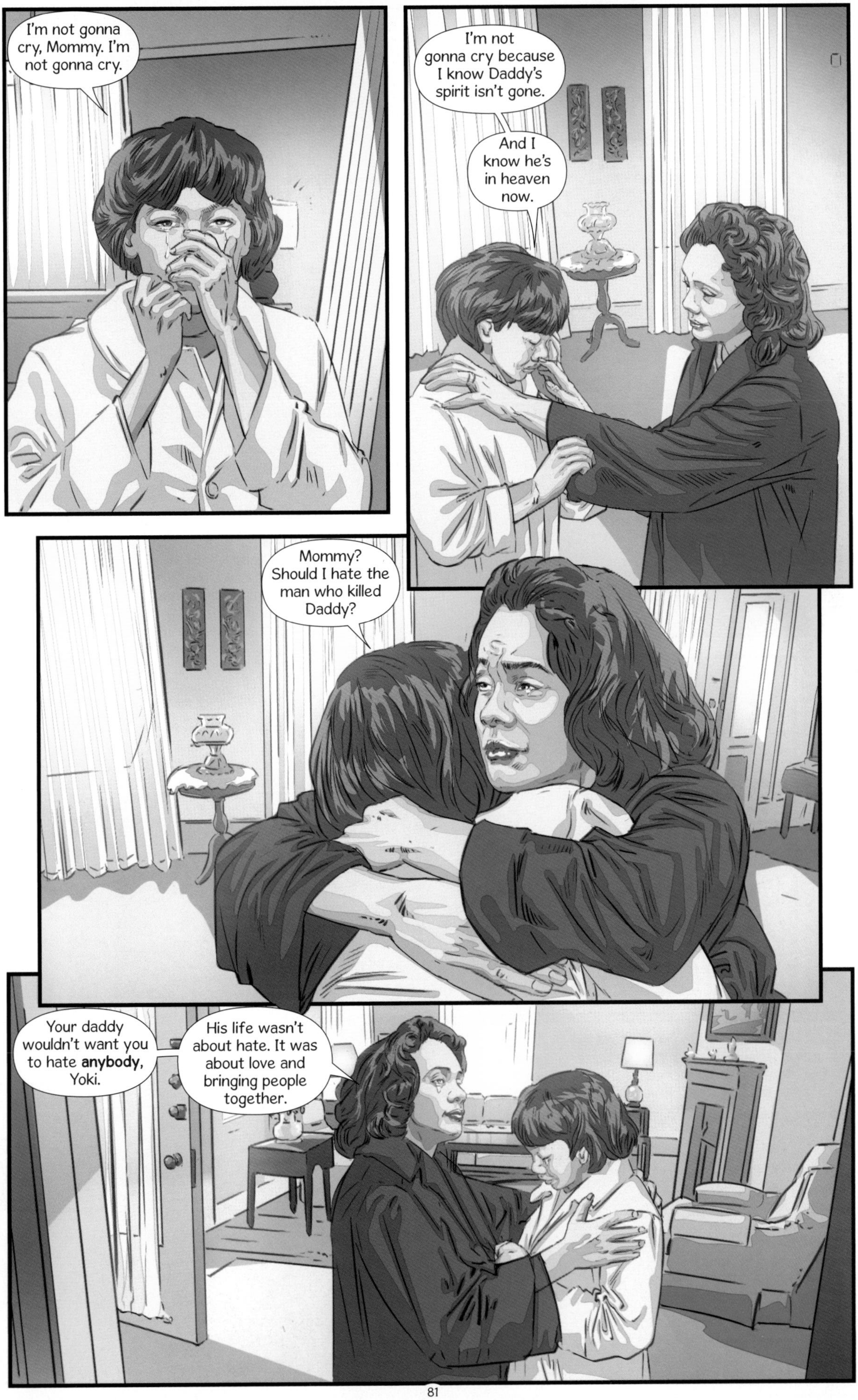

I'm not gonna cry, Mommy. I'm not gonna cry.
I'm not gonna cry because I know Daddy's spirit isn't gone.
And I know he's in heaven now.
Mommy? Should I hate the man who killed Daddy?
Your daddy wouldn't want you to hate **anybody**, Yoki.
His life wasn't about hate. It was about love and bringing people together.

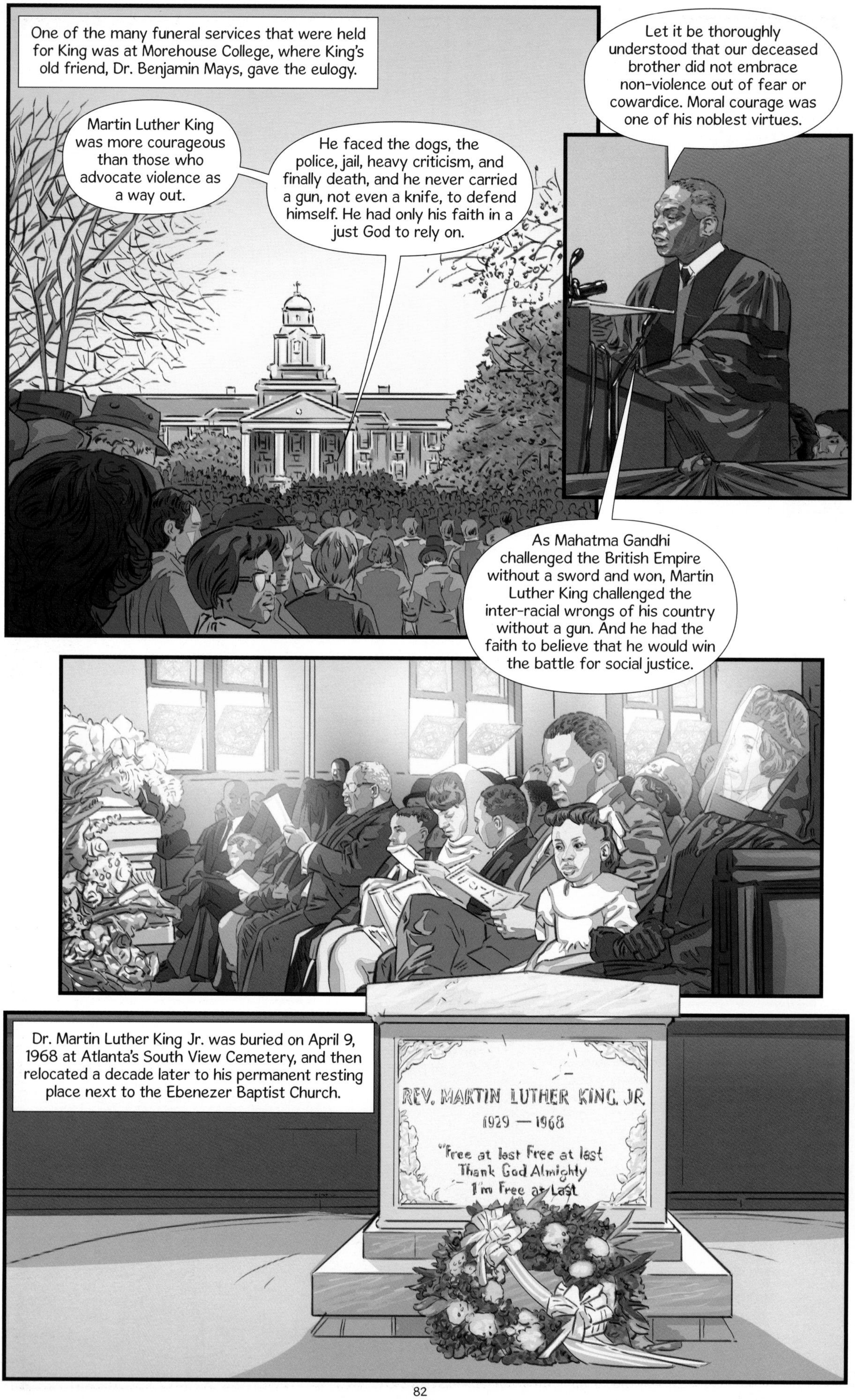
One of the many funeral services that were held for King was at Morehouse College, where King's old friend, Dr. Benjamin Mays, gave the eulogy.
Martin Luther King was more courageous than those who advocate violence as a way out.
He faced the dogs, the police, jail, heavy criticism, and finally death, and he never carried a gun, not even a knife, to defend himself. He had only his faith in a just God to rely on.
Let it be thoroughly understood that our deceased brother did not embrace non-violence out of fear or cowardice. Moral courage was one of his noblest virtues.
As Mahatma Gandhi challenged the British Empire without a sword and won, Martin Luther King challenged the inter-racial wrongs of his country without a gun. And he had the faith to believe that he would win the battle for social justice.
Dr. Martin Luther King Jr. was buried on April 9, 1968 at Atlanta's South View Cemetery, and then relocated a decade later to his permanent resting place next to the Ebenezer Baptist Church.
REV. MARTIN LUTHER KING, JR
1929 — 1968
"Free at last Free at last
Thank God Almighty
I'm Free at Last

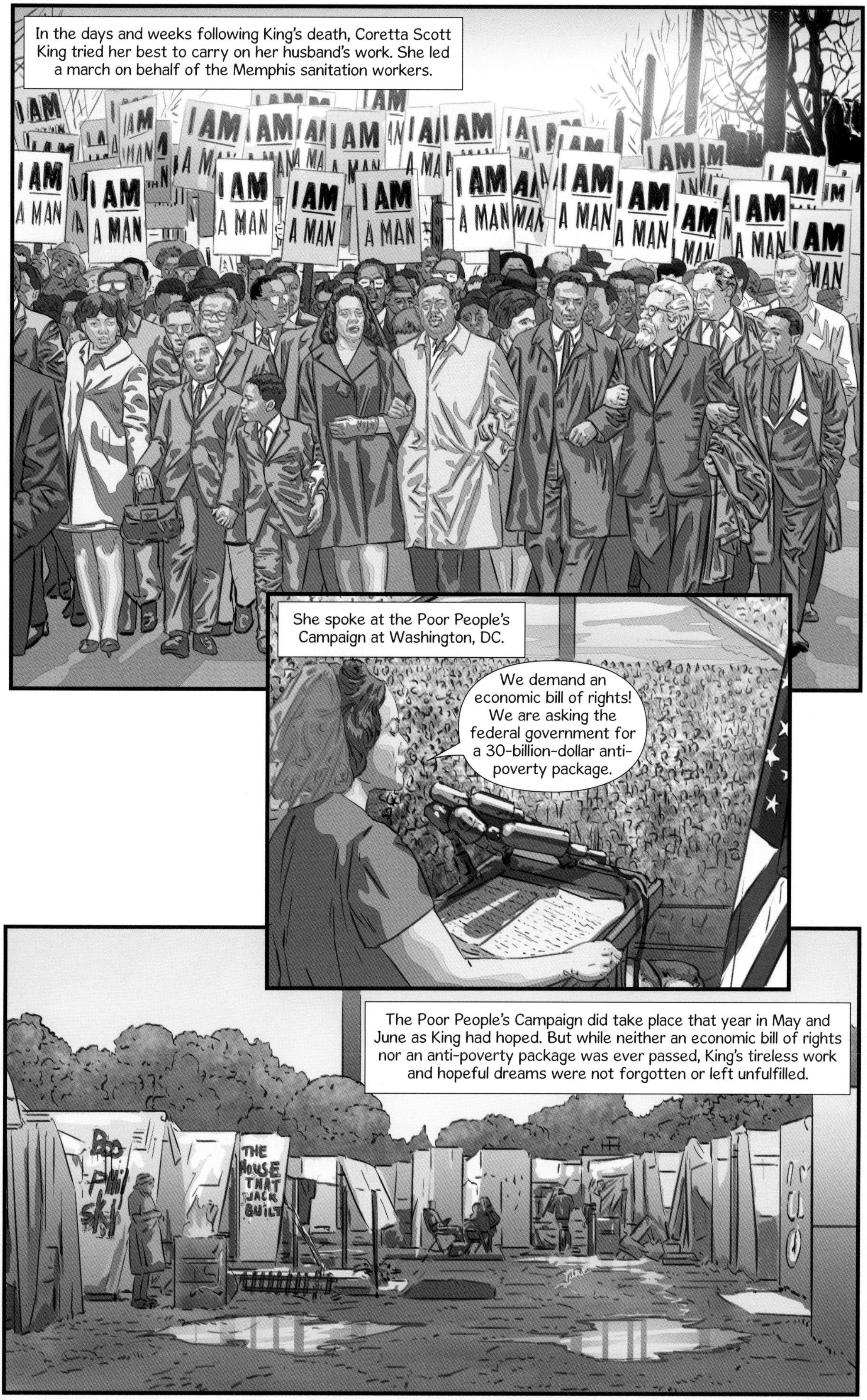
In the days and weeks following King's death, Coretta Scott King tried her best to carry on her husband's work. She led a march on behalf of the Memphis sanitation workers.
I AM A MAN
She spoke at the Poor People's Campaign at Washington, DC.
We demand an economic bill of rights! We are asking the federal government for a 30-billion-dollar anti-poverty package.
The Poor People's Campaign did take place that year in May and June as King had hoped. But while neither an economic bill of rights nor an anti-poverty package was ever passed, King's tireless work and hopeful dreams were not forgotten or left unfulfilled.
THE HOUSE THAT JACK BUILT

Shortly after King's death, President Johnson signed the Civil Rights Act of 1968 into law. Also known as the Fair Housing Act, it prohibited discrimination in the sale, rental, or financing of housing, something King had long lobbied for.

In Memphis, the site of King's final efforts before his assassination, the sanitation workers got an increase in wages and formed a union.

King's work lived on without him. The hope was that the memory of this great man would live on as well.

So on November 2, 1983, in Washington, DC, with Coretta Scott King looking on, President Reagan signed a bill establishing a federal holiday in honor of Martin Luther King Jr.

Today, on the third Monday of January every year, Americans pause to think about and pay tribute to the man who did so much for the freedom and equality of all people.

But King's legacy goes far beyond a single day of remembrance.

WE DEMAND END SEGREGATED RULES IN PUBLIC SCHOOLS

WE DEMAND EQUAL RIGHT FOR ALL FREEDOM

WE DEMAND VOTING RIGHT NOW

NO MORE SEGREGATION

ALL PAY NOW!

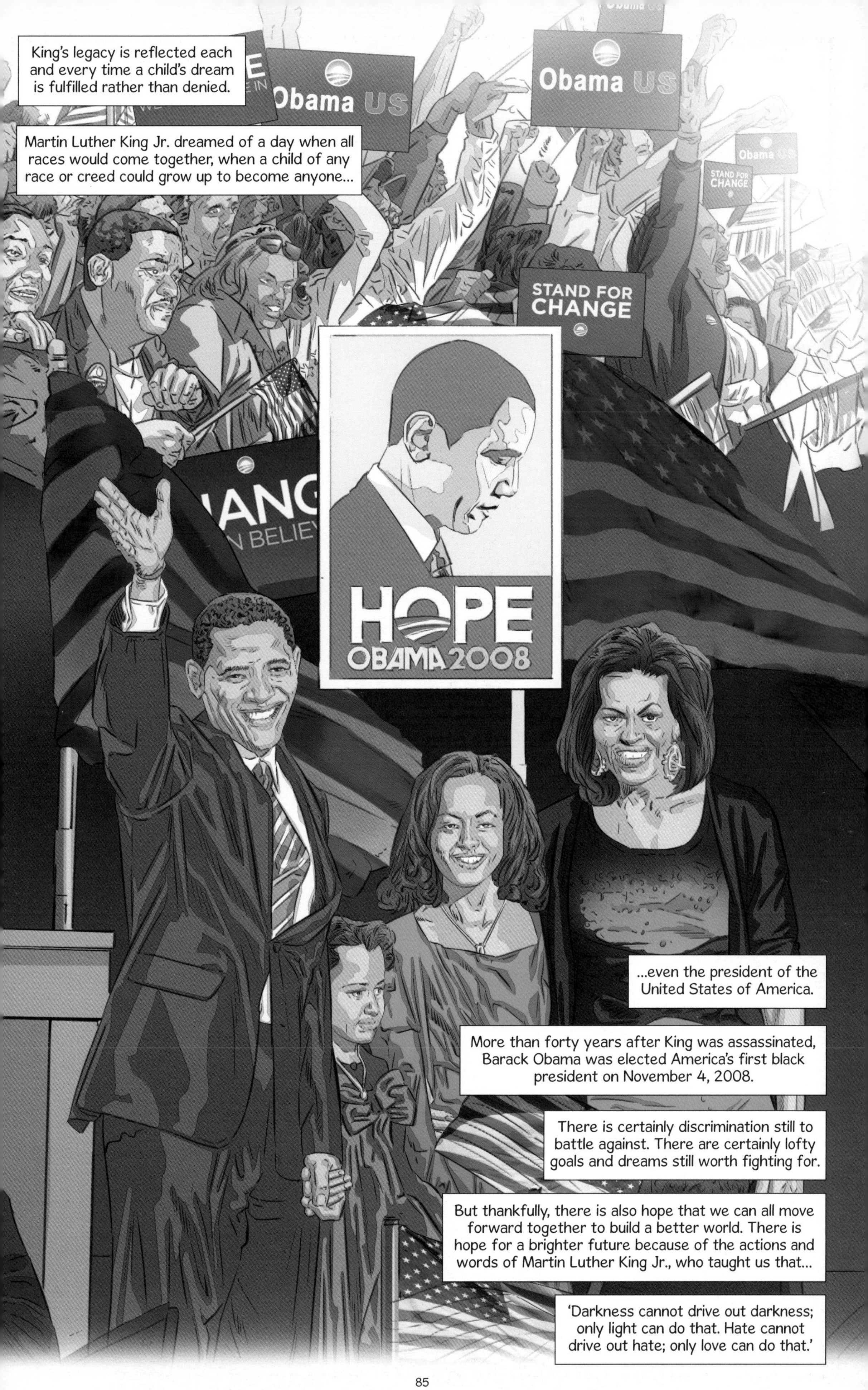
King's legacy is reflected each and every time a child's dream is fulfilled rather than denied.
Obama US
Obama US
Martin Luther King Jr. dreamed of a day when all races would come together, when a child of any race or creed could grow up to become anyone...
Obama US
STAND FOR CHANGE
STAND FOR CHANGE
HOPE
OBAMA 2008
...even the president of the United States of America.
More than forty years after King was assassinated, Barack Obama was elected America's first black president on November 4, 2008.
There is certainly discrimination still to battle against. There are certainly lofty goals and dreams still worth fighting for.
But thankfully, there is also hope that we can all move forward together to build a better world. There is hope for a brighter future because of the actions and words of Martin Luther King Jr., who taught us that...
'Darkness cannot drive out darkness; only light can do that. Hate cannot drive out hate; only love can do that.'

Born to illiterate parents in the untamed frontiers of America and raised with virtually no formal education, Abraham Lincoln often questioned his future. But he took comfort in knowing that at least he had the freedom to choose his own path in life. Freedom, he believed, was a precious thing, and he was certain that no man had a right to enslave another.

Unfortunately, not everyone in America shared that belief. In the mid-19th century, America was a nation with more than 4 million slaves; it was a nation that had lost its moral compass, a nation that was desperate for a leader to step forward. That leader was Abraham Lincoln.

Thrust into the national spotlight when his conscience would not let him turn away from injustice, Abraham Lincoln took control of a shattered nation at the cusp of a civil war. And he helped ensure that the idea of freedom for all did not perish, and that America lived up to the dream of its Founding Fathers.

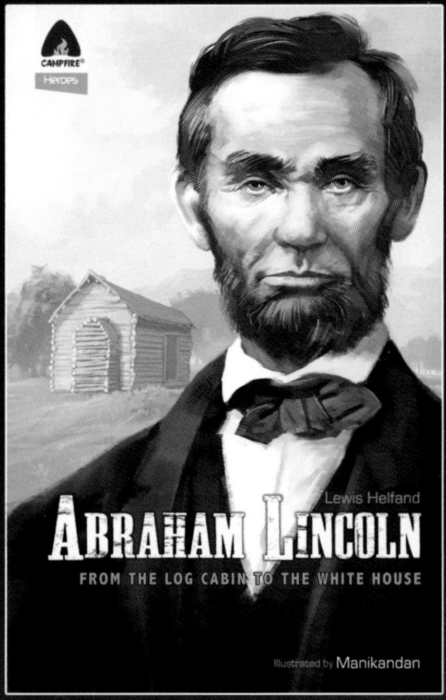
CAMPFIRE
Heroes
Lewis Helfand
ABRAHAM LINCOLN
FROM THE LOG CABIN TO THE WHITE HOUSE
Illustrated by Manikandan

ABRAHAM LINCOLN

FROM LOG CABIN TO WHITE HOUSE

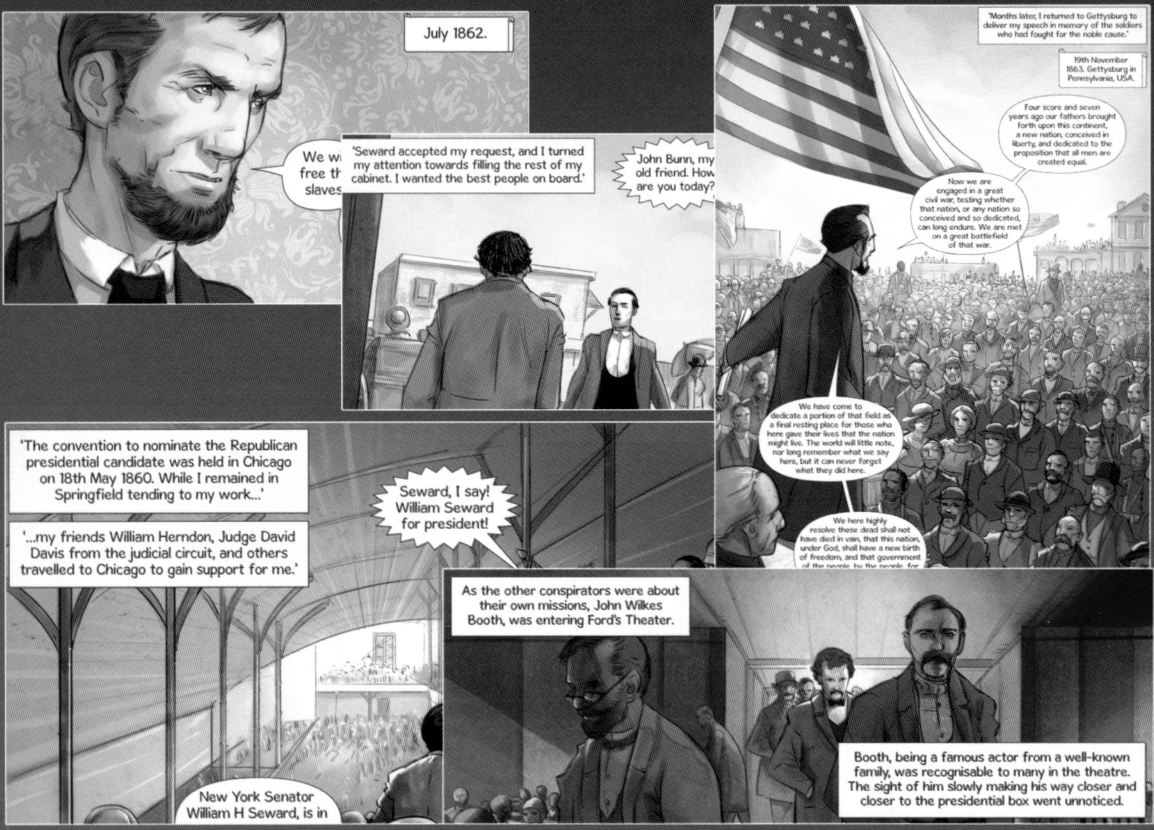
July 1862.
'Seward accepted my request, and I turned my attention towards filling the rest of my cabinet. I wanted the best people on board.'
'Months later, I returned to Gettysburg to deliver my speech in memory of the soldiers who had fought for the noble cause.'
19th November 1863. Gettysburg in Pennsylvania, USA.
Four score and seven years ago our fathers brought forth upon this continent, a new nation, conceived in liberty, and dedicated to the proposition that all men are created equal.
Now we are engaged in a great civil war, testing whether that nation, or any nation so conceived and so dedicated, can long endure. We are met on a great battlefield of that war.
We have come to dedicate a portion of that field as a final resting place for those who here gave their lives that the nation might live. The world will little note, nor long remember what we say here, but it can never forget what they did here.
'The convention to nominate the Republican presidential candidate was held in Chicago on 18th May 1860. While I remained in Springfield tending to my work...'
'...my friends William Herndon, Judge David Davis from the judicial circuit, and others travelled to Chicago to gain support for me.'
Seward, I say! William Seward for president!
New York Senator William H Seward, is in
As the other conspirators were about their own missions, John Wilkes Booth, was entering Ford's Theater.
Booth, being a famous actor from a well-known family, was recognisable to many in the theatre. The sight of him slowly making his way closer and closer to the presidential box went unnoticed.

Muhammad Ali. His ferocious skill inside the ring made him a champion, his gentle spirit outside made him a hero, and his courage in life made him a legend.

Like David taking on Goliath, he fought against the biggest and the strongest and managed to come out on top. Like a modern-day Robin Hood, he gave his wealth to the poor. He had the good looks of a movie star and the words of a poet, and left his fans and critics absolutely spellbound every time.

He soon became the champion of the world, but gave it all up by standing for what he believed in. Refusing to abandon his Muslim faith and refusing to fight in the Vietnam War cost him the best years of his career, and nearly stripped him of his freedom. But Muhammad Ali survived it all, and fought his way back to the top all over again.

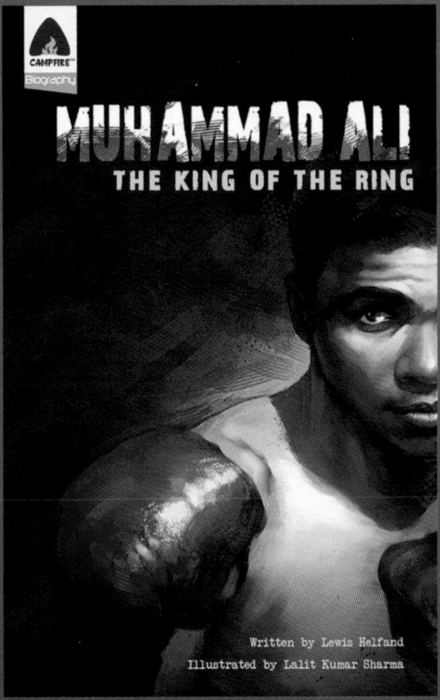
CAMPFIRE
Biography
MUHAMMAD ALI
THE KING OF THE RING
Written by Lewis Helfand
Illustrated by Lalit Kumar Sharma

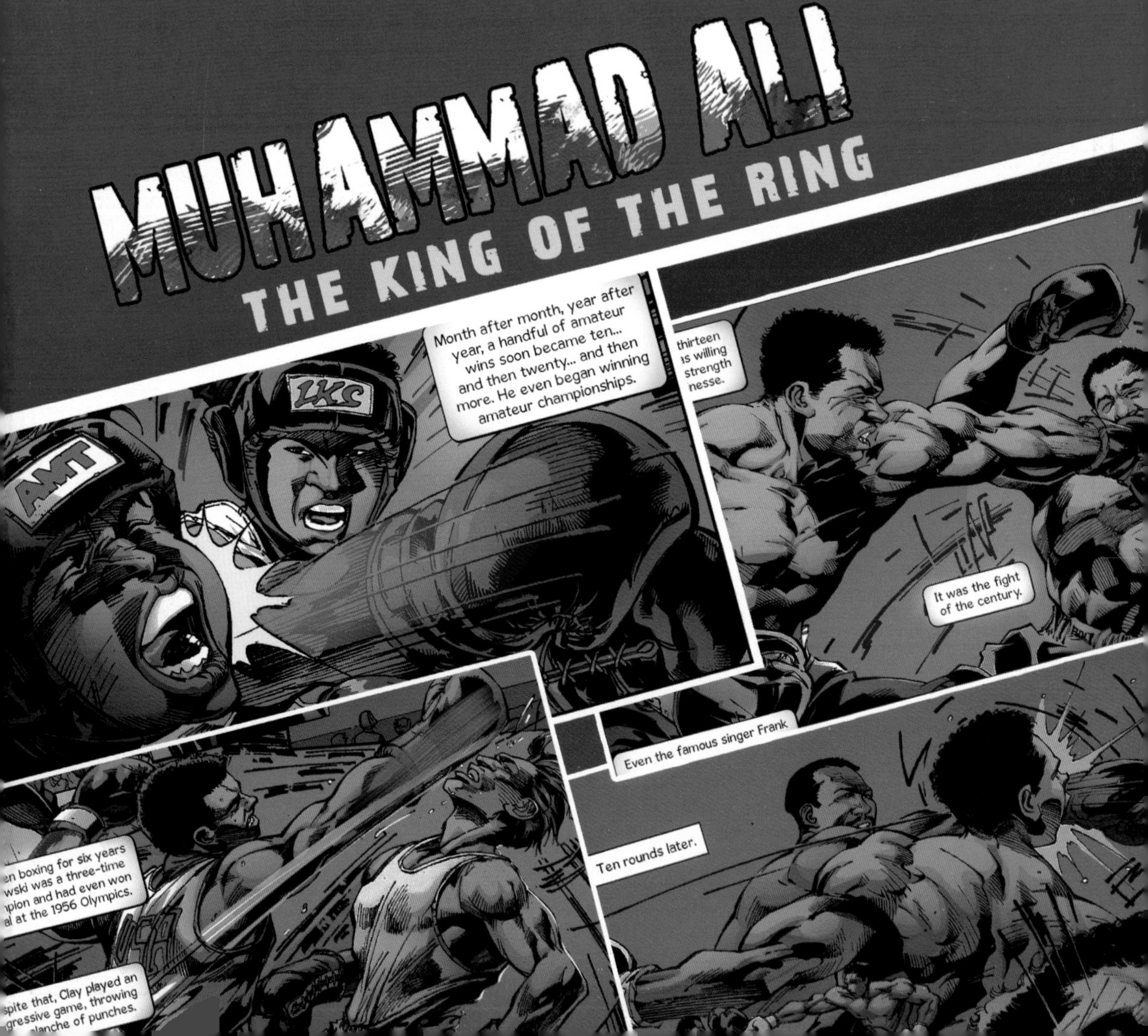
MUHAMMAD ALI
THE KING OF THE RING
Month after month, year after year, a handful of amateur wins soon became ten... and then twenty... and then more. He even began winning amateur championships.
thirteen
as willing
strength
nesse.
It was the fight of the century.
en boxing for six years
wski was a three-time
pion and had even won
al at the 1956 Olympics.
Even the famous singer Frank
Ten rounds later.
spite that, Clay played an
gressive game, throwing
lanche of punches.

You may also like to read other titles from our

HEROES SERIES

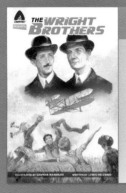

THE WRIGHT BROTHERS

THE WRIGHT BROTHERS

Orville and Wilbur Wright were just two seemingly average brothers from the American city of Dayton, Ohio, without even a high school diploma. Like so many others, the two creative and inventive brothers harbored a secret fantasy since childhood—a dream to be able to fly. In the late 1800s, the world's leading scientists were trying to construct a machine that could soar above the earth. One by one these brilliant scientists failed, some even falling to their deaths, victims of their own winged contraptions. So, how could Orville and Wilbur even think of succeeding when no one else could?

CONQUERING EVEREST

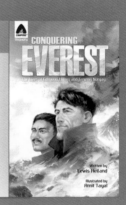

Tenzing Norgay was the son of poor Tibetan immigrants living in Nepal. He longed to see the world but was told he could aspire to be little more than a servant. On the other hand, Edmund Hillary was a humble beekeeper from New Zealand, who spent his youth dreaming of adventures he could never hope to experience. And Everest was the ultimate adventure. Alone at the top of the world with their oxygen running low, they were armed with little more than their courage and determination. But would that be enough to achieve the impossible—what no man had ever done before?

CONQUERING
EVEREST
Written by
Lewis Helfand
Illustrated by
Amit Tayal

LEONARDO
DA VINCI
The Renaissance Man

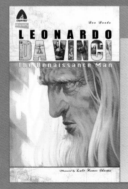

LEONARDO DA VINCI

Leonardo da Vinci has captivated the world's imagination for nearly 500 years. Yet, from the day he was born, the fates were against him. Torn from his mother and happy life in the Italian countryside, Leonardo was again uprooted by his father, whom he barely knew, and moved to Florence. The future seemed to hold little hope for this young boy. But Leonardo rose against impossible odds to embrace a destiny unlike any man's before or since. His is the amazing story of an illegitimate son, rejected by Renaissance society, who makes his own groundbreaking path in the world to claim an identity envied by all.

NELSON MANDELA

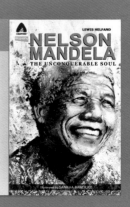

South Africa was a nation ruled by an oppressive and discriminatory set of laws known as apartheid. Black men and women could not have certain jobs or live in certain neighborhoods, or even walk down the street without being arrested or assaulted by the brutal police force. South Africans desperately needed their freedom, and Nelson Mandela answered the call. Sent to the harshest prison in all of South Africa to die, Mandela's spirit could not be broken. From his tiny prison cell, Mandela not only rallied the entire world to his cause, he even taught his oppressors the value of tolerance and compassion.

LEWIS HELFAND
NELSON
MANDELA
THE UNCONQUERABLE SOUL